# THE MAN WHO WROTE THE TEDDY BEARS' PICNIC

How Irish-born lyricist and composer Jimmy Kennedy became one of the twentieth century's finest songwriters.

## J. J. Kennedy

authorHOUSE®

*AuthorHouse™ UK Ltd.*
*500 Avebury Boulevard*
*Central Milton Keynes, MK9 2BE*
*www.authorhouse.co.uk*
*Phone: 08001974150*

*First published by AuthorHouse      07/08/2011*

*ISBN: 978-1-4567-7811-8 (sc)*
*ISBN: 978-1-4678-8569-0 (ebk)*

# What they said about Jimmy Kennedy and his songs

**The Faber Companion to 20th Century Popular Music.** 'An emotional directness and dramatic power rare in British songwriters outside music hall and rock music.'

**Sir Tim Rice:** 'I was, indeed am, a great fan of Jimmy's work. I don't remember coining the phrase "The Great Jimmy" but I am sure everybody called him that one time or another.'

**Dame Vera Lynn:** '*Red Sails in the Sunset* was the first song I ever broadcast.'

**American National Academy of Popular Music's Songwriters Hall of Fame:** 'While Jimmy Kennedy was a true son of Ireland, the appeal of his music is lasting and universal and stretches far beyond the Irish Sea. If music indeed is international, Kennedy's many memorable songs are living proof of the fact. He wrote more than 2,000 songs overall and their sales in sheet music and records reached into the millions – and they all had a memorable story.'

**Sir Terry Wogan:** You don't need a litany from me of the succession of huge hits he wrote that rang around the world, but a nicer, gentler man would be hard to find.

**Bing Crosby:** 'What songs he wrote – *Red Sails in the Sunset, My Prayer, Harbour Lights, South of the Border* – I'd like to have a bob for every time I sang *South of the Border*! Great, great songs.'

**Hal David:** 'I met him in New York. I was a professional songwriter in my twenties and I'd had hits. I thought I'd like to write like him. A great writer, ripe for rediscovery.'

**Don Black:** 'What a great catalogue of songs Jimmy Kennedy had – little nuggets, all of them.'

**Gene Autrey:** 'Jimmy was a class act. *South of the Border* is one of my favourite songs.

**Sir Denis Thatcher:** 'Jimmy Kennedy had an indefinable quality which made an irresistible appeal to those who came to know him.'

**Jonathan Channon:** Executive Vice-President EMI Music Publishing: 'He rivalled the best of the great American songwriters; an all-rounder with an unerring sense of what people wanted. He was the consummate Tin Pan Alley writer and justifies his place alongside the greats from that era.'

### *The Teddy Bears' Picnic*

*If you go down in the woods today*
*You're sure of a big surprise*
*If you go down in the woods today*
*You'd better go in disguise.*
*For ev'ry Bear that ever there was*
*Will gather there for certain, because,*
*Today's the day the Teddy Bears have their picnic.*

*Ev'ry Teddy Bear who's been good*
*Is sure of a treat today*
*There's lots of marvelous things to eat*
*And wonderful games to play.*
*Beneath the trees where nobody sees*
*They'll Hide and Seek as long as they please,*
*'Cause that's the way the Teddy Bears have their picnic.*

*If you go down in the woods today*
*You'd better not go alone*
*It's lovely down in the woods today*
*But safer to stay at home.*
*For every Bear that ever there was*
*Will gather there for certain, because*
*Today's the day the Teddy Bears have their picnic.*

*Picnic time for Teddy Bears,*
*The little Teddy Bears are having a lovely time today*
*Watch them, catch them unawares*
*And see them picnic on their holiday.*
*See them gaily gad about,*
*They love to play and shout,*
*They never have any care;*
*At six o'clock their Mummies and Daddies*
*Will take them home to bed,*
*Because they're tired little Teddy Bears.*

**Jimmy Kennedy**

# Acknowledgements

I have been helped and supported by many people. The first person to thank is Jean Billington, a dealer in ephemera who used to supply me with sheet music covers and who chanced upon Jimmy Kennedy's lost private papers for sale at a Fair at the Russell Hotel in London. She telephoned me about her discovery one day and thanks to this tip-off I was able to get the papers back. Without them I would not have been able to write the book.

I should also particularly like to thank Brian Willey, for many years vice-chairman of the British Academy of Songwriters, Composers and Authors (BASCA), who read through a draft version of the book and made many helpful corrections and observations.

Two songwriters, the late Bob Barrett and the late Ronnie Bridges, both of whom were members of the Council of BASCA during the 12 years my father was chairman, provided me with first-hand information about Jimmy Kennedy's professional life and the music business of his time. So too did songwriter and producer Guy Fletcher, a former chairman of BASCA, and ex rock singer turned businessman, Tim Hollier, another contemporary BASCA Council member. John Baskin, a cousin from America, supplied me with information about the possible origins of the Baskins, my grandmother's family from County Donegal. Heather Wisener, another cousin from Coleraine, was a mine of information on the origin of the Kennedys in Ulster. Ian Kennedy and his sister, Heather Pitchforth, supplied information about their father, songwriter, performer and BBC producer Hamilton Kennedy, my father's younger brother. I met the late Constance Carpenter-Kennedy, my father's second wife, several times in New York and she told me about her relationship with Jimmy Kennedy, especially during the 1950s when she starred in *The King and I* on Broadway. Eileen Williams, my father's close friend in the 1950s and 1960s, provided additional personal background. The late Leslie Mann, from Belfast, who did so much to promote the life and works of Jimmy Kennedy, sent me a stream of information during the 1980s and 1990s, much of which provided helpful background for this book. The late Sir Denis Thatcher kindly made available the eulogy he gave at Jimmy Kennedy's memorial service together with other useful comments about their long friendship. The late Sir Bill Cotton Jnr added an anecdote and general advice and support as did Sir Tim Rice. Irish RTE presenter John Bowman was also encouraging and gave me practical support. He also introduced me to the Dublin literary agent, Jonathan Williams, who most helpfully edited a later draft of the book. I would also like to thank Sir Terry Wogan for his tribute, Val Doonican who wrote such a lovely foreword and Jonathan Channon from EMI Music Publishing.

Of many supportive and knowledgeable friends, I would like to single out a former colleague, Brian Johnson from Manchester who proof read the last draft of the book. The illustrations were improved by the photographic skills of my wife, Saskia. Encouraging family members include my ex-wife, Dee Jones, my elder daughter, Joanna, and my son, Robert. Finally, my younger daughter, Lucienne, read through the first draft with an eagle eye, making useful suggestions and correcting the many grammatical errors.

# Author's Introduction

Readers of contemporary books on the popular music scene could be forgiven for assuming that before The Beatles pop music in Britain did not exist – that the group was pop music's Big Bang, exploding somehow from apparently empty space. Nothing could be more wrong. America certainly led the way in the development of popular music through the first half of the 20th century: gospel, blues, ragtime, country, rock 'n' roll and more all fused into a kaleidoscope of different American musical genres and the pop music universe all this engendered continues to expand today. But Britain also produced a rich popular song culture which went back to before the beginning of the 20th century and was built upon by later generations. This book celebrates the life and work of someone who helped develop that culture, my father Jimmy Kennedy. He could rightly be described as the leading light of a colourful band of around 20 writers who together wrote songs of such quality during the 1930s that the period is universally known as the 'golden age' of popular song.

Kennedy is famous for writing the words for *The Teddy Bears' Picnic*, a lyric which transformed an old American tune into one of the world's most famous children's songs. But he did much more than this. He wrote or co-wrote ballads like *Red Sails in the Sunset, Isle of Capri, Harbour Lights* and *South of the Border*; party dances like *The Cokey Cokey* and *The Chestnut Tree*; novelty numbers like *Istanbul (Not Constantinople)*; and a host of other commercially successful songs including

*My Prayer, April in Portugal, Did Your Mother Come from Ireland, Serenade in the Night* and *Love is Like a Violin.* They topped hit parades all over the world, each selling records and copies of sheet music by the million. The century's greatest popular music stars recorded his output throughout his fifty year career. In the 1920s and 30s music hall artists such as Florrie Forde and entertainers like Gracie Fields performed and recorded them; then came big bands from both sides of the Atlantic – Joe Loss, Ambrose, Lew Stone, Ray Noble, the Dorsey Brothers, Guy Lombardo, Louis Armstrong, Glenn Miller, Herb Alpert and many others. Overlapping and following on from the big bands came a galaxy of great vocalists, singers and groups, including Bing Crosby, Vera Lynn, Frank Sinatra, Perry Como, Fats Domino, Patsy Cline, Tom Jones, Roy Orbison, Ken Dodd, Val Doonican and The Platters. But there were hundreds more. Even The Beatles included a Jimmy Kennedy song at an early concert in Hamburg.

My father had talent, worked hard, had luck on his side and his output of 2000 or so published songs was rewarded with something like thirty No.1s and innumerable chart entries. But he also did his best to give something back to writers who were less fortunate. He was chairman of the British Academy of Songwriters, Composers and Authors for 12 years. After his death in April, 1984, an annual Ivor Novello award, for the craft of song writing, was named after him and, despite not being American, his huge success over there led to him being posthumously inducted into the American Popular Songwriters Hall of Fame in 1994. There he took his place with the all-time greats of the genre.

I hope this book will appeal to some of the millions who continue to enjoy his compositions, especially his fellow countrymen from Ireland. Although popular music has changed almost out of recognition since the golden age, I hope that there will be sufficient insight into the creative mind of one of Britain's best professional songwriters for it also to appeal to some of today's budding authors and composers and encourage them to follow in his footsteps.

**J. J. Kennedy, Céret, France, June, 2011**

# The Jimmy Kennedy I knew
## By Val Doonican

*Courtesy of Val Doonican*

I suppose my first experience of Jimmy Kennedy's songs must have come when I was still a teenager in Ireland, trying to make my way on the fringes of the music world. I sang so many of them while performing in small vocal ensembles and dance bands. They were the standards of the day and all the great singers I admired so much had them in their repertoires. This really was a vintage era for song writing and Jimmy was right in the centre of it. At a time when so much popular music came from the USA, it was with great pride that we listened to the top American vocalists singing numbers written by an Irishman.

Some years later, when I became a regular broadcaster, BBC radio invited me to present a three-part biography called *The Jimmy Kennedy Story*. Perhaps I was chosen because of the Irish connection. Who knows? As a result, the man himself sent me a song he had written with me in mind. It was a lovely, light-hearted number called *The Jarvey was a Leprechaun* and it was through this project that we first met. Through the years that followed, we became both professional and personal friends. My wife Lynn and myself came to know Jimmy as a warm, kind and very generous man.

I recall one evening when he came to our home and presented our very young daughters with a signed and dedicated piano copy of *The Teddy Bears' Picnic*, something that has remained a family treasure. I must admit that up until that moment, I had not realised that it was yet another of his compositions, but then Jimmy's canon of work is quite astonishing in both its variety and popularity.

Jimmy was always a most generous and entertaining host. His knowledge of good food and wine made every meeting a special occasion, but it was so much more than that. I was starting to become successful in the business at this time and I will be forever grateful to Jimmy, who was full of concern about the fleeting nature of success and the importance of keeping your feet on the ground when everything is taking off around you. Coming from someone who had achieved as much as he had, this was valuable advice indeed and the time I spent with this elegant, modest and gentle man was all the incentive I needed to take on board.

While I was presenting my own Saturday night television shows, I wondered whether Jimmy would agree to join me as a special guest, the idea being that he would sit at a grand piano with the large BBC orchestra and our resident vocal chorus. A special medley of his world-famous hit songs would then be shared with the studio audience and the viewers. Self-effacing as ever, Jimmy was flattered, but concerned about his skills as a performer and solo pianist. He need not have worried. It was a lovely 'spot' and the audience immediately joined in, singing along and marvelling at how he had written so many well-loved melodies.

In later years, Jimmy spent most of his time at his home south of Dublin and we saw each other less often than we would have liked. We were never forgotten, however, as each Christmas a fabulous whole Irish smoked salmon would be delivered, making him a part of our family celebrations even in his absence.

Sadly, as the saying goes, all good things come to an end and in 1984 I found myself among Jimmy's friends and family attending his memorial service in the heart of London's West End, close to his old stomping ground of Tin Pan Alley. A most affectionate eulogy, delivered by Denis Thatcher (one of Jimmy's oldest friends, I believe) recalled a man who was full of honour, modesty and concern for others. I can only concur.

Having now spent more than 60 years singing thousands of songs, one thing has always struck me as strange. The public will warmly remember the singer and the song, but rarely the person who made the whole thing possible. So, I'll end with the hope that when you read the pages to follow, you may have good reason to remember the songwriter, too.

**Val Doonican**

# CONTENTS

# 1: Celtic roots

Jimmy Kennedy was born on 20 July 1902, in Omagh, County Tyrone, on a cool Irish summer's day. With temperatures barely getting into the 60s and a chill wind blowing in from the north, I expect that Jimmy's mother Anna, wrapped in a shawl she had knitted herself, would have lullabied her baby to sleep with a favourite Irish or Scottish folk ballad or, perhaps, one of the year's most popular songs, *Just Like the Ivy (I'll Cling to you)* – written by Harry Castling, who was later to write music hall and novelty numbers with Jimmy early in his career.

The birth made few waves, even in the rural backwater of Omagh. But on the other side of the Atlantic something else was happening which did. Songwriter Harry von Tilzer opened up a publishing office on New York's West 28th Street in 1902. It was an event, practically unnoticed at the time, which for many marks the early beginnings of America's 'Tin Pan Alley'. After Tilzer set up his business, more and more publishers, producers and musicians moved into the district, and it developed to become the heart of America's commercial popular song industry right up to the 1950s, one which had a profound effect on the development of musical taste right round the world. Coincidentally, at around the same time, music publishers in London began to form the nucleus of a British Tin Pan Alley in an area centred round tiny Denmark Street in Soho.

Nobody would have thought that, in a glittering 50-year song writing career, the gurgling Kennedy baby would grow up to occupy centre stage in both. Surrounded by lush Irish countryside, sleepy turn-of-the-century Omagh – no tractors, no cars, just birdsong, barking dogs and mooing cows - was about as quiet a backwater as you could imagine. Yet somehow it nurtured a talent in Jimmy which enabled him to become one of the all-time popular music business greats. The question that has always intrigued me as his son was how and why did this happen? I looked up our family trees to see if I could find any evidence of artistic ability because that sometimes runs in families. But there was little evidence of anything out of the ordinary on his mother's side, the Baskins of County Donegal, or his father's, the Kennedys of County Londonderry. There is, however, a possible family link with the arts. Though I have found no proof, the Baskins were supposedly related to the leading late 19th century poet, William Allingham, the 'poet of Ballyshannon'. A friend of Tennyson, William Allingham wrote poetry about the cottagers, fishermen and ballad singers of Donegal and the myths that surrounded them. His best known poems include *The Fairies* (*Up the airy mountain/ Down the rushy glen /We daren't go a-hunting /For fear of little men...'*) and *Four Ducks on a Pond*. At one time Allingham's poems were in all the anthologies and would certainly have been among the books my father read when he was young, so it is likely he was at least influenced by their natural rhymes and rhythms even if there were no family ties.

Who were the Baskins? There are four of five theories, the first of which was his mother Anna's favourite. She had inherited some beautifully-wrought antique gilt spoons, so soft you could bend them with your fingers, saying they were handed down to her by members of the family, probably Huguenots, who had fled from France to Ireland to escape religious persecution. The name 'Baskin' proved that the family's origins were originally from the Basque country in the south-west of France, she insisted. My father was so enraptured by the romance of the story that when he was in his twenties, he used to say he was 'part Irish, part Huguenot'.

But there are other ideas about the family's origins. One was that the Baskins were descendants of Abraham Baskin, the sole survivor of a ship chartered during the mid-17th century by wealthy Russian Jews from Murmansk who were escaping attacks by Tsarist troops. The refugees hoped to reach America but were shipwrecked in Donegal Bay not far from the ancient monastic settlement of Glencolumbkille, where they married into local families. Another improbable theory is that the family is descended from a German officer who commanded a ship during the Spanish Armada in 1588. Some of the ships from the attempted Spanish naval invasion were carried by the winds and tides onto the west coast of Ireland and the one commanded by 'Herr' Baskin was, like Abraham's boat, also shipwrecked near Glencolumbkille. It is said he too married into a local family, settling near the small town of Ardara in the south west of the county.

A fourth and fairly convincing story is that the name Baskin is Irish and is derived from the Irish name Ó Baiscinn, an ancient family originally from west Clare. The Ó Baiscinns are reputed to have been there when St Patrick visited the area in the middle of the 5th century and were still there 600 years later because the name 'Baskinn' is mentioned in a poem attributed to MacLiag, the court bard of Ireland's High King Brian Boru, written after his victory at the battle of Clontarf in 1014. The fifth stanza reads:

*And where are the chiefs with whom Brian went forth,*
*The ne'er vanquished sons of Erin the Brave,*
*The great King of Onaght, renowned for his worth,*
*And the hosts of Baskinn, from the western wave?*

But, so the story goes, by the 14th century, the Baskins had fallen out with their local allies, the Macmahons, and resettled in County Donegal.

But perhaps the most likely origin of the family is simply that the Baskins were Scots who came over to Ireland during the 17th century plantations and were either granted sufficient land to scrape a living in Donegal or rented it. Coming down to more modern times, to fact rather than fable, early 19th century local records show that around 1800, our branch of the Baskin family was established in Donegal and that William Baskin was farming a 62-acre plot of townland called Garrawort a few miles from Ardara and Glenties, which he leased from a Thomas Connelly. Furthermore, the records show that he married a lady called Margaret Carson in Ardara Parish Church in 1830. My grandmother came from this branch of the family. Her father, James, farmed the same land in Garrawort, when she was born, the youngest of 12, in 1875.

As for the Ulster branch of the Kennedy family, they certainly came from Scotland. The Kennedys of Ayrshire were an old lowland clan who, not content with fighting against the English with distinction, spent a good deal of time fighting with their neighbours, among themselves, and supposedly 'roasted' at least one abbot (of Crossagruel Abbey). Unsurprisingly quite a few were expelled or escaped from Scotland and emigrated to Ireland. The contacts between Ulster and south-west Scotland were historically close, so Kennedys, along with other Scots, may have come over to Ireland at almost any time, though early members of our branch probably settled around the middle of 18th century. There is evidence to show that a Thomas Kennedy came to Belfast at around that time before heading west to find work, going first to Fermanagh, then on to Derry. What happened to Thomas is not known but parish records show that James Kennedy, probably a grandson of Thomas, was a tenant farmer at Teenaght near Claudy – then a tiny village not far from Derry – in the early 19th century and it is known that the family moved two miles down the road to a modest one-storey farmstead at Upper Binn in 1834. Meanwhile other members of the family used Ireland as a launch pad to cross the Atlantic – without doubt spurred on by the consequences of the mid-19th century potato famine. With practically no employment in rural areas, emigration was the only option available for many thousands of people to get away from the hardships they faced. Some of the Kennedys went to Canada, settling in New Brunswick, while others moved on to more westerly parts of North America

My cousin, Heather Wisener, whose mother, Sadie Kennedy, was a first cousin of my father, believes the first Kennedys came to Ireland following the Battle of Culloden in 1745, where they had supported the mainly catholic Jacobites – the followers of Bonnie Prince Charlie. After the battle, the 'butcher' Duke of Cumberland, the English general, took no prisoners, so all those connected with the opposition had to escape or face execution. Heather's theory is drawn from an unusual fairy story related by a Canadian relative, Mary Anne Kennedy, who was born in 1827. She heard it from her father. Here is her fairy tale which she headed 'A True Story':

In Erin's Isle on the banks of Faughan stream in the early part of the 19th century lived a family by the name of Kennedy. One evening, Mr Kennedy, a weaver, was working in his room, when, glancing out of his window overlooking Faughan Water, he saw light suddenly twinkle in all directions, and float in and out among the houses along the river and twinkle through the sloe bushes in the glen. Then all the lights gathered together and went floating down the river about six roods away while strains of the sweetest music he had ever heard floated up from the river, played by unseen hands. He could whistle the tune which was played – 'Blue Bonnets over the Border' – and the fairy light shone so brightly that the smallest objects in the dooryard could be easily seen. He didn't inform his wife just then of what he had seen as he had to journey to Derry, eight miles away, and didn't wish to give her any unnecessary anxiety on his account. About this time, a lady acquaintance died across the river and Mr Kennedy always believed the fairies had stolen her away and it was a common belief that if a nude woman died, the fairies took her. One of his kinsfolk said she had seen fairies in her garden as often as she had fingers and toes and they were always dressed in green. *As told by Mary Ann Kennedy (1827-1921) to her family*

How does the fairy tale give a clue to Jacobite sympathies? Says Heather, 'The fairy our great-great-great-grandfather "heard" was whistling a tune, *Blue Bonnets over the Border*, a (Scottish) Jacobite song. And I think that is a fairly good indication that the Kennedys came over to Ireland in the second half of the 1700s. The next generation down, she added, always referred to themselves as Irish, so would probably not have known it.

I think that the Scottish Kennedy side of the family was considered as our true lineage despite the fascination of the Baskin past. Members of the family had clothes – skirts, hats, dressing gowns, ties etc – made from the very attractive Kennedy tartans, both ancient and modern. I even had a tartan waistcoat at one time. Culzean Castle, the Ayrshire seat of the leader of the clan, was still thought of as our spiritual home.

In Ulster, the Kennedy tenant farm at Binn was cut off from the hamlet of Claudy by a mile-long drive. But the family were eventually able to buy and slowly improve and extend the property down the years and descendents are still farming there. William, Jimmy Kennedy's grandfather, was born the year the family moved from Teenaght and married a local girl, Frances (Fanny) McKinley from Dunamanagh. They had 10 children, five boys and five girls. (If you add up all the Baskin and Kennedy siblings of that generation, my father had something like 22 possible uncles and aunts – though this never happened because some of them, mainly on the Baskin side, died when still young). Joseph Hamilton, Jimmy Kennedy's father, was born in 1873 and was the second eldest of William's five boys. With only a small farm and so many children to feed, there was little money about, and rural thrift, with a tough vein of religious discipline, underpinned everything. Perhaps it was not surprising that when William died, neither young William (the eldest son) nor Joseph Hamilton wanted to scrape a living running the farm. The two sons next in line died prematurely (one following an inebriated cycle crash) so it was left to the youngest, Robert, to take over. William and Joseph Hamilton, however, had prospects of getting a job outside farming. This came about because their teacher, noting they were brighter than average, gave them free extra coaching after school hours, something their parents would not have been able to afford. Thanks to this help, they were able to consider jobs that were more congenial than the gruelling round-the-clock work on the land.

*Jimmy Kennedy's grandparents, William and Fanny, centre, surrounded by their children. His father, Joseph Hamilton, is second from the right, top row.*

The reward for the extra academic work was that they both passed exams to get into the Royal Irish Constabulary (RIC) in 1900 and were soon earning a steady income, some of which, as was customary in those days, they would have sent home to help support the farm, though I think Robert probably later bought out the two of them. Policing in rural Ireland at the turn of the century was very different from today. When the brothers joined up, it is quite likely that an important part of their job would have been as 'revenue' police, searching the Sperrin Mountains for the illegal tax-avoiding stills used for making poteen, a cottage industry that exists even today. It is said that poteen was also made at the farm at Binn in the early days. It was described as 'good stuff' by one family member. Joseph Hamilton's first posting was to Ardara in late 1900 and it was there that he met Anna Baskin for the first time – not at a local beauty spot on the Donegal coastline, but in church. The tall, slim bachelor officer with the farming background might well have stood out among the congregation as a perfect catch for Anna, who by then was a 26-year-old teacher. They must have got to know each other quickly: they cannot have courted for more than a year before he proposed – a decision perhaps speeded up because he knew that his job could easily take him away to some other part of Ireland at any time. They were married at the Parish Church of Ardara on the 5th of September, 1901.

A few months later, Joseph Hamilton was indeed sent to another posting, to Omagh, County Tyrone. The two newly-weds had not even time to find a permanent house when, 10 months after they were married, Jimmy Kennedy was born in a room 'over the shop' – the police station in the town's Pretoria Terrace, an unlikely start to a career as an international songwriter! Years later, Anna still shook her head in disbelief. Like most mothers, she would brag about her children – she had three more after Jimmy – and she was particularly proud that he began to walk when he was only nine months old. Perhaps it was the daily snipe of Guinness her doctor prescribed her when she was pregnant that did it. She used to joke that her toddler looked so determined when he first climbed out of his cot and headed for the door of the sitting room that he must already have decided he wanted to make it all the way to Tin Pan Alley. He used to say she was right – but it took him a quarter of a century to get there! Proud though she was of his achievements, she would much have preferred him to have gone into the Church.

Anna was a very strong and forceful – some might say domineering – person with definite views about most subjects, especially if there was a moral issue at stake. Despite belonging to a moderate wing of the Church of

Ireland, for her things were either right or wrong – and there was little in between. Her views were built on the unshakeable conviction that whatever you did, 'God will know', a catchphrase that must have instilled a feeling of perpetual God-driven anxiety in her children. You had to be pretty sure of your ground before you argued with her because she seemed to have a direct line to Him. Sunday was the Lord's Day and no singing or boisterous games like football were allowed. No pop music could be played on the piano – only hymns. The children used to have false dust jackets inscribed with the words 'Holy Bible' to disguise books which she might have considered unsuitable Sunday reading. Fifty years later, when she was living with her grandchildren in Somerset, I remember playing a game of indoor French cricket one rainy Sunday morning with my cousin, Ian, who at 11 was about the same age as me. We were ultra quiet, but 'granny', who was by then well into her seventies and extremely deaf, must have guessed what we were up to because she swept into the study where we were playing, confiscated the tennis racket we were using as a bat, grabbed my hair and proceeded to bang my head against the wall. The wrath of heaven – or was it hell! I suspect my father had to put up with similar rough justice when he was a boy. Anna ran a commando course in growing up, something that must have helped him a lot in dealing with the tough types he later met in the music business.

Anna's occasionally intimidating personality gave her a presence that everyone noticed. The family used to call her 'The Duchess'. But despite frequently playing the role of moral matriarch, my grandmother's bark was worse than her bite and I suspect that some of her apparent inflexibility was a cover for shyness, the natural diffidence of someone who had been brought up with the traditions, prejudices and poverty of a 19th century Donegal farming family. I remember that she had a contrary streak which would sometimes break out into a major argument and it was best to make yourself scarce to avoid any consequences of her temper. But she would soon calm down, become reasonable, and when the storm had blown out, that was the end of it. Her attitudes were rooted in the Victorian era or even earlier. It is sometimes hard to believe that as I write this book in the early years of the twenty-first century she used to tell me first-hand stories about one of her uncles who was in the British army at the time of Napoleon, a human link going back 200 years, to before Victoria came to the throne. Her farming background had its positive side. She produced food from the garden all her life – fresh vegetables and fruit, and fresh eggs and a chicken or duck for the pot – a good wife and mother to have when money was tight.

Joseph Hamilton was very different from Anna in temperament. He was quiet, with a good sense of humour, unassuming, wanting to do a good job rather than to get to the very top of his profession – with something of the friendly qualities of the traditional village bobby. As time went by, his normally peaceful job became increasingly dangerous, especially in the 1920s, when the Troubles meant that if he went out to work, there was a chance he would not come back. Strangely enough, despite the fact that the IRA was mainly Roman Catholic, Anna always said she hated the Presbyterians much more than the Catholics. At home, Joseph's idea of relaxation was to take his pipe and stick and go for a walk. He retired as a head constable (equivalent to a station sergeant in the UK) in 1928 because of ill health and thereafter spent many hours in the garden of his house in Portstewart growing flowers. When he died of a heart attack aged 64 in 1937, the local paper wrote an appreciation which included the following:

He found great delight in the simple, beautiful things of life. He had a wide intellect, appreciating everything that was good and eschewing everything that was unwholesome. The depth of his friendship was unlimited and this help was readily given to those in need of advice or encouragement. His fitness of character will never be forgotten by those, who, while not of his family circle, were intimately acquainted with the hospitality of his household and were privileged to enjoy his close friendship. Mr. and Mrs Kennedy took a great interest in the welfare of the people – an interest that was rewarded by the esteem in which they were held.

Although the quiet, reserved, side of Jimmy Kennedy's character came from his father, he also inherited some of the more prominent traits of his mother – the flashes of temper quickly over, the strong convictions, and a doggedness which meant he was always prepared to stand his ground if he believed he was right. He had his mother's presence and could quietly command a room if he was so minded. He also had an ability to get on with just about anybody, an understanding of what made people tick and a great sense of humour. As the eldest of four children, (Nell, born in 1904; Hamilton, born in 1908; and Nina, born in 1912), he also took his personal responsibilities seriously, looking after and caring for various members of the family in later years. I think his mother's strong personality meant he would have been admonished many a time as a child growing up. So perhaps some doubt, some insecurity, lurked behind his usually urbane personality. I think this insecurity occasionally expressed itself in his family life and in his job where he often made threats which he had no intention of carrying out. Like his mother, he had a softer, sentimental side (though it was usually well hidden). And this artistic side, the escapist, the dreamer, came out in his songs – where else would he have been able to find so many words of romance to write the ballads on which his reputation was to be based? His gentlemanly charm was legendary in Tin Pan Alley, his amusing story telling making him seductively attractive to women.

# 2: Coagh's one-man Tin Pan Alley

For much of Jimmy Kennedy's school days, the family lived in an old rectory at Tamlaght, near Coagh, a tiny village on the banks of the river Ballinderry, about six miles from Cookstown and not far from Lough Neagh. Now ruined, the rectory was an imposing grey stone five-bedroomed house overlooking the village. It had a big garden and an impressive stand of chestnut trees, a wonderful mine of conkers for generations of Coagh children. When the family lived there, Joseph had just been promoted but it is still hard to imagine how anyone could maintain a house of that size on a police sergeant's pay. Perhaps in those days, the cost of living – whether rates, rents, food, clothing or any of the basics needed by the average family – was proportionately much cheaper than now. You could buy a hundredweight bag of potatoes for 5p – enough to feed a family for several weeks – and a dozen fresh eggs for 2p. Coagh in those days was practically part of a peasant economy, with plenty of informal barter trade. The rectory garden produced enough fresh produce for family basics and free labour was provided by the children. If you wanted to top that up you could try the neighbours or the shop in the village.

As to where people lived, outside of the village many of the surrounding farms were leased from the local landowner, the grandly styled Sir William Lenox-Conyngham. Coagh had some facilities - a store, a hotel, a blacksmith, a saw-mill, an award winning creamery, a flax mill and a corn mill. The nearest town of any size was Cookstown. With a population measured in thousands rather than hundreds, it was famous not only for its agricultural market but for its linen. Jimmy Kennedy went on from his elementary education in Coagh to The Academy secondary school (now Cookstown High School) when he was 11, cycling six miles each way in all weathers from Coagh, with his chums Eddie and Hugh Flack and their sister Mary. There he would while away maths lessons surreptiously gazing out of the school windows, watching the rain washing the town and its countryside clean, humming the latest tunes in his head, dreaming of a life writing them himself. He was good at arts subjects and was sporty enough to become captain of football. A boy at the school, albeit briefly, was Ernest Walton. He was outstandingly bright then and later turned out to be a scientific genius. Twenty years later, in 1932, he and John D. Cockroft were the first scientists to split the atom and they went on to share the Nobel Prize for Physics in 1951. But Walton's abilities were not appreciated by the bucolic spirits of Cookstown Academy: Walton always had his head in a book so they nick-named him 'Stew'.

A social and commercial highlight of Cookstown in those days would have been the Saturday market. The famous main street, said to be the longest and widest in Northern Ireland, was not made up so it was dusty when it was hot and muddy when it was not – which was most of the time. Horse and cart, perhaps the jaunting car, would have been important modes of transport, though I expect Jimmy would have used his faithful bicycle. In those pre-supermarket days you bought virtually everything you could not get locally for the home at the market where there was produce of all kinds on display on stalls or carts or, in many cases simply laid out on straw on the ground. A contemporary account lists a range of country products for sale: potatoes, fruit in season, vegetables in season, meat – beef, sides of bacon, pork hacked on the spot from pig carcasses laid on straw (but covered in clean white cloth) – bread, flour, bran, home-made ice creams, fizzy drinks, cockles, herrings, second-hand clothes and much more. Then there would have been numerous speciality stalls including a music stall from which, no doubt, Jimmy Kennedy, accompanied by his youthful brother Hamilton, would have purchased supplies of sheet music for their gigs. Trade produce, some sold at markets held on different days of the week, included grass-seed, flax, live pigs and cattle and potatoes, most of which was for transportation by train or lorry to Belfast. There was plenty going on behind the trading stalls, as well. Cookstown and its markets provided a weekly social forum where people would have a few convivial drinks in the pubs, gossip about their neighbours and the headlines of the day, and more importantly make friends, including of the opposite sex before heading home through the gas lit streets. There would, too, have been live music – folk singers, fiddlers and other entertainers would have vied for attention and the hope of earning much-needed income.

Jimmy Kennedy would have loved the bustle of the market and, as he grew older, would surely have used the opportunity to escape the watchful eye of his mother, to make secret assignations with the girls of the surrounding villages. Like all teenagers, he led an increasingly active social life. From the age of 10 he had provided piano accompaniments for local teenage concerts, sing-songs and other ad hoc social get-togethers. This youthful music-making received a further boost during the World War, which began in 1914, when his mother began to organise local concerts to raise money for the Red Cross. Who better to fulfil the role of provider of the music than her elder son! Young Jimmy found himself being pushed forward into the spotlight for adult audiences, something he did not enjoy so much as he was not a particularly talented pianist, more a writer. Anna also got him involved in church activities so that, by the time he was 14, he had to play the organ at his local church in

Tamlaght, 'something that ruined my piano playing for life', he used to say. Along with this he began to make his own arrangements of the popular tunes of the day, blissfully unaware that he was contravening the nascent copyright laws on which he was later to rely. But he got a big thrill when he wrote his own material: 'I decided that if these things could be written by other people, they might as well be written by me so I sent off my rather amateurish efforts to well-known music publishers like Chappell's and Francis, Day & Hunter... and got them back!' The Jimmy Kennedy name was being posted off to publishers 15 years before he arrived in person – from Ireland's one-man teenaged Tin Pan Alley, Coagh!

He also started to dabble in 'versification' as he called it. Indeed, when he was very young, he aspired to take on the William Allingham mantle and become a poet. This ambition was fuelled by victory in a school sonnet-writing competition featured in the local newspaper, *The Mid-Ulster Mail*, when he was 12. My father would never have published these poems himself – though they were a good deal better than the average Tin Pan Alley lyric: I suspect the sonnet 'Spring' contained his first use of the word 'charms' (though not rhymed with 'arms'!). I found the two winning poems tucked way with his papers in a tiny booklet called *The Poets' Own Library*, published in London by Arthur H. Stockwell, Ludgate Hill. So here they are, for the first time since 1914.

### Spring

*O joyous season, is thy advent near?*
*How I delight to listen to thy charms!*
*And as I see thee creeping o'er the farms*
*The voice of Nature then I seem to hear.*

*The lark so merrily will sing his song,*
*The birds will build their nests and hatch their young,*
*And all the world will seem from Heaven sprung*
*And purified throughout the winter long.*

*Thou hast thy time, and when thy race is run*
*Thy closing days will fly with wondrous speed;*
*Till waning, waning, thou wilt pass away,*
*Thy work performed, as heaven hath decreed:*
*Thou fadest fast until thy days are done*
*And Summer then in order will hold sway.*

**St Patrick**
*O Patron Saint! An era new did shine*
*When first thou landed on fair Eden's shore*
*Our pagan sires had never heard before*
*The gospel story of our Lord divine.*

*Thou drovest heathen pests from out our land*
*Nor snakes nor pois'nous reptiles didst thou leave*
*'Twas then at length the heathen did believe*
*That thou wast aided by th'Almighty hand.*

*For ages long our island has been known*
*A place of sanctity and Christian lore*
*And saints and scholars flock from distant climes*
*To seek the wisdom which the wide world o'er*
*Renowned in song and legend thou hast grown*
*And reverently worship at thy shrines.*

The publication of the two poems got the Jimmy Kennedy name into the newspapers for the first time but, as he said in an article many years later: 'Fortunately, I had a commercial instinct and decided that there was no money in writing verse, so I turned to lyric writing instead.' He added, 'I had always been able to do an odd spot of piano playing and so by combining these two hobbies I became an amateur songwriter. As it happened, I retained my amateur status for a very long time before I became a success!'

17

Music-making and poetry were, then, the twin foundations of Jimmy Kennedy's artistic development from an early age. But as he got older there was a third ingredient - romance. He fell head over heels in love with a local girl on his 16th birthday when they danced together to an old song called *The Twilight Waltz*. She said she admired him for his writing as much as for his dancing and, spurred on by the comment, he was inspired to write his first ballad. 'It was the kind of thing you do when you are very young which you can recall vividly in later years,' he once told me. 'It was very, very sad. I was in the sentimental stage which one strikes at the mature age of 16, when your heart has been smitten by a wide-eyed, blue-eyed blonde. I called it *A Rose That Has Faded Away*, hammering it out on the old piano at home line by line. But when I played it over to the family they said it was terrible - a real "miss"!'

He refused to accept the verdict of the family juke box jury and sent the song to a firm of London publishers with a long explanation as to why they should take it. It came back with a short explanation as to why they would not. These were early steps towards a career in song writing, but they were enough for mother Anna to realise that young Jimmy was not going to be persuaded to enter the Church. So he was prepared instead for Trinity College, Dublin. A degree from there was an entrée for a good career in any profession in Ireland or Britain - a lawyer, diplomat or administrator, perhaps.

Jimmy Kennedy's hobby meant that he developed a deep interest as a young teenager in what was going on in the world of popular music well beyond the shores of Ireland. Though popular songs had been created, sung and sometimes later sold on printed sheets in Europe for centuries, they were not produced commercially on a very wide scale until well into the second half of the 19th century. Early European popular music, carried mostly by immigrants, originally had a big influence on

American popular song, but by the end of the 1890s, just a few years before Jimmy Kennedy was born, the flow had started to reverse, especially after New York began to emerge as the driving force for the mass market. America's dynamic and ever-changing output was responsible for a huge variety of genres over the next 50 years and came to symbolise modern popular music, producing during the 20th century some of the most famous writers and performers of all time, and greatly influencing popular music in Britain and Europe. My father spent many hours studying the American masters, learning from them and all about Tin Pan Alley. This is his version of its American origin taken from an article he wrote in the early 1930s:

Tin Pan Alley originated in the United States, and owing to its attractiveness and 'glamour', the name was later adopted in London. It all began in 1902, when a certain American songwriter-publisher called Harry von Tilzer had his office in a small building in New York mainly occupied by non-musical firms, who strongly objected to his perpetual pounding on the piano. Mr von Tilzer could not afford to take other premises but something had to be done to appease his disgruntled fellow tenants.

So he hit on the idea of cutting up a newspaper and putting the strips of paper between the hammers and strings of his piano. The result was a dulcet tinkling noise which did not penetrate very far beyond his room. One day a journalist, Monroe H. Rosenfeld, who was writing an article on songs in an adjacent office, was stuck for a title. In the silence of thought the muffled sound of a piano filtered through to his ears more like a jangle than a tinkle. 'That blessed noise sounds like a tin pan,' he grumbled to a colleague, who retorted, 'Well, they're all like that down this alley.' 'That's an idea,' thought the journalist, 'I'll call the article 'Tin Pan Alley'.

That was Jimmy Kennedy's take on the US origins of Tin Pan Alley. But he was to start his career in the London version in Denmark Street where, one of the first commercial popular music publishers, Lawrence Wright, had opened up in a basement at Number 8 in 1911. The real importance of both Tin Pan Alleys was not so much when they were started or where they were located but what they represented: a music business that produced and promoted the professionally written commercial popular song that people sang, listened and danced to up until the 1950s.

In the first decade of the 20th century, with commercial popular music in an early stage of development on both sides of the Atlantic, the piles of sheet music on top of the Kennedy family's upright piano was very eclectic. To please Anna, there would have been some collections of the lighter works of classical and romantic composers such as Mozart, Beethoven, Dvorak, Mendelssohn and Chopin, perhaps. Jimmy himself did not care for this 'heavy' music, but liked music with a good singable tune. He liked some of the music from the operettas – Franz Lehar (*The Merry Widow*), Offenbach (*La Vie Parisienne,* famous for the *Can-Can*), and, a particular favourite, Johann Strauss. He also liked the American Stephen Foster, who was of Irish descent, and who had written *Jeannie with the Light Brown Hair, Beautiful Dreamer* and minstrel songs such as *Old Folks at Home (Swanee River)* and *My Old Kentucky Home.* Irish songwriters such as Michael Balfe (*Come into the Garden, Maud*), Thomas Moore (*Believe Me, If All Those Endearing Young Charms*), and Percy French (*The Mountains of Mourne, Phil the Fluter's Ball*) were favourites, as were the old Irish, Scottish, English and Welsh folk songs. They would have had an important place mixed in with other traditional and community songs like *Londonderry Air, Cockles and Mussels, Loch Lomond, The Skye Boat Song, Swing Low, Sweet Chariot, Greensleeves* and many others. And there would also have been a selection of drawing room ballads and miscellaneous popular songs recently arrived from America such as *A Bird in a Gilded Cage* and *After the Ball*. I expect he would also have had a good selection of music hall numbers. Some of these were close to folk but there were hundreds of songs dating back 50 years or more which had the music hall trademarks – a story with a topical twist, sometimes funny, sometimes sad, a touch sentimental, maybe satirical, something to engage an audience and to be a vehicle to show off the talents of the star variety performers. Songs like *Champagne Charlie, The Man who broke the Bank at Monte Carlo,* and *Polly Perkins* were immensely popular in Britain (though nowhere else). I can well imagine that from all this varied sheet music came the addresses of the publishers to whom my father used to send his early output. Last and perhaps not on the very top of the pile but on the piano nevertheless, there would have been a hymn book, not just to keep his mother happy but to practice for playing the church organ on Sundays.

Of all the various musical sources that interested Jimmy Kennedy, I think that folk songs with a 'story' had the most direct influence on him. Some of his biggest hits, such as *South of the Border* and *Red Sails in the Sunset* were based on the ballad idea and his lyric-writing ability is perhaps closely related to the fact that words are crucial to tell the stories. He interpreted the importance of Irish folk music in an article he wrote in 1968 for Dublin-based *Folk Magazine* (Volume 1, Number 6):

I was more or less brought up on Irish folk songs and, like so many other children living in Ireland in the days before radio, they were my first acquaintance with musical sound, apart from what I heard in church. This early impact had a great deal to do with the trend of my own output, as more often than not when evaluating something I had written, I compared it, rather boldly, with well known songs in the traditional field, wondering to myself how did it compare with a master work – a very exacting task it used to be.

Folk songs were stories going way back, with lyrics commemorating battles or other events, and these lyrics were frequently brought up-to-date with fresh stories, legends or news. It was a continuous process and what we know as street ballads were regularly grafted on to older musical stock and benefited considerably from the popular strength of the older tunes. This was particularly true of the 18th century and the process is still going on. What I often think is remarkable, and it's an equally remarkable tribute to the Irish, is the fact that in spite of there being no written music, the original purity of these ancient melodies has somehow preserved itself. Although its survival has depended on being handed down from generation to generation, and even allowing for embellishments and changes, the basic melody is still there. The passing on from fiddler to fiddler, or harpist to harpist was, one supposes, the only way to keep the tunes alive as the chroniclers of those days were monks without much knowledge or interest in song, their minds being on more spiritual things.

An Irish melody is always easily identifiable; it has retained its purity, whereas a Rumanian tune, for instance, may have traces of Russian, Hebrew or gipsy overtones. Perhaps our island's geographical isolation, 'lost in the western mists', may account for this. And, of course, Irish folk had a big influence on American music. When you look through collections of say, American folk songs, such as those recorded by Alan Lomax [who introduced American audiences to Huddie Ledbetter, Woodie Guthrie, Muddy Waters and many others], or Carl Sandburg [who published an early collection of American folk song], it is surprising to read in footnotes that such and such a song was known and sung in Colorado in the early 1940s and we, knowing quite well that the tune is as Irish as shamrock, can be forgiven for being a little irritated by the American claim. So despite the early influences of French, Italian and Spanish folk tunes, American popular music, especially country and western, owes a lot to Ireland.

What the Irish immigrant, carrying his songs home into the mining camps and the wilds of the west, was also doing was to give them a new life in a new world. I did the same sort of thing when I adapted the Canadian mining song, the *Cokey Cokey*! Now everybody dances it all over the world. Songs don't care who sings them and great songs never die, especially those with the sentiment and poignancy of the Irish folk tradition, living on in the hearts of the people of Ireland – and the world beyond – up to this very day, wherever they may be. So it was natural for us to play and grow to love our cultural traditions, and that meant I was brought up on a lot of old Irish and Scottish melodies with their balladian lyrics!'

Though he was steeped in folk and other traditional musical forms when he was a teenager, my father would have followed all the latest musical fashions as new increasingly commercial popular songs came out, especially from America, so the pile of sheet music on the piano would have kept growing throughout his boyhood. A highlight must have been Irving Berlin's *Alexander's Ragtime Band*, still claimed to be one of the fastest best-sellers of sheet music in history, which came out in 1911. It introduced a completely new genre of popular music to Britain, ragtime, and made a huge impact. But there were so many more great songs published around that time and they helped set the standard for commercial popular music for the rest of the 20ᵗʰ century. *Oh, You Beautiful Doll, Some of These Days, My Melancholy Baby, You Made Me Love You, The Sunshine of Your Smile, St Louis Blues, If You Were the Only Girl in the World, Rock-A-*

*J. J. Kennedy*

*Bye Your Baby with a Dixie Melody* and countless others transformed sheet music publishing into big business with a mass market – and for the first time made popular music something that aspiring writers and composers could consider seriously as a career.

Where would the youthful Jimmy Kennedy have heard this music? Flat disc recording, played on a gramophone, was patented in 1888, only 14 years before he was born. Moreover, most of the early recordings were either of classical music, scratchy but wildly successful recordings of famous opera singers like Dame Nellie Melba or Enrico Caruso, or traditional songs sung by people like Harry Lauder. There were very few recordings of commercial popular songs at that time, so there is nothing to suggest that he could have heard very much recorded popular music of this type until he was older. He must have heard commercial popular music 'live', from folk singers, from bands at public entertainments, local dance halls, from the musical accompaniments to films, and from hearing music at local fairs and any variety shows he was able to get to. The bands would have played arrangements of the latest numbers and the dances that went with them. Live music, then, must have been what he heard most and what must have influenced him most and that is the music he made with his friends when they went off to play at a local gig.

# 3. Salad days

With all these influences chiming away in his head, in 1921 Jimmy Kennedy went up to Trinity College, Dublin to complete his formal education. When he took the entrance exam just four days before his 19th birthday, on 16 July 1921, he did well and his marks were among the highest of the entry for that year. However, in those days, specialist honours degrees were not considered to be as important as they are now, so he did a 'pass arts' degree made up of a range of subjects that he thought would be useful and interesting – ethics, psychology, education, Latin, French and English.

It was a time of change. Beyond the front gates of the College, Ireland was undergoing enormous political upheaval. The 1916 Easter Rising and the occupation of the General Post Office had occurred less than a mile from Trinity College's front gate. In 1920, an Act of Parliament was passed partitioning Ireland North and South. Civil unrest, political turmoil, the sending over of British forces to intervene in the fighting between republicans and home rulers, the setting up of the Irish Free State, the very nasty civil war of 1922/23 – all these outside events made the Kennedy years at Trinity a time which profoundly changed the political map of Ireland. He hardly every referred to them, but those years must surely have had an unsettling effect. As a member of the RIC, his own father was in the front line during this period because the force bore the brunt of heavy attacks, including one on the police barracks at Cookstown in June 1920. It was a far cry from what Joseph Hamilton had expected when he joined the RIC

– to keep a loose rein on what little crime there was in his rural patch.

However, although I believe troops did enter Trinity, student life seems not to have been seriously affected. My father told me it was usually reasonably safe to walk the streets of Dublin, though everyone had to be careful going into some areas. He recalled once having a frightening experience when he took a wrong turning and met a band of armed men waving pistols! But the men let him pass.

He made the most of his time at Trinity. He had great fun writing articles for the College journal, *TCD*, which he later edited. *TCD* was a miscellany of topics – student affairs, university politics, personalities, humour, the arts, sport, gossip and so on. He used a pen-name, Jay Kay, and mostly contributed verses and stories. Reading through the back copies of *TCD*, you can see how they reflected the student humour of the time and doubtless gave rise to many a laugh. Here's an example of one of my father's verses, cocking a snook at college life:

**Porters Know**
**An indigestible tale – with a moral**

*Have you heard about the man who used to live in 22?*
*Who was an awful glutton? – Here's what he used to do:*
*At night when all was still he used to satisfy his greed,*
*And creep down to the kitchens to have another feed.*

*To him it did not matter if the soup was cold as ice.*
*And frozen vegetables he considered very nice.*
*He much preferred potatoes with his supper than at lunch,*
*And he didn't mind the weevils which he often had to crunch.*

*Now there was a College porter who was cute as cute could be.*
*He used to walk about at night to see what he could see.*
*And one night as he chased a cat around the dining hall,*
*He spied our friend a feeding and he promptly paid a call.*

26

*He caught him swilling College beer; he gave him quite a 'sell',*
*He took his name, his standing and his tutor's name as well.*
*But strange to say, he didn't send for Junior Dean or Proctor;*
*He considered that the best thing was to go and get a doctor!*

Student diners gave the Knights of the Garter motto, 'Evil be to him who evil thinks', new words: 'Weevil be to him who weevil eats'! Apart from the set meal times for Commons, there was nowhere else to eat in College apart from rooms, though many young scholars needed little encouragement to spend their meagre allowances in the pubs – perhaps on a steak at the Dolphin if they had a win on the horses or an unexpected birthday cheque. Students liked to patronise The Stag's Head, which is little changed and still popular. But, according to 'Jay Kay', drinking in the pubs was not restricted to the students:

It was Sunday afternoon, with a cold and drizzling rain. The time was just ten minutes to two. A well-known and reverend Fellow was walking down the street with his overcoat collar turned up, hiding the sign of his calling. Evidently he had forgotten his watch, for accosting a member of the Dublin Mounted Police, he said solicitously: 'Can you tell me what the time is, officer?' 'Oi can, Sur,' said the officer. 'Err, what is it then?' asked the Fellow.

'Well now,' promptly began the guardian of the law, 'Oi'll tell yer.' And putting his hand to his mouth, at the same time lowering his voice to a confidential whisper, he remarked in his most unofficial manner, 'They'll be open in 10 minutes.'

Although *TCD* absorbed much of my father's youthful writing output in the intervals, as he put it, 'between rags, lectures, binges, girls, and football matches', he still continued to write songs and send them off to

London publishers, just as he used to do at home. Few of them bothered to reply and, of those that did, the answer was always no. He had a habit of thinking of ideas and then putting them in the back of his mind until he found an opportunity to use them, so some of his early efforts were reworked in material published in later years. He told me, however, that after he became a professional songwriter he recycled only one of his tunes more or less as he had originally composed it at Trinity – a comedy number called *Why did She Fall for the Leader of the Band?* , a Tin Pan Alley best seller in 1935.

Academic terms took up less than half the year. During the holidays, my father would go back home to visit the family, study, socialize, take long country bike rides and work away at his songs. His younger brother Hamilton was still at school so it meant that the two could team up at local concerts and try out a few of their own compositions. 'Hammie' could pick up any stringed instrument – guitar, banjo or ukulele – and play and sing; he was already on the way to becoming a polished performer.

Throughout his four years in Dublin, my father lived in Botany Bay, an L-shaped granite terrace of lodgings which formed two sides of a square just off to the left of the university's front square. Forming a third side was the much grander Graduate Memorial Building which housed the celebrated college debating societies, The Philosophical Society (The Phil) and The Historical Society (The Hist). The Hist was founded in 1770 by the philosopher Edmund Burke and is said to be the oldest university debating society in Britain or Ireland. Botany Bay's fourth side was the College bath house, so its inhabitants were possibly among the cleanest people in College. Botany Bay was originally, the College vegetable garden.

Despite its rather grim Georgian façade, the sets of rooms inside Botany Bay were comfortable and homely, albeit threadbare – the university had a good academic reputation but no money. Each had a sitting room with a decent open gas fire (ideal for making toast), basic cooking facilities and individual bedrooms. The rooms were kept reasonably tidy by cleaning ladies and the College servants, or 'Skips'. Rooms in College were 'men only', so the College porters used to keep a sharp look out for lady guests, who could not be inside the precincts after 7 p.m. No hanky panky after dark! My father shared rooms with R. B. D. French. Bob French also edited *TCD* and later went on to have a distinguished career as a university lecturer in English. Apart from writing, my father's other main interest was football, and he played a part in reviving the university football club, which did not field a team for two years or so from 1922. In October 1924, he sent the following letter to *TCD*:

Dear Sir,

It is the wish of many soccer enthusiasts in college that the DU Association F.C. be re-formed. Up to the beginning of 1922, there was a strong and successful club in College, but during the last two and a half years there has been no activity and as far as is known to 'the man in the square', there is now no soccer club.

Many are convinced that if soccer were again to be taken up, it would do credit to Trinity.... If more of those who are interested (or members and supporters of the old club) will send in their names to me at once, a meeting will be held to discuss prospects.

I write this letter solely as a lover of the game and with the idea of putting the matter before college.

I am, Sir,
Faithfully Yours,
J. Kennedy

Thanks to my father's letter, the authorities decided to re-form the club and gave it funding but I do not know if Jimmy Kennedy actually played for it or not.

Trinity always had a reputation for being egalitarian. It was relatively easy to pass the matriculation exams and enter the university, but not so easy to leave with a decent degree. My father's various leisure interests meant that his academic work suffered. I suspect he would have been as anxious as anyone waiting outside the Exam Hall in the Main Square of the College for the results to be posted in July 1925. Unfortunately, they were not what he had hoped for. He scraped through with only an unclassified degree. His father and mother and the rest of the family would have been expecting a much better result from him and I expect he too must have been disappointed. I think it was then that he had the bright idea of placating his parents by agreeing to take the entrance exam for the British Colonial Service, as a fall-back for a 'respectable' career: it definitely was not the time to announce at home that he was thinking of spending his life as a songwriter, even though that was what he was secretly hoping to do. The fear of failure concentrated his mind wonderfully and he passed the Civil Service exams with flying colours, so regaining his credibility in the family. The Service wrote to offer him an administrative post in northern Nigeria but added that he would have to wait for at least a year before he could take up the appointment because priority had to be given to applications from ex-servicemen still unemployed after the War. I expect my father was heartily relieved to hear the news. You could sell a lot of songs in a year. But first he needed to earn some money and, with few opportunities locally, he found his first job as a trainee in the Dublin branch of a large insurance company. Although there are no records of his employment, he must have been with the firm for a large part of 1926, possibly longer. A highlight of his new job, he told me, came in February of the same year when he was sent over to the 'palatial' London head office of the company on a two-week familiarization course. As soon as possible at the end of the first day's training he was off to Denmark Street, gazing through the windows of the music publishers he had been writing to for so many years, excitedly reading the posters advertising the latest dance sensations: 'I could hardly believe that I was actually walking the pavements where so many illustrious feet had trod and where I hoped I might follow,' he wrote later. But there was little spare time in the insurance company for a budding songwriter to get to grips with the music publishing world so he found a teaching job at a little school in the heart of Dublin, St Stephen's Green School, a job which gave him more time to write.

He soon realised that he needed to be even closer to the Denmark Street centre of the music business if he was to sell his songs to publishers in person. So, before long he was again scouring the papers for a job in England. Eventually he found a post teaching French at Shaftesbury Grammar School in Dorset. It was not as close to London as he would have liked, over a 100 miles, but at least it was in England. Despite being at St Stephen's Green School for only a few months, the head master gave him a handsome reference: 'He is a most satisfactory colleague keeping good discipline in his classes and at the same time being extremely popular with the boys. He has done excellent work for me being endowed with the gift of imparting knowledge.'

# 4: *P'liceman! P'liceman!*

The Shaftesbury Grammar School post was quite simply a means to an end for Jimmy Kennedy, giving him steady income and spare time to learn his trade. At night he used to sneak downstairs to the piano in the draughty school hall and try out ideas he had thought up during the day, muffling the notes so that he did not wake anyone up. Then at weekends and at half-term he would take a train to London and try to interest publishers in his latest creations. Dressed in his well-worn schoolmaster suit, a rose in the buttonhole, a striped TCD Association tie, and with his black wavy hair smoothed down under a fashionable felt hat, he must have appeared more a fresh-faced young Irish country gentleman than an aspiring songwriter – quite a contrast to some of the brasher types who frequented Tin Pan Alley at the time.

Telling stories, especially on a one-to-one basis, was a Jimmy Kennedy trademark. But it was his way of hiding his country shyness. Moreover, though he was full of new ideas for the next hot number and could compose melodies, his piano playing was not as good as many of the other budding songwriters hoping to make the grade in the music business and that was a handicap when it came to playing over his songs and selling them to publishers. There were no pre-recorded demo tapes to showcase songs in the 1920s. So the routine of visits to publishers was a big effort for him. He used to compare his trips to Denmark Street with the well-known story of the Scottish king, Robert the Bruce, hidden in his cave watching a spider as it attempted and eventually succeeded in climbing up its silk thread: 'If at first you don't succeed, try, try, try again.' Following the spider's example, he kept up his stream of visits to publishers, learning more and more about what they wanted as he did so: 'Although I was getting rejections, I began to feel they were increasingly sympathetic,' he wrote at the time. 'Wishful thinking perhaps, but you know instinctively sometimes that you are gradually getting nearer to the target well before you've hit it.'

Early in 1927, when he was almost 25, his determination at last paid off. He managed to sell a publisher two comedy songs with in-vogue themes and a music hall flavour, *My Cleopatra* and *Mothers are Wonderful!* He got £2 for each. Even then, it was not much money. But if a publisher was prepared to buy not just one but two songs, why not more? It made him even more certain that song writing was what he wanted to do: 'Contrast the rewards of a songwriter with those of a schoolmaster! Somehow I could not face the idea of knowing that my salary would go up by a certain small amount each year until it reached the top of the scale – a dizzy £1000 a year! And there I would stick until I retired. But, if I got a few decent hits, I could make more in a year than I'd earn in a lifetime at Shaftesbury Grammar School.' So, at the end of the 1927 summer term, he resigned, threw all his textbooks into his classroom desk and set off like Dick Whittington minus the cat for London, filled with burning ambition, a case full of newly-minted songs and some meagre savings bolstered by his final one-week salary cheque. It was just enough to finance a couple of months in cheap theatrical digs in Brixton, found for him by the rector of a church in Tooting, a family friend from Northern Ireland. The goal now was song writing fame or bust and a successful full-time career in the popular music business. But what would life be like when he made it? Here is how he later described Tin Pan Alley in a contemporary newspaper article:

Through the open first-floor window the tinkling of a piano filters into the narrow city street. The tune halts suddenly in the middle of a bar, and voices chip in, arguing...But, where are you? In Denmark Street, London's Tin Pan Alley, and a new song is being born. It may sell a million copies, make a fortune for someone whose name you have never heard, be sung by famous stars, whistled by errand boys, strummed on pianos in the five continents. Or its writer may take it to a score of those music-filled first-floor rooms in Tin Pan Alley and hear his song played through, discussed, dissected – and walk out with the crumpled sheets of paper back in his pocket. Between those two extremes, lie all the triumphs and heartbreaks, the clinging hopes and dull disappointments of the Alley.

Just imagine yourself in a business where 20 minutes' work may make a £1000 for you...or weeks of struggle and concentration mean – NOTHING! Where your empty pockets may compel you to sell outright the results of your labours for a few pounds only to see it make a fortune for someone else!

That was not just the dream, it was the reality. Day after day in the misty autumn of 1927 he would set out from his Brixton digs and travel up to Denmark Street with new ideas, new songs and old songs reworked. In the evenings he would return, with the voices of the publishers explaining why they had to reject his work ringing in his ears. But despite the lack of success, he was supercharged with hope. He loved the life. It was a new and exciting world. Though flat broke for most of the time, it did not seem to bother him. For the first time in his life he was mixing with 'charming, lovable, theatrical people' who had the same kind of talents and interests as he had.

Then, out of the blue, Jimmy Kennedy had a lucky break. Years later he recalled the moment when he came out of Charing Cross tube station with just tuppence in his pocket, wondering where his next meal was going to come from. It was one of those rare beautiful October days, sunny and warm, and he felt optimistic and full of youthful bravado despite his dire financial position. Barely a hundred yards up the road, he ran into an old-time publisher called Maurice Scott who had achieved a big success a few years previously with *Oh! It's a Lovely War.* Soon he was telling him about his own songs and this enthusiasm captured Scott's imagination, so much so that he handed over £5 on the spot for half shares in three of them. You could live for a month on a fiver! My father spent the next couple of weeks going up to Scott's Charing Cross Road office to find out when they were going to be published and who was going to record them. But Scott would not tell him what, if anything, was happening to the songs. Eventually, he realised why. They were never published! Instead, Scott did what many publishers used to do at the time and sold them direct for a quick profit to a music hall artist looking for new material for a variety show. Ergo, there were no recordings, no sheet music and, most important for a hungry young aspiring songwriter, no royalties.

Despite not publishing the material, Scott had seen some Irish promise in the youthful Kennedy and a few weeks later he bought another song, again for £5. It was called *Hear the Ukuleles* and this time Scott asked him to sign his first contract, which he did with jubilation. Within a fortnight, two big music hall stars of the day, Lillian Carmen and George Elliott, had recorded *Ukuleles* and it went on to sell 150,000 records and even more copies of sheet music. It was Jimmy Kennedy's first 'hit'. Soon, he was listening to something that was entirely his own – words and music – on the radio. What a thrill! Broadcasting was still new – the BBC was less than five years old – so to hear a song live on air would have been hugely impressive to him and his theatrical friends. I have no doubt that he entertained more than one young actress-to-be to a nice dinner on the expectation of his first royalty cheque.

*Hear the Ukuleles sold 150,000 records and even more copies of sheet music in 1929 but only made money for the publisher.*

Full of hope and expectation, he once more went up to Scott's offices to find out how much he was likely to earn from the success of *Ukuleles*. But he was in for another shock. He was to get nothing: Scott told him the contract he had signed made over all the author's rights to him, the publisher, in exchange for £5. Despite his diffidence Jimmy Kennedy had quite a temperament. One can but imagine his mood and frustration over the next few weeks as he heard the song on the BBC, knowing that it was also being played in hotels and clubs he could not afford to go in to, imagining all the performance and sheet music royalties going into Scott's pocket, while he dined on a sandwich. And Scott did *very* well. He sold half the rights to Francis, Day & Hunter, who published and promoted the song and paid him a reputed £800 in royalties – serious money in those days.

Losing out on much needed income was bad enough but Kennedy was even more annoyed to see that Scott named himself as the composer on the printed sheet music, though he had not written a note. This was an old trick publishers used to play to gain more royalties and they continued to do so well into the record era. Getting writers to sign so-called 'phoney' contracts was also a common practice which continued for years. One publisher used to have a pile of such contracts for 'mugs' and another pile of straight contracts for 'experienced' writers. There was a lot to writing a good popular song but learning all about the business side, including the legal tricks of the trade, was almost as important. Kennedy later said that he had been naïve to sign the *Hear the Ukuleles* contract, so it was his own fault. But he never forgot the lesson he learnt from that incident. In the early days of the popular song business, there was not much protection for writers, many of whom were amateurs never likely to earn a decent living out of writing. Indeed, some still sold what they had written for a few pounds, a meal or a pint of beer – a practice going back centuries – and did not even think about long-term royalties: hence the expression, 'Going for a song.' A man called Charles Sloman, who turned out a few hits not long before that time, actually advertised his song 'poems' at 'Five shillings for 20 lines, and three pence after that.' The Copyright Act of 1911 improved and extended protection for writers because, among other things, it covered recorded music. Soon after, in 1914, the Performing Right Society was set up to collect royalties from live performances. However, in 1927, when Jimmy Kennedy started out, there was still much further to go to fully protect and remunerate writers for their creative efforts. It was still early days for authors and composers in the music business.

Nearly everybody thinks they can write a popular song. It looks so easy! My father used to buy an occasional pound of sausages in London's Smithfield market, where meat was cheap but good, to take home for his supper. There he became friendly with a stallholder, who confessed that he hated being a butcher and that he really wanted to become a songwriter. He had done well in the meat trade, he argued, why not Tin Pan Alley? My father takes up the story:

It was December 1927, just before my first Christmas in London, and I was so badly broke that I hadn't sufficient money to go home to Ireland or to buy a present. But the meat merchant came to my rescue by buying a half share in a musical comedy song I had written called *P'liceman! P'liceman!* For £10! That was enough for me to go home for Christmas, buy presents and a badly needed overcoat. Meanwhile, possibly spurred on by his investment in my song, the man decided to quit his job at Smithfield to try his luck in Tin Pan Alley. Alas, he did not last long. Within months he had lost everything trying to buy up other people's songs without having a clue about the business.

Whilst this was happening, I was trying, among other things, to sell *P'liceman! P'liceman!* 18 months went by and still I had not been able to persuade anyone to take it. Then came a stroke of luck. One of the gramophone companies liked it and offered to record it. Six months later, when I opened my first royalties letter, there was a cheque for £48, a vast sum for me at that time.

Among the first things I did was to hurry round to Smithfield to see if my meat merchant friend had gone back to his trade and pay him his share. After all, it was thanks to his kindness and confidence in me that I had managed to survive. When I went along to his old stall, I found that it was now occupied by another firm and the people there told me that he had left the meat business altogether and gone to Southampton, though no-one had his address. I made exhaustive inquiries to find him and eventually tracked him down via the phone book and was very pleased to be able to post the £24, his share of the profits. He had got another job by then but wrote back later to say how touched he was that I had remembered how he had helped.

As Jimmy Kennedy, the meat merchant and many more amateur and professional aspiring songwriters struggled to get their material accepted by publishers, three important technological changes, which were to have a dramatic influence on how music was disseminated and how people listened to it, were taking place in the entertainment world – radio broadcasting, sound film, and records. Although live music in theatres, dance halls and other places of entertainment, continued to be the most important route for music to reach the public, these three new technologies started a revolution affecting millions from the early 1920s.

The BBC began radio broadcasting in 1922 and gradually attracted big audiences, many of whom did much more than sit and listen. Thousands rolled back their living room carpets to party and dance at home to the latest hot sounds broadcast live by their favourite bands. Instead of reaching perhaps a couple of hundred people at a local palais, broadcasting meant the top bands could now reach hundreds of thousands via the airways, making them more influential and important to music publishers and writers than ever before.

Films had been silent (often with musical accompaniment) up until the 1920s, but momentous change took place after feature films with synchronised speech, music and sound effects came in during the mid 1920s. *The Jazz Singer*, starring Al Jolson, was perhaps the most famous of these and it marked the beginning of a revolution in the motion picture industry and had a profound effect on entertainment as a whole. The public loved the new American and British 'talkies', and going to the cinema soon became a regular and affordable form of entertainment for millions. It opened up huge new possibilities for Tin Pan Alley writers and publishers and there was quite a scramble to satisfy the huge demand for songs for the new medium.

At the same time, gramophone sales began to take off as people competed to be the first to play and dance to their favourite songs at home. Though classical and traditional music still dominated the genre – Beecham conducting Elgar, for example (The biggest-selling British record of the period and the first million-seller was Mendelssohn's *Oh for the Wings of a Dove* in 1926), as the 1920s progressed, popular music record sales increased rapidly. But the Depression drastically slowed sales for all but the well off. Millions of people were out of work at that time and had little enough cash to feed their families, let alone buy gramophones and records. So record companies had to wait nearly 20 years, until the early 1950s, before they came to truly dominate the music industry. Meanwhile, sheet music kept up strong sales through the decade and continued as the main way for songwriters and publishers to earn royalties, something they did not complain about since the royalty percentages were better than they were for records. Some of the world's most popular and enduring standards and some of the best shows of all time were produced in those years.

# 5: Lyrics make the difference

In general, the lyrics of individual commercial popular songs in the 1920s and 1930s were more important than they were in later years. People sang words when they listened to the wireless or danced at the local palais, when they gathered round the front room piano or when they joined in community singing at the seaside. And when they did so, they wanted simple, memorable, words. Fortunately, this was Jimmy Kennedy's speciality and he used it for quite a long time to earn some money – though barely enough to live on – dashing off lyrics on a freelance basis to the music of other people. But it was just enough to make him think he could do better if he moved closer to the centre of London, nearer to the action. So he left his Brixton lodgings and moved to a flat at 25, Cambridge Gardens, Ladbroke Grove, a fairly cheap area near Portobello Road, the long winding lane filled with a market famous for antiques and bric-à-brac, low-priced clothes and food. I am sure he used to saunter past the shops and stalls, joking and chatting with the owners and got to know many of them well. He had an interest in history and antiques – and in bargains – so the tremendous variety of items on display would have fascinated him. My guess is that this interest and his cheerful personality were probably why he was offered some part-time work on one of the market stalls, an offer he accepted to help supplement his earnings. From there he graduated to renting his own stall on a Saturday, the biggest day for the market – and a day when music publishers did not work! He sold household items such as glass, crockery, cutlery and smaller items of furniture which he bought from dealers or house clearance sales and auctions. It was a tight operation because he had little capital and I do not think he made much money. Eighty years on I still have a collection of some of his unsold glassware and crockery.

The fun of buying and selling seems to have stimulated his entrepreneurial spirit because at around the same time he started a stamp collecting service, Kennedy Enterprises, following in the footsteps of his mother Anna, who was a keen collector and reputed possessor of a Penny Black. He mailed packs of mint stamps to collectors 'on approval'. If they liked them, they would pay for them. If not, all they had to do was to send them back in a pre-paid envelope. But most people kept the stamps, whether they wanted them or not, and did not return anything. Faced with a loss, Jimmy soon gave up. A third enterprise was more closely linked to his writing abilities, a monthly magazine to which he gave the rather grand Kiplingesque title, *The Empire*. He thought there might be a market for the publication because the British Empire still existed at that time and there was a huge civil service devoted to it, one he had almost joined when he passed his colonial service exams a few years earlier. He prepared a launch edition of *The Empire*, designing a full-scale mock-up with articles, appropriate diagrams and photos, and hawked it round periodical and book publishers. But no one was interested.

Along with these unsuccessful money-making attempts, he kept up his regular tramp to Soho, maybe in the rain or in pea-soup London fog, to knock on the doors of music publishers. On a typical day, he would leave his rooms in Cambridge Gardens with a briefcase full of brand new songs, walk nearly a mile down Portobello Road to Notting Hill Gate and get a tube or catch a bus to the end of Tottenham Court Road. From there, Denmark Street and the other publishers in the area would be only a short walk away. After a fortifying cup of tea he would then steel himself for his first visit, knock on the door, go up the stairs with optimism but a beating heart and try and talk his way into seeing a publisher or at least a publisher's demonstration pianist or musical director. Publishers might have up to eight or ten rehearsal rooms, supposedly soundproofed, all with a piano manned by these musical doormen so if you could persuade one of them that you had a song that could become a hit he might play it to the publisher in person and get a favourable decision for you. Jimmy Kennedy was joined in his quest by many other writers, some successful, some in the same position as he was, chain smoking nervously before knocking on the same doors. This is how he described the scene:

...Performing artists would be there, too, along with recording company representatives and the all-important arrangers for the dance bands – each looking for good new material. The performers, in particular, were constantly on the lookout for something novel and exclusive to show off their talents so the writers would often try to speak to them personally without a publisher getting in the way, in the hope they could sell them a song directly. Artists wanted songs for the pantomime season and again before concert party time so they were to be found in publishers' offices at almost any time of the year. If a songwriter managed to interest them in something new they had written, they might rehearse it on the spot with one of the pianists until they knew it and this would be a key argument for getting it published. And the performers might come from anywhere in the world. I remember Fats Waller coming into a studio when I was at Feldman's. He wasn't looking for a song: he had plenty of his own. He was just enjoying himself and the atmosphere. I remember him putting a bottle of gin on the top of the piano and playing all afternoon. He didn't get up until the bottle was finished – but what a player! The sound proofing in the studios was very minimal, so you can imagine the noise! Especially when the windows were open! All those pianos mingling with the voices of composers and artists singing their latest with conviction and hope, as if their lives depended on it! The background roar of the traffic with the guttural growl of the red London buses and the hoot-tooting of the taxicabs must have provided a uniquely discordant counterpoint. Tin pans might have sounded quite harmonious by comparison!

Everybody followed the band leaders and their favourite performers, but few people outside the music business knew much about the songwriters who wrote the numbers they played, even though they had a higher profile than now because their names were on the sheet music. Something which would make them stand out from many writers of today was their relatively well-dressed formality: suits, ties, hats, perhaps a rolled umbrella. Their dress code gave them a respectable air – reflected in much of the material they produced. In addition to professional songwriters and musicians, Tin Pan Alley was home to many hopeful amateurs ranging from the song writing meat merchant through to people like lawyers or teachers – slices of society from all walks of life. What they had in common was the belief that they could write a hit. But where did they come from? What were they like?

Some were already established and the most successful even managed to combine writing with publishing which meant they owned the copyrights of the songs they produced and could reap far greater rewards than writers on their own. Lawrence Wright, for example, was respected as a founding father of Tin Pan Alley. But before he opened up his business in Denmark Street, he had sold sheet music from a market stall in Leicester where he also used to entertain customers by playing the latest best sellers on a piano next to his stall. After his move to London, he wrote big 1920s hits, such as *Wyoming* and

*Babette*, both of which sold a million copies. Other big successes included *Shepherd of the Hills* and *Say a Little Prayer for Me.* He also had a flair for publicity stunts. Once he flew members of Jack Hylton's band around Blackpool Tower in a light aeroplane showering people underneath with sheet music copies of a new song, *Me and Jane in a Plane.*

Jimmy Campbell and Reg Connelly also combined writing and publishing. Their road to success had started in 1925 with *Show Me the Way to Go Home.* No one was interested in the song when they first hawked it round publishers of the day, so they borrowed enough money – £10, so it is said – and published it themselves. It went on to sell an incredible two million copies of sheet music, making today's equivalent of £30,000, more than enough to set up Campbell, Connelly & Co, a firm my father was to work with a decade later. Two other worldwide best sellers of theirs from around this time were *Good Night Sweetheart* (with Ray Noble) and *Try a Little Tenderness* (with Harry Woods).

A well known writer – though not a publisher – was Tolchard Evans, a close friend of Jimmy Kennedy's brother, Hamilton, whose most famous song was *Lady of Spain* (1931). Evans's first job was as an office boy in Lawrence Wright's publishing firm. He also had a spell as a cinema pianist. His highly-successful composing career went on into the 1950s, finishing with *My September Love* (1956), a flourish that earned him a song writing Ivor Novello award. According to my father, some people found it hard to pronounce his Christian name, so they called him 'Tortured' (though his songs were anything but). Others called him 'Tolch'. He regularly teamed up with Stanley Damerell, an ex-army officer, and Ralph Butler. The trio were one of the leading song writing teams of the period. Contemporary newspaper cuttings describe Butler as a plump, red-faced, jovial man who invariably greeted people 'Hallo laddie, how are you?'

His first job had been a bank clerk but, so he said, did not see the fun in looking after other people's money, so decided to make some himself. He tried his hand as an actor but, the story goes, someone threw a cabbage at him, so he went into farming! After that failed, he wrote a song about the incident called *Down on Misery Farm* and its success encouraged him to take up song writing full-time.

Harry Leon was another leading writer. His first job had been in a hat factory in the east end of London. Then he ran away to sea, working on oil tankers, tramp steamers, whalers – doing just about anything to earn a wage. When he came back, he found various jobs as a pianist and got into the music business that way. He wrote Gracie Field's biggest hit, *Sally,* with Leo Towers. Harry and Leo never got on and were always quarrelling, dissolving their partnership and then getting together again, but they were very successful during the 1930s. Unfortunately for Harry, he sold his interest in *Sally* for £30 and then had to spend the rest of his life listening to it gathering in royalties for other people. Top Alley lyric writer Tommie Connor, best known, perhaps, for later writing the lyrics for the Second World War hit, *Lili Marlene,* started as a 16-year-old call boy in the Theatre Royal, Drury Lane, before becoming a ship's steward for a few years. Then, like Jimmy Kennedy, he spent five years trying to get his songs accepted by publishers. He said that he was eventually successful because he was so persistent. He just kept going back with more and more new songs and ideas, which was exactly Kennedy's philosophy. Tommie Connor had many other big hits including *I Saw Mommy Kissing Santa Claus* and *The Chestnut Tree* (with Jimmy and Hamilton Kennedy).

But there was such a throng milling around the Tin Pan Alley hub. Take Eltom Box and Desmond Cox, unmistakeable because both were about 6 feet 4 inches tall. Their hits included comedy numbers such as *Horsey,*

*Horsey* and *In the Quartermaster's Stores*. Box had been a lumberjack in Canada and Cox a mining engineer who had prospected for gold in Australia. The pair tramped Tin Pan Alley for three years before they had any luck. Then there was Paddy Roberts, who wrote some great songs on his own but had a well-known partnership with Box and Cox. Roberts was a qualified barrister who had sailed to England from South Africa in a 40-foot ketch, a journey that took three and a half months. He continued his long career into the 1950s with UK hits such as *Softly, Softly* and *The Ballad of Bethnal Green*. But there were many more…

Of those who were more on the fringe of Tin Pan Alley and so not central to this book, perhaps five should be mentioned because, in addition to their huge successes on stage and screen, they had enduring popular song hits. Most famous were Noel Coward and Ivor Novello both of whom wrote dozens of world-famous songs but mainly for the stage. Vivian Ellis (*Spread a little Happiness, This is My Lovely Day*), a classically trained pianist and composer who wrote musical comedies, was also among the most popular composers of the era, though his output was less recorded than might be expected. Then there was Eric Maschwitz (*These Foolish Things, A Nightingale Sang in Berkeley Square*) and Noel Gay (*The Lambeth Walk, Leaning on a Lamp-post,* and *Run, Rabbit, Run),* who both specialized in English-style musical revues. Maschwitz also worked for the BBC. Gay, who came from a middle-class background and went up to Cambridge University, where he got a degree in music, was, like Lawrence Wright and others, wise enough – and successful enough – to set up his own publishing company.

There were also talented songwriters who worked within the music publishing business. Wally Ridley, for example, was a demonstration pianist at Feldman's in 1928, playing tunes from the firm's catalogue to music hall and radio artists. In a very long career, he collaborated with many Tin Pan Alley lyricists, including Jimmy Kennedy's early co-writer, Harry Castling. Later, he moved to Peter Maurice and then after the War had a major career on the production side of the record business.

Writers, singers, arrangers, artists and performers of all kinds would not only meet at the publishers' offices to hear and practise the latest creations. There were favourite cafés, such as The Dairy, and pubs such as The Royal George, just across Charing Cross Road from Denmark Street, or you could take your pick from scores of eating and drinking establishments in near-by Soho. My father used to say that if he had a pound for every chicken sandwich he ate sitting in one of them, it would have added up to the income from another hit. But they were good places for making contacts in those early freelance days and it was in The Royal George, he once told me, that he landed his first staff job. In 1929 he was introduced to the proprietor of a small publisher called Lareine & Co. which had offices in Green Street (now renamed Irving Street) just off Leicester Square. The company was not doing well - publishers needed hits, too - but Lareine had high hopes for it to take off into the big time. What he needed was a young professional staff songwriter who could also turn his hand to publicity and act as the firm's sales manager. Would Jimmy be interested? With the Portobello Road stall making very little money and the stamp enterprise a failure, Lareine's offer could not have come at a better time. Accepting it meant a steady job that would give him all kinds of opportunities to do more writing and at the same time make more contacts without the constant worry of where the next meal was coming from. It was also a great opportunity to learn about music publishing, especially its commercial aspects, from the inside.

Jimmy Kennedy's main job at Lareine's was to meet the demand for the film, dance and jazz songs that were then coming into fashion. In the year or so that he was with the firm he wrote about a hundred, usually words and music. The idea for one of his very first came indirectly from his girlfriend, an attractive dark-haired young woman called Peggy, who had a room in the same building as him in Cambridge Gardens. He was due to meet her for an evening drink once when, at the last minute, he was asked to rehearse film actress Mabel Poulton for songs he had co-written for her 1929 musical film, *Taxi for Two*. By the time he got to his rendezvous in Leicester Square, Peggy had been waiting outside for over an hour in the cold – at the time, women would not enter a pub or club unaccompanied. The incident gave him the title of an extra song for the film, *Little Lonely Lady:*

> *Little Lonely Lady I'm in love with you*
> *Little Lonely Lady*
> *Can't you see it's true*
> *All day long my heart sings a song about you*
> *And it seems I never have dreams without you*
> *Little Lonely Lady, say we'll never part*
> *While true love ever lives in my heart.*

The song turned out to be a rather original chat-up line and the friendship between them continued to grow. She even had a go at writing lyrics herself:

> *I may forget the sunshine*
> *I may forget the dew*
> *I may forget the folks I've met*
> *But I'll always remember you...*

I am sure my father was flattered. I expect he would also have advised her gently not to go into the music business.

At around the same time, he began to give serious thought to his image as a writer and experimented with a professional pen-name, James Bascoigne – after the supposedly French origins of the Baskins, the theory favoured by his mother. A year or so later, he had a change of mind and reverted back to Jim, sometimes Jimmy, Kennedy, but he kept the B for Bascoigne as an initial. When he joined the songwriters' royalty collecting agency, the Performing Right Society in January 1930 it was as James B. Kennedy. It was also around this time that he got to know someone who was to be his best known future collaborator, Michael Carr. Carr's family name was Cohen – though his mother was Irish – but he felt he had to camouflage his origins in those days for fear of anti-Jewish prejudice, a growing and sinister development in Europe, though less so in England. Carr's father had been a fly-weight boxing champion when he was young, moving to Dublin where he ran a restaurant called The Kitchen in the early 1920s, when Jimmy Kennedy was a student at Trinity College – though he never remembered eating there. Carr's boyhood ambition was to be a songwriter but he had a wild streak in him and before he began his assault on Tin Pan Alley he had a go at just about everything else. People used to say that in his early days he had more jobs than hits. In about 1924, he went to America where he was successively a stage-hand, an actor, a rancher in Montana, a stunt man, a morgue attendant, a bell-hop, a porter, a drug store assistant, a cook, a boxer (following in his father's pugilistic footsteps) and a pianist in a Las Vegas bar (where he was called the 'Rhyming Limey').

A favourite Carr story came from his time in Las Vegas. 'One day,' he said, 'a young singer came in to the rehearsal studios where I was working, took off his jacket, threw it on the floor and listened intently to the band, running his fingers through his hair as he did so. Then he got up and said: "Hey, you guys, you're all out of tune! Say, don't you know the music of your own songs?" No one knew who the singer was so we said: "OK, let's hear *you* sing!" As soon as he did, we realised the stranger had a special voice so I asked him: "What's your name?" The reply? "Bing Crosby"'.

*Wife-to-be Margaret (Peggy) Galpin in 1931.*

When he eventually got back to Dublin after his adventures in America, Carr's desire to get into the popular music business made him so restless that his family clubbed together to lend him £200 so that he could seek his fortune in London. Then he talked a Dublin band leader into writing an open letter of introduction praising his abilities and a few days later was in the front of the queue of the hopeful songwriters in Tin Pan Alley. Like everyone else, he found success hard to come by: 'I tried my hand at composing but was not very successful. I think I must have been kicked out of music publishers' offices at least twice a day: they were heartily sick of me.' From time to time he would drop in to Lareine's to try to sell his new material and to reminisce about Dublin with Kennedy and it seems that a relationship developed between the two men, strengthened by their shared Dublin backgrounds and the fact that Carr was mainly a musician, Kennedy more a lyricist. However, after a few months there was a falling out and Kennedy claimed in a 1936 newspaper article that Carr had been instrumental in getting him the sack. Why? He never revealed the reason. My guess is that Carr persuaded him to collaborate on a couple of songs (possibly using his Bascoigne pen-name), which he then tried to sell to a rival publisher. Though Carr also sometimes used Maurice Beresford as a pen-name, in the small world of London's Tin Pan Alley this 'initiative' may have got back to Lareine's. As it happened, the firm was losing money, so it is unlikely it would have been able to employ Kennedy for much longer. Less than a year after he left, it went into liquidation.

Commenting about Michael Carr many years later my father said that 'Michael is still rather proud of the fact that he got me the sack! He says it did me good. I am now inclined to agree. Though I was plunged back into the uncertain world of freelance writing, it spurred me on and eventually I did very well. I doubt I would have made the big time, if I had stayed where I was.' But the period immediately following his departure from Lareine's was tough. He had little luck plugging his songs – making only around £90 in 1929, mainly small advances on songs that never saw the light of day. He tried freelance journalism, sending off humorous articles to Fleet Street newspapers. But Fleet Street did not want his brand of humour. It was a year, he used to say, 'of short commons with few steak dinners and many cup-of-coffee lunches.' He worked hard to expand his portfolio to include every style he could think of so that he had something for every occasion. His facility for music hall comedy numbers stands out. He wrote many of these: *Tilly Took a Tramp in the Woods, Felix is Walking Back Again* and *They Never Go to Bed in China* (revived by Billy Cotton in the 1950s).

*Jimmy Kennedy's first hit sold half a million records thanks to recordings by Gracie Fields, Sandy Powell and Florrie Forde. It was given an unintended boost in popularity in 1930 because it was banned by the BBC's teetotal boss, John Reith.*

But though music halls were a big tradition in Britain, they were beginning to go out of fashion as the public started to go increasingly to the pictures where they became captivated by sophisticated, romantic, and usually American, film songs, a genre he was still inexperienced in writing. So it was not surprising that in the end it was not a film song that gave Jimmy Kennedy his first real success. One day, after finishing yet another depressing foray into Denmark Street, he stopped for a cup of tea in a Lyons Corner House in Oxford Street. It was not exactly the road to Damascus but he did see the light, that he should play to his strengths and write something in a style he was familiar with, and give music hall or a Blackpool-style community song a final fling. A few days later, he popped into his local in Notting Hill for a nightcap and at the end of the evening the barmaid called 'Time, Gentlemen, please!' What a punch-line for a comedy song! It was completely different from anything else at the time but was an exhortation that everybody knew! Walking back to his flat, the phrase grew into the lines of a chorus and by the time he had got there, he had worked out the bones of a tune, with an old-fashioned polka style rhythm, to fit the words. 'I decided I would have to call it *The Barmaid's Song*', he told me many years later. 'Once the idea had come to me I had this feeling that I had at last done it and that I had the makings of my first real hit. I could see it going down well with the crowds at Blackpool. I was so excited, I sat up that night until I had the whole thing finished.'

The Blackpool angle was very important because the resort was the biggest honey-pot for the entertainment business in Europe, every year attracting millions of day-trippers and holiday-makers, especially from the cotton towns of Lancashire. The town hosted all kinds of musical seaside entertainment on its three piers, in the pubs, the music halls, theatres, clubs and hotels, with everybody joining in singing from song sheets. The town was hugely important as an outlet for sheet music sales. There even used to be music demonstrations in its many music shops encouraging customers to buy the latest numbers. Several dance bands played there during the summer months. Many are now forgotten – Bertini at the Tower Ballroom, Laddie Clark at the Imperial, Larry Brennan at the Winter Gardens – to name just three. Some entertainers carried on for many years. For example, organist Reginald Dixon, still famous for *I Do Like to be Beside the Seaside*, was a household name. He played on the Wurlitzer cinema organ (which he had designed himself) at the Tower Ballroom and later had his own radio show and was still going strong thirty years later. The upshot for writers and publishers was that the resort gave their songs big exposure to millions of holiday makers so that if you had a success there, it could easily sweep the country – a kind of 'Blackpool effect'. It was the same at the other holiday resorts, such as Brighton, but none were as big as Blackpool.

With these thoughts in his mind and full of hopeful enthusiasm, Kennedy took *The Barmaid's Song* to every publisher in town. But they all turned him down. Then, following a chat with Michael Carr, he went to see Bert Feldman, head of a publishing firm with a track record in musical comedy, but who had also made his name by taking up the rights of older American songs like the turn-of-the-century *A Bird in a Gilded Cage*. That sold a million copies – a huge hit by the standards of those days. Feldman had also introduced ragtime to Britain with Irving Berlin's *Alexander's Ragtime Band* and published *If You Were the Only Girl in the World* and *It's a Long Way to Tipperary*. When Feldman saw *The Barmaid's Song*, he was lukewarm about its prospects but, said my father, realised it had possibilities because 'He immediately offered me a contract and paid me a desperately-needed royalty advance.'

It turned out to be a very good deal for both. The holiday crowds in Blackpool loved it. Soon there were recordings by Gracie Fields, Sandy Powell and Florrie Forde, selling half a million records between them and generating even higher sheet music sales. It was the hit of the 1930 summer season. The words of the chorus of *The Barmaid's Song* could not have been simpler:

*Let's all sing the barmaid's song,*
*Let's all sing the barmaid's song,*
*Let's all sing the barmaid's song,*
*'Time, Gentlemen, please!'*

Harmless words, most people would have thought, but the BBC's boss, John Reith, who considered himself the guardian of the nation's morals, saw them differently. He said the middle eight bars – *Ev'ry evening singing this refrain/Ev'ry night at ten o'clock, singing it again. Oh!* – encouraged the evils of drink and he banned it from being played by the BBC Dance Band. Though many more songs got banned by the BBC in later years, *The Barmaid's Song* may have been the first. It also had the opposite effect of that intended by Reith, encouraging more people to buy sheet music copies to play and sing on their pianos at home. As the sales went up, the royalties started to roll in and Feldman and Kennedy laughed all the way to the bank.

There was a properly drawn up contract for *The Barmaid's Song* so Kennedy got a fair share of royalties by the standards of the day. But what was in the contract that he signed? The brief original contract below, on Feldman's headed notepaper, was a typical example of how (little) songwriters used to be paid:

Having this day (2 October 1929) purchased from you the Copyright in your composition entitled *The Barmaid's Song*, we agree to pay you royalties at the following rates on copies sold by us:

£1 per thousand sold of sixpence edition (250 copies to be free samples),

12 shillings and sixpence per thousand sold of Foreign Colonial or American editions,

25% of the amount received by us in respect of Mechanical reproductions [i.e. records].

Signed B. Feldman and Co

By my calculations, Feldman grossed 25 times as much as the author on the half million sheet music sales alone – £12,500 compared with £500 for Jimmy Kennedy. Even allowing for the printing and publishing costs, not a bad profit! Even so, having earned only around £90 in 1929, *The Barmaid's Song* rocketed Kennedy's income in 1930 to £600, enough for him to feel that he had at last arrived. From now on publishers knew Kennedy had the talent to write a genuine hit song, essential recognition if he was to succeed as a freelance or get another salaried job in the industry.

Lyons, in whose famous Corner House on Oxford Street he had begun to get the germ of the idea for a Blackpool-style song, leapt onto the bandwagon of its popularity and used it in a company press advert: *Let's all sing the tea-time song/Let's all sing the tea-time song/Let's all sing the tea-time song/More Lyons Swiss Rolls!*

# 6: Blazing Away into the music business

Bert Feldman now asked Jimmy Kennedy to write an English lyric for an Austrian tune, a Continental tango which he called *Oh! Donna Clara*. It quickly became a British best seller and has continued to earn royalties ever since. Shortly after that he wrote the lyrics for what was later to become among the most famous of all children's songs, *The Teddy Bears' Picnic*.

There is quite a history to how and why teddy bears became so popular. Modern stuffed teddy bears were made at the beginning of the 20th century in both Germany and the United States, though there are examples of stuffed bears which considerably pre-date this. However, the first commercial American bear and the 'teddy bear' name was inspired by the story of President Theodore (Teddy) Roosevelt, who, when visiting the state of Mississippi to sort out a border dispute in 1902, was invited to a bear hunt. The hunt was not a success – only one old bear was found. The President's hosts, however, captured it, tied it to a tree and invited the President to shoot it and claim a trophy. He refused and the story of the incident got out to the American papers. Various articles and cartoons sympathetic to Roosevelt were published illustrating the incident, including a cartoon in *The Washington Post* in November 1902. The story captured the imagination of the public and inspired the wife of the owner of a Brooklyn novelty shop to make a couple of stuffed bears and put them on sale in her shop window. Both were snapped up immediately by customers. Sensing there might be a demand for more, she and her husband started the first mass production teddy bear manufacturing company in America – having got the President's permission to call them 'Teddy's bears' (they soon dropped the apostrophe). At around the same time, the German stuffed toy manufacturer Steiff also cashed in on the idea, manufacturing more finely-crafted upmarket teddy bears, some of which were also exported to America. It was not long before there was a worldwide teddy bear craze, so much so that Roosevelt used teddy bears as part of his campaign publicity when he ran for re-election in 1905.

Composers – and lyric writers – frequently got ideas for their works from actual events, just like cartoonists. American composer John W. Bratton used the popular teddy bear idea for a topical instrumental composition which he called *The Teddy Bears' Picnic*. The music was published in 1907, during Roosevelt's second presidential term, and soon became a popular standard for bands and light orchestras. In Britain, the music was often used in pantomimes where its element of mystery made it ideal for announcing the entry of the giant, ogre or some other 'baddie'. When Jimmy Kennedy was starting his career, pantomime producers used to join writers and artists milling around Tin Pan Alley music publishers to look for good material for the coming Christmas season. These producers were very influential because successful pantomime songs by popular performers sold lots of sheet music and could easily be taken up by the bands. Late in 1930, one of them came up with the idea of writing words to the Bratton *Teddy Bears' Picnic* tune. Feldman did not see commercial prospects in the idea but asked Jimmy Kennedy to do a lyric, gratis. The whisper in the Alley was that Feldman was thinking of setting up a very desirable new post in his firm as lyric editor so, hoping he might get the job, Kennedy treated the assignment seriously. His main idea was to appeal to children but make it fun for grown-ups as well:

*If you go down in the woods today*
*You're sure of a big surprise.*
*If you go down in the woods today*
*You'd better go in disguise.*
*For ev'ry Bear that ever there was*
*Will gather there for certain, because,*
*Today's the day the Teddy Bears have their picnic...*

The first-ever performance using the lyric is believed to have been in a Manchester panto around Christmas 1930. After that it went into a desk drawer somewhere in the Feldman building. That did not matter to Jimmy Kennedy because Feldman gave him the lyric editor job on the strength of it anyway. A permanent job with a top publisher now gave him real security for the first time since he had arrived in London, a basic salary of around £7 a week (which has to be multiplied by over 50 to get any idea of its value today) and, more importantly, first choice to go through a constant stream of material sent in by Continental publishers – from waltzes, marches and polkas to tangos, foxtrots and other styles, including ballads, children's or novelty songs – whatever was in vogue at any moment. As the daily post bag arrived, Jimmy, sitting in his Charing Cross Road office, would sift through his in-tray looking for a hidden gem to turn into the next Tin Pan Alley sensation. He would have the original lyrics and titles of anything that looked interesting translated, pick out the tunes on the piano, and try to think up a catchy new idea. Then he would rewrite it with a new lyric and, where needed, a new musical arrangement. It was not long before he was supplying a stream of new material that was broadcast regularly, played by bands up and down the country and sold plenty of sheet music. Just what Feldman was looking for! And it was a big boost to Jimmy Kennedy's income because he earned royalties on everything he wrote. At the same time, he soon found himself involved in other aspects of the business including publicising the whole Feldman publishing catalogue and helping on the technical side as a copyist for orchestral and band parts.

Though about 3,000 popular songs were published each year in London in the early 1930s, less than 100 were best sellers. Feldman and Kennedy were in a business that was outwardly one of charm, humour and romance but under the surface it was tough and competitive and only the strongest survived. There was a lot of hard selling to do. Jimmy Kennedy threw himself into the commercial side of publishing as editor and author of the firm's monthly publicity magazine, *Feldmanism*, with relish. The journal was sent out to bandleaders, performers, record company producers (there were more than 20 record companies in London, some of them still producing wax cylinder rolls) as well as to the retail trade and others connected with the business. It promoted the firm's latest sheet music and recordings, together with snippets about the music business, background stories, jokes and gossip – an opportunity Kennedy also shamelessly used to plug his personal output on which he also earned royalties. The March 1931 edition, for example, starts with a puff for his adaptation of *Oh! Donna Clara:* 'This is the slack season of the year,' he wrote, 'but nothing can stop the demand for, *Oh! Donna Clara*...it's the most popular hit of the day and proving a success with a host of band leaders including Jack Payne, Billy Cotton, Herman Darewski, Sid Bright, Henry Hall, Jerry Hoey and many more...Feldman hits are world hits!' And, again, 'Cecil Hurn, whose popular band broadcasts from the Esplanade Hotel, Porthcawl, writes in glowing terms of *Oh! Donna Clara*, which he says is stupendous as either a fox-trot or a tango...' Then, there is a reference to the early song part-financed by the Smithfields meat merchant: 'Al Tabor, the wonder leader, now playing at Cricklewood Palais de Danse with his famous Transatlantic Band, specialises in making a novel presentation of comedy numbers. His present hit (which has been running for some time) is *P'liceman! P'liceman! Hold my Hand* and Mr Tabor introduces many novel effects, including a comedy policeman. Needless to say, the show is a riot (of fun) and Mr Tabor's fans include North London *en masse*.' *Feldmanism* also included the following story: 'A news item, headlined "Still Going Strong" reads as follows: "*Let's both sing the Barmaid's Song* was the concluding sentence of a letter found on a burglar convicted recently in Winchester. Sentencing him, Mr Justice Swift remarked that it would be a long time before he heard *The Barmaid's Song* again. For him, *Time – Gentlemen, please!* has taken on a new meaning." We sympathise with Jimmy Kennedy in the loss of one of his fans.' Then, a plug for another Kennedy adaptation, *Blaze Away*: 'A newspaper states that the London Fire Brigade successfully extinguishes every big blaze. Let them try stopping *Blaze Away*!'

They seemed to be innocent, almost carefree days. But in the background was the most serious economic recession Britain had ever experienced. This is occasionally reflected in some of the items which have the common theme of 'Keep your chin up – things can only get better':

The coming winter season has not been looked forward to by many bandsmen, but the trend of recent events appears to be towards more prosperous times. After all, political events have really very little bearing upon the affairs of the band world. Our personal opinion is that at a time of crisis, musical fare is more essential than ever and we should not be surprised to see dance halls and similar venues doing enormous business this winter. During the War, in spite of all our troubles and hardships, we danced and sang. It will be the same now.

A job with such wide scope gave Jimmy Kennedy the chance to learn about almost everything connected with the industry. *Feldmanism* is full of comment, advice and exhortation:

To the hypercritical few who turn up their noses at six-eights may we remind them that they are expected to please the public – *not themselves*! It is the bands featuring commercial programmes that get the jobs nowadays. Such leaders have a fan mail! – while 'hot merchants' are left cold!... .

Some little time ago there was a quite a spate of interviews with persons supposed to have superior knowledge of popular music. And one and all of those knowledgeable chaps stated boldly that the life of a popular song was three months. As we said at the time, it all depends on the song and the manner of handling it. The continued popularity of *I'm Alone Because I Love You* [a Feldman song] after more than six months of public favour and the continued steady sales of this number, both in sheet music and gramophone records, is one instance of the success of our system...

We feel certain that it is not in any band's interest, and it is against public desire, to ring the changes too frequently. Listeners like to 'get hold' of a tune and, having done so, they are pleased to hear it again. After all, most people prefer to hear a good tune played on 20 occasions rather than 20 different songs played once each. *And there are far more poor tunes than good ones...*

We are convinced that while fox-trots are fine to dance to, the great stronghold of melody is the waltz...also to get away from the sameness of the average fox-trot which in many cases suffers from over-orchestration in which melody and tone-colour are frequently sacrificed in order that as many changes of instrument and other variations can be introduced...Discerning readers will have noticed that many crack American bands are turning to waltzes and even hillbillies in their search for melodic freshness...

Jimmy Kennedy's new job at Feldman's was featured in the October 1931 edition of the music business journal *Metronome.* Under the heading of 'B. Feldman signs J. Kennedy' is the paragraph: 'Kennedy has acquired the knack of writing like American lyricists and is capable of turning out a good hillbilly. He did several of this type for the recording companies in London. Feldman vouches for the fact that Kennedy at one sitting turned out 36 ditties for the Crystalate Record Company which sold in large quantities in the Woolworth Stores. Kennedy, an Irishman, looks like the best coming writer of English lyrics in England.'

A song my father wrote in 1931, *The Twilight Waltz,* gave him a more than usual feeling of nostalgia. It was a new version of *A Rose that has Faded Away,* the sad and sentimental waltz that had welled up in his romantic imagination when he fell for a local Coagh girl as a 16-year-old boy. Things were a lot different now and she was 10,000 miles away: 'I used to get a lot of mail from aspiring writers, fans and so on, and along with these came a letter from her, quite out of the blue, from Australia. Apparently she had been hearing my songs over there on the radio and that reminded her of our teenage years. "Do you remember the song we used to dance to together when we were 16?" she wrote. It inspired me to write a completely new version, one which evoked those teenage memories: *Lights are low while it's playing/ Hearts aglow as we're swaying/ And we'll know the bliss of a sweet stolen kiss/ In The Twilight Waltz.* When the song was recorded, it became the ballroom waltz of the season, so I sent her a record and she wrote to tell me she played it a lot. I wonder if her husband ever knew why!'

1931 continued to be a very productive year for Jimmy Kennedy as he settled into his new job at Feldman's. Not all the music was from Continental Europe: a couple of interesting tunes came from America, including *Blaze Away,* a world-famous military march composed by Abe Holzmann in 1901. Kennedy wrote a straightforward chorus to the tune:

*We'll make a bonfire of our troubles*
*And we'll watch them blaze away*
*And when they've all gone up in smoke clouds*
*We'll never worry should they come another day.*
*And as the bonfire keeps on burning,*
*Happy days will be returning,*
*While the band keeps playing,*
*We'll let our troubles blaze away.*

But the fact that it was a march written for the instruments of a military band meant that it was hard to write a lyric suitable for the human voice and the awkward trio in the middle required nifty vocalisation:

*Start and throw them right into the fire*
*Watch the flames going higher and higher:*
*Blazing away, blazing away,*
*So come along bring your worries round today.*

With its new lyric, the march sold well when it was first published in 1931 but it sold even more records nearly a quarter of a century later when the great Irish tenor and entertainer Josef Locke recorded it in 1955.

*Blaze Away, an American march with a Jimmy Kennedy
lyric, later made famous by Irish entertainer
Josef Locke.*

Jimmy Kennedy also had a go at beating the Americans
at their own game by writing what was claimed to be the
first British hillbilly best seller, *In the Mountains of the
Pine.* Meanwhile, partly to increase the firm's output of
material for performers in live variety and music hall,
Feldman got him to team up with Harry Castling, who,
in addition to writing *Just Like the Ivy*, had also penned

a music hall smash called *Let's all go down the Strand* and many others of that ilk. Castling died only two years later, in 1933, so the association between the writers was short. However, their output was recorded by most of the early 1930s music hall stars, including Florrie Forde and Ella Retford. One of their most-played collaborations was a popular comedy song called *Oh! Nicholas (Don't Be So Ridiculous)*, which was recorded by comedian Tommy Trinder in 1938 and Billy Cotton in the 1950s. The idea came, indirectly, from Bert Feldman himself (though he never realised it!). Despite being nearly 60, Bert was having an affair with an attractive young actress called Nita Croft, who used to visit him in his private office at work. One day Kennedy popped up to see him to talk over some ideas about a comedy lyric he was writing and, forgetting to knock, he accidentally walked in on them in a 'romantic embrace.' To cover his embarrassment, he read out the lyric and jokingly asked Feldman if he had any ideas for a title. Before Feldman could reply, Nita Croft said: 'What about "I don't like it in the day time!"' My father was amused by the *double entendre* and it became the punch line of the chorus:

*Oh! Nicholas! Don't be so ridiculous!*
*'Cos I don't like it in the day time!*

# 7: *The Teddy Bears' Picnic*

In the bustle of the office, *The Teddy Bears' Picnic* lyric was still lying forgotten in the desk drawer where it had been filed after the Manchester pantomime the year before. It might never have been heard of again but for band leader Henry Hall, (known by everybody in the music business as 'HH'), who had taken over from Jack Payne as the conductor of the influential BBC Dance Orchestra in 1932. He had a programme which went out at the peak hour of 5.15 p.m., a time when children might be listening, usually with their mothers. Henry Hall wanted to play something to interest both audiences but did not have anything he liked in his repertoire so he despatched his arranger, Tony Lowery, to talk to the publishers in Denmark Street to see if he could find something suitable. When Lowery got to Feldman's, he went to see Jimmy Kennedy who racked his brains but could think of nothing until he remembered *The Teddy Bears' Picnic* lyric. Showing it to Lowery, he said as a joke that Feldman was going to promote it. Lowery knew the J.W. Bratton tune but not the unpublished words. However, he thought HH might like them and took away a copy to show him. Without saying anything to Feldman or his lyric editor, he also did a new musical arrangement that night to go with the words and this brand new version was on Henry Hall's rostrum the next morning. HH loved it. So much, in fact, that he broadcast it live the same day – to several hundred thousand BBC listeners. The whole process had taken less than 24 hours.

Jimmy Kennedy knew nothing about the new musical arrangement or the broadcast and had not thought it necessary to tell Feldman he had given the lyric to Lowery.

He was about to learn a painful lesson. Within minutes of Henry Hall's broadcast, the phones started ringing at the BBC and Feldman's asking for sheet music and records of *The Teddy Bears' Picnic*. The calls intensified the next day. Some came directly to the office and some were passed on by the BBC, where the switchboard was jammed. Then came telegrams and numerous personal and trade calls to the office. Feldman wanted to know what was going on and who had given permission for HH to broadcast the song before it had even been published or any sheet music had been printed. He had thousands of orders but no immediate way of meeting them. He also had no deal with the American publishers of the J. W. Bratton music score. It meant he would have to do a special print run, rush out copies and hold back other work – with no guarantee that *The Teddy Bears' Picnic* would end up being profitable. The upshot was that instead of being praised for his initiative, Jimmy Kennedy was reprimanded and Feldman refused to give him a contract for the lyrics. That meant no credit for it on the sheet music and no royalties.

Kennedy was naturally disappointed and upset but he had to accept the situation. If he had argued too much, he might have lost his job. He did not know if the lyric would be a success either. Most children's songs lasted a season and that was that. It took a few months and then a few more before he realised that *The Teddy Bears' Picnic* wasn't just a children's pot-boiler, but a song in a million. Henry Hall's recording, made on 28 September 1932, was the most famous he ever made, selling between three and four million records by the end of the decade. Kennedy commented a few years later: 'Tony Lowery did a marvellous arrangement of the song that the publisher never wanted to publish and it became a national favourite. It is still Henry Hall's most requested song, as popular as Little Miss Muffet.' Despite its success, Feldman's refusal to pay royalties or acknowledge Jimmy Kennedy's authorship meant that no one at the time knew he had written the lyric which made the tune famous. People thought both words and music had come from John W. Bratton's pen. It was not until 14 years later, after Feldman died in 1945, that the new boss at Feldman's, Eddie Firmani, righted the wrong and gave Jimmy Kennedy a contract. By this time, though still a big standard, the song had peaked and he lost out on thousands of pounds of royalties. He once told the story to band leader Frank Chacksfield on a Canadian radio show: 'Why didn't you sue?' said Frank. 'I hadn't been to New York in those days!' my father riposted.

Henry Hall's recording of Tony Lowery's arrangement was so well regarded by engineers at the BBC that for many years hundreds of special copies were pressed for use as a sound test recording. There have been many other versions – Bing Crosby recorded it twice – but everybody knows the Henry Hall recording. When I was going through my father's papers, I came across what purports to be a version by Noel Coward, written in the late 1950s when Teddy Boys were in fashion:

*If you go down in the woods today,*
*You'd better go in disguise,*
*With drainpipe trews – and fancy shoes*
*And something intense in ties.*
*Don't bother to wash – it's sure to rain*
*But take your cosh and bicycle chain*
*For this is the day the Teddy Boys have their picnic.*

I don't suppose Coward got any royalties for that either!

There are now numerous original 'productions' of *Teddy Bears' Picnic* on YouTube and in other corners of the internet, many accompanied by very creative animations – including cartoons and films, some of which are very funny. A member of an internet blog (Jarvis Cocker's) forum is quoted as saying that when he was a child he thought it was the scariest children's' song ever! Jimmy Kennedy would have been amused.

Apart from the contretemps over *The Teddy Bears' Picnic*, Jimmy Kennedy's first three years with Feldman's went very well. His income rose steadily so much so that he felt sufficiently secure to marry the girl he had almost stood up when he was at Lareine's and who had inspired *Little Lonely Lady.* Peggy Galpin and Jimmy Kennedy were married by the family friend who had helped him find his first flat in Brixton, the vicar of St Augustine's Church, Tooting, on 11 June 1932.

*The Teddy Bears' Picnic* incident showed what little protection song writers had, an important reason why they also had to monitor their affairs personally – there was no one else to do it. They listened to broadcasts and live performances of their work and checked sheet music and record sales and royalty payments. I recently came across an early letter to Jimmy Kennedy from the Performing Right Society (PRS) which illustrates how closely he was monitoring the performances of everything he had written. Dated 4 October 1931, it said:

'With reference to our telephone conversation yesterday afternoon, when you informed us that your composition, *Song of the Fly* was broadcast on 12th of January last (National Programme) and the 14th January (London Regional), on referring to the programme in question, we find that these songs are duly shown, but unfortunately no composer's name was given and as you notified this composition under the title of *The Fly Song*, we were naturally unable to trace it. However, credit has now been given to you in respect of these performances and will appear as an adjustment in our next Distribution of Broadcasting Fees.'

The lyrics of *Blaze Away* and another less important song, *Serenade*, were also not credited to Jimmy Kennedy in a royalty statement from the PRS at the time. When he tackled the Society about this, it said it would check with Feldman's to ascertain that he really had written the lyrics. Then it wrote back to say: 'Feldman's have notified us that you have indeed written the lyrics and you will be duly credited with the fees. In the case of *Blaze Away*, this will be, as you say, the full author's share.'

Late in 1933, the budding songwriter's hard work scripting lyrics for continental imports gave him his first world hit. His ballad *Play To Me, Gipsy*, based on a continental tango written by Karel Vacek, sold over a million sheet music copies and more than a million records.

Lyrics of the 1930s look simple. In fact most people then (and probably now) thought they could do as well or better than the professionals, given the chance. This gave pianist Billy Mayerl, who also wrote for *Melody Maker*, the idea for a regular column inviting amateurs to submit songs they had composed themselves for him to comment on professionally. The idea was that the best would be offered to a publisher and this would set the would-be songwriter on the road to fame and fortune. Mayerl expected he would be sent ten songs a week, enough for an interesting weekly feature. In the event, he was deluged by hundreds of manuscripts. He was so overwhelmed, he could not cope and had to abandon the idea after just three weeks. What were most of the songs like? 'Terrible!' said Mayerl. 'That's the other reason I had to abandon the column!' Writing a catchy tune with a simple lyric was harder than it seemed. The British popular song format of that time made it difficult to be original, something that David Day of Francis, Day & Hunter used to joke about. When asked by an enthusiastic writer if he liked his new song, he replied, 'Like it? I've *always* liked it!

*Jimmy Kennedy's marriage to Margaret (Peggy) Galpin at St Augustine's Church, Tooting, London, on 11th June 1932.*

# 8: Controversy over a golden ring

*Picture courtesy of the Grosz family*
*Dr Wilhelm Grosz collaborated with Jimmy Kennedy on
many famous songs, including Red Sails in the Sunset.*

In 1934 a Jewish artistic director and composer from Vienna called Dr. Wilhelm Grosz arrived at Feldman's offices in Shaftesbury Avenue. Not a typical Tin Pan Alley type at all, Grosz had a considerable reputation in his native Austria for light classical compositions. Four years earlier he had written music for the German translation of a cycle known as the *Afrika-Songs*. Most of the lyrics for these had been written by Langston Hughes, the black American poet from Joplin, Missouri, and came from a book of poems he had published in 1926 called *The Weary Blues*. Grosz's music needed a large chamber orchestra with jazz capability, including a saxophone, trumpet, trombone, sousaphone and jazz percussion – very different from a normal big band line-up.

Grosz had many other compositions to his name and he had also been director of the Ultraphone Gramophone Company in Berlin. After the Nazis came to power in 1933, he knew he had to get out of Germany and so returned to Vienna. There he continued his successful musical career for a time, conducting at the Kammerspiele Theater. However, life as a Jew became increasingly dangerous there too and a year later he left for the relative safety of London. With his musical background he decided he might be able to make a career writing more commercial popular music and, like all the other debutantes, he soon found himself knocking on the doors of Tin Pan Alley music publishers, just as Jimmy Kennedy had done five years earlier. When he reached Feldman's, he received a sympathetic reception. Grosz's light classical style was very melodic and Feldman, who still had one foot in the 19th century, thought it might be possible to adapt his relatively highbrow creations to the commercial tastes of Tin Pan Alley by working with an established lyricist and musical editor who knew what the public wanted, Jimmy Kennedy. 'See what you can get out of him', he said. It was to be the start of a very fruitful four-year partnership. The two writers worked well from the start – my father described Dr Grosz as 'an agreeable, cultured and very charming gentleman' – and together they produced a string of Kennedy/Grosz hits among which were three world standards, *Isle of Capri, Red Sails in the Sunset* and *Harbour Lights.*

When Grosz came to England, Continental tangos, which had been so popular in the early 1930s, were beginning to give way to more escapist songs, especially ballads, about faraway places or romantic situations – as writers tried to help people forget the hardships of the Depression years. Only well-off people could afford to go abroad. Most people stayed at home for their holidays or, if they could afford it, went to the seaside. France, Spain or Italy were the romantic settings people could only dream about. Sheet music with attractive designed covers depicting exotic locations decorated and cheered up many a living room piano reinforcing the idea, selling dreams and romance. The challenge for Dr Grosz was to adapt to these trendy low-brow commercial requirements and it seems he had little difficulty doing so, helped doubtless by his knowledge of the light classical Viennese musical tradition. Here is how my father remembered his first meeting with him:

The first time we met, I sat down and picked out a selection of songs like *Play to Me, Gypsy* that were popular at the time. Then Grosz sat down and started 'fiddling' with the keys, strumming half a dozen phrases, halting, and then starting again. Suddenly, his fingers pressed out a phrase which had me on my feet in a flash. In one second, after those many undistinguished bars of music, he had struck out a snatch of melody which was going to sell over a million copies of sheet music and millions of records. And I knew it in the moment of time it took for his finger to pass over the keys.

But it wasn't easy to work out what the song would be – a foxtrot, perhaps? Or, maybe, a tango? I wasn't sure. It was unusual, unlike any other tune of that time. As

Feldman's lyric editor, I had the problem of trying to get a different, commercial, idea for it. It wasn't the overall structure, which was a fairly normal ABA - a main tune or chorus (A), a contrasting middle section (B) and then a repeat of the chorus (A) - it had a different 'colour'. First, though, I had to recast it into an eight-bar format - which is what the band arrangers always wanted - and add a verse. Then I needed to come up with an idea for the title. That was always the hardest thing to do when working from raw music. It stumped me until the following weekend when I picked up a newspaper and read an article by Christopher Stone, who, in the days when most broadcasts were of live bands, played records and has always been credited with being the first disc jockey. He was writing about Gracie Fields, who was far and away the top British entertainer. In fact, she was the most famous person in the country after royalty and everything she did was followed avidly by her fans through the columns of the popular press. According to Stone's article, "our Gracie" was making some recordings in London before going off to her villa on the Isle of Capri. Isle of Capri, I thought. Could that romantic Italian island make a good title?

It was an idea which would fit neatly into the current vogue for romantic, escapist songs. The more I thought about it, the more I felt that Capri, with its Gracie Fields association, could provide an ideal backdrop for a ballad lyric. But as I tried to fit the words "Isle of Capri" to the Grosz melody, I realised that the word Capri, which was usually (and correctly) pronounced with emphasis on the first syllable, would not work - unless I changed the stress to the second syllable and made it Capree: *'Twas on the Isle of Capree that I met her* ...became da da da dum da da <u>dum</u> da da dum dum. That worked. And with this problem overcome, I completed the lyric, verses and chorus, in a matter of hours. I think, eventually, the vast popularity of the song led to nearly everybody pronouncing

Capri the new way because you rarely hear the 'correct' pronunciation any more, in England, at any rate:

*'Twas on the Isle of Capri that I found her*
*Beneath the shade of an old walnut tree....*
*Oh! I can still see the flow'rs blooming round her*
*Where we met on the Isle of Capri...*

Jimmy Kennedy knew that old-fashioned Feldman would like the lyric because it began with 'Twas'! But part of the rest of the lyric got him into a furious argument which eventually led to his resignation from the firm:

*Summer time was nearly over*
*Blue Italian sky above*
*I said "Lady, I'm a rover,*
*Can you spare a sweet word of love?"*

*She whisper'd softly "It's best not to linger"*
*And then as I kiss'd her hand I could see*
*She wore a plain golden ring on her finger*
*'Twas goodbye on the Isle of Capri.*

But why should the lyric be a resigning matter? Feldman insisted that the reference to the 'plain golden ring' on her finger made it obvious that the 'rover' was making a pass at a married lady. The BBC would ban it, he said. But Kennedy thought the ring idea was a key point of the lyric and refused to have it taken out and there was a big argument between the two men. Realizing the impasse could go on for some time and that Grosz needed to earn a living, my father advised him to forget his lyric and try to sell the music to another publisher. So he hawked the music around the publishers in Denmark Street, eventually finding the Peter Maurice Music Company, where the new general manager, Jimmy Phillips, offered him a contract for the music. Phillips tried to find another lyricist to produce words to go with the song, but could not find anything he liked. In the end he had to go back to Feldman for the original lyric. However, he, too, thought the 'ring on her finger' line could cause problems with the BBC and wanted it removed. But Jimmy Kennedy once again refused to take it out. The dispute over the line eventually reached the ears of Alec Kraut, an influential executive who picked the songs for Regal Records. He liked the lyric and did not think the BBC would ban the song. He was so convinced the song had potential that he promised to record three different versions, provided the line was kept. That was an offer Jimmy Phillips could not refuse.

*Jimmy Kennedy's first important collaboration with Will Grosz topped the list of sheet music best sellers for three months.*

Though the nuns in the convent schools in Ireland banned it – the girls had to read the illicit lyrics of the year's best seller by torchlight under the bedclothes – after all the fuss, the BBC did not. *Isle of Capri* was first broadcast in 1934 by Lew Stone and his Band, from the Monseigneur Restaurant in London. After the broadcast, the BBC switchboard was jammed with people requesting it to be played again. Most callers were not certain about the title; some thought it was *I Love Capri*, for example. What did they ask for? The one about the 'lady with the golden ring on her finger'! *Isle of Capri* topped the bestsellers list in the UK for more than three months with recordings by all the big bands. Lew Stone followed up his broadcast with the first recording (with a Nat Gonella vocal) and he was quickly followed by the London Accordion Band, Roy Fox, Geraldo, Billy Cotton, Jack Payne, and Ray Noble (vocalist Al Bowlly). Thanks to her villa in Capri, Gracie Fields made it one of her pet songs. It was also one of the best sellers of the year in America: Ray Noble's version was No.1, followed by Freddy Martin at No. 2 and Lew Stone at No. 3. Xavier Cougat and his orchestra had a hit version and a jazz recording by the one-armed trumpet player Joe 'Wingy' Manone (Vocalion) was also hugely popular. My father told me he hated this version. He told me that it sounded as if Manone had heard the song too many weeks before and had forgotten the words: 'I thought this will kill it. But, strangely enough, it didn't. In fact it did a lot of good. For one thing, the black population loved it. They took to it in a big way and it sold very well. In fact it's still selling, this old, old record.' Jimmy Kennedy was not a jazz enthusiast generally. He hated Louis Armstrong's version of the 1935 Kennedy/Grosz's ballad, *Red Sails in the Sunset,* for example. He felt that jazz musicians went their own way too much and could ruin the intentions of the songwriter.

*Isle of Capri* went on to become one of the great standards and down the years many more recordings were made by leading performers on both sides of the Atlantic. In addition to many big band versions, solo recordings include Bing Crosby (with Rosemary Clooney), Frank Sinatra and Fats Domino. Jimmy Kennedy may not have liked jazz particularly, but Duke Ellington, Chris Barber and many other jazz bands featured the song. It reached the American Top 20 again in 1954 thanks to covers by The Gaylors and Jackie Lee. It has been in several films. My father was amused to discover it was No.1 in the Soviet Union and in India during the 1950s, though there were no royalties on offer from these countries! To this day, there are still at least thirty versions in albums you can order in the shops and many are available on the internet. For example, there is a 1934 Pathé Pictorial film of Greta Keller singing it on YouTube, with Will Grosz at the piano. I think it may be the only extant film recording of Will Grosz. Also on YouTube is a great up-tempo 1994 Chris Barber jazz version. Interestingly, crooner Rudy Vallée, a huge American star in the 1920s and 1930s, never recorded the song. Band leader Henry Hall said Vallée did not consider it to be 'a good popular song'.

But he was wrong. *Isle of Capri* was so popular and played so much it not only topped hit parades all over the world, it generated interest from all sorts of people unconnected with the music business or the sheet music/ record buying public. Compton Mackenzie, for example, then among Britain's best-known writers, and later famous for *Whisky Galore*, wrote in an article that he had lived on Capri but had never seen a walnut tree, so it should not have been mentioned in the lyric. Jimmy Kennedy had never been to Capri. In fact, he had not at that time even been to Italy. The reason why he used a walnut tree in the chorus was because he had an idea that walnuts came from Italy and he wanted to get away from 'the sort of tree you usually found in ballads of the time, something really old-fashioned like a linden tree or a willow tree.' But he had to check to find out if Mackenzie was right, so he contacted a music dealer on the island of Capri. Were there walnuts on Capri? 'Of course,' came the reply. 'We even export them to the mainland. They're sold as Sorrento walnuts.'

Then someone wrote to a paper called *The Star* (a middlebrow paper, quite different from today's *Daily Star*) to complain about the line, *And tho' I sail'd with the tide in the morning*. 'There are no tides in the Mediterranean!' said the writer. This was a little harder to refute. Most people would agree there were no tides in the Mediterranean, so it was a genuine slip. However, Jimmy Kennedy, with his university background, was nothing if not resourceful and decided to check this, just in case. Looking up the tidal tables for the region in the local library he found that there was a tide – almost two inches!

*Isle of Capri* established Jimmy Kennedy as a leading lyricist but he felt Bert Feldman's refusal to give him any royalties for *The Teddy Bears' Picnic* was unjust, as was the absurd squabble over the *Isle of Capri* lyric. Other aspects of his work at Feldman's were beginning to become rather irksome too. For example, as part of his contract as lyric editor, he had to produce run-of-the mill comedy material and extra verses for artists, none of which were productive for him personally. British performers working in Variety always wanted a second or third verse so they could repeat the chorus to plug the song – and themselves. But the material that came over from New York and Hollywood usually had only one verse to accompany the chorus. This meant that my father had to keep ghost-writing extra verses without getting the credit and it ate up time he needed for other income-generating work. Though the £7 a week he earned from his staff job as lyric editor was a useful basic wage by the standards of those days, he still needed his own royalties to pay the rent.

So, despite the fact that Jimmy Phillips had also originally turned down the 'golden ring' line (though he did get the song recorded), Kennedy accepted an offer to join him at Peter Maurice in late 1934. It seems that Jimmy Phillips managed to poach him by persuading him that the kind of problem he had had over the *Isle of Capri* lyric would not occur again and that he would have more freedom and more progressive ideas with a younger team. Furthermore, at Peter Maurice, Kennedy would also be able to renew his partnership with Will Grosz, someone he respected and who was now under contract.

Shortly afterwards, Phillips also signed up Michael Carr, who had been having a moderately successful time at the publisher, Irwin Dash. The song writing team Phillips assembled had plenty of promise – a leading lyric writer and music editor, a composer and, in Carr, despite being a maverick, someone who could write good tunes and lyrics.

# 9: The Peter Maurice Hit Factory

*Will it be a hit? Publisher Peter Maurice (left) and his general manager Jimmy Phillips mull over a song.*

The Peter Maurice Music Company had been founded by a wealthy Belgian Old Etonian called Peter Maurice Jacques Koch de Gooreynd, who had gone into publishing after failing to make the grade as a songwriter. He set up business in the heart of Tin Pan Alley at 21 Denmark Street, registering the company after his first two Christian names, which were much easier to remember than his surnames. De Gooreynd was not only a songwriter and publisher, he was an inventor. One of his ideas had been a device which he had attached to the grand piano in his office which could record all the notes played, the sound going down special tubes onto a Dictaphone apparatus. When Kennedy joined, the company appeared to be very successful but contemporary accounts suggest that was far from the truth. De Gooreynd had hired Jimmy Phillips to save the company from going bankrupt. Phillips, who had built up a reputation as an ace song picker with Lawrence Wright, started to pay his way by buying some important American songs, including *Lullaby in Blue* from New York publisher Shapiro, Bernstein & Co. Snatching *Isle of Capri* from Feldman's produced an even bigger hit. With Will Grosz, Jimmy Kennedy and Michael Carr under contract, Phillips had assembled possibly the strongest contemporary song writing teams in British popular music. It was the master stroke that led to a stream of best sellers that changed the fortunes of the firm, soon turning it from a loss maker into one of Tin Pan Alley's most successful publishers. Only a year after he had assembled his new team, Peter Maurice became the first British music publisher to sell an advance catalogue of British popular songs to America where it was snapped up by the Chappell-Harms Group. Usually the musical traffic went the other way, so this was a significant coup by a British music publisher.

However, the two Jimmys, Phillips and Kennedy, both of whom had strong personalities, never got on during the decade they worked together at Peter Maurice. Jimmy Kennedy constantly complained that Phillips interfered with his titles and lyrics and refused to give him credit for all the behind-the-scenes work he did in thinking up ideas and writing musical adaptations. For example, he not only wrote all the words, he usually wrote some of the music, especially for the verses, of the songs in his collaborations with Carr and Grosz and for the Continental tunes he adapted. Despite this contribution, he was usually only credited with the words.

There were also frequent arguments with Phillips over marketing his songs. The 'golden ring' line in *Isle of*

*Capri* was not just an artistic concept, it was commercial, said Kennedy. It was the memorable idea that listeners caught on to. If they forgot the title, they remembered the line and quoted it when they rang up the BBC request line or went into a music shop. But Phillips, like Feldman, could not see this or did not want to see it. Commercially, said Kennedy, there would be battles over just about everything: 'A regular argument was over plugging. Sometimes Phillips would get halfway through plugging a song, and then something else would come along which looked a greater certainty, so he would drop the first song and switch to the other. That happened to me many a time.'

Another example was the refusal by Phillips initially to promote three of Kennedy's later compositions – *Red Sails in the Sunset*, *South of the Border* and *The Chestnut Tree* – because he did not think they would sell. Yet all three turned out to be world hits. But what my father complained of most in his later years was that many of his songs, written on his own or in collaboration, were never published at all. They were buried somewhere in a filing cabinet and he never got them back.

There is always the chance of discord between successful people with strong personalities, especially if one is creative and the other a businessman. Jimmy Kennedy's job was to produce successful songs and Phillip's job was to pick the best and sell them. Both thought they knew what would do well and what would not. I think, too, that looking at the history of conflict between the two men, there is more than a suggestion that Phillips, like De Gooreynd, was also a frustrated songwriter. It has even been alleged that, using pen names, he put several songs he had written or co-written on the 'B' side of records, knowing he would profit from the much better songs on the 'A' side. According to Wikipedia, using the pseudonym John Turner, he also made suggestions for changes to several Geoffrey

Parsons lyrics during the 1950s, so getting a cut of the royalties. These included lyrics to smash hits such as *Auf Wiedersehn*, Charlie Chaplin's *Eternally* and *Smile* (from the film *Limelight*) and *Oh My Papa*. My father frequently called him a 'crook' and over the years developed a long-standing sense of injustice in the way his own material was treated. Even though as a revered freelance songwriter he was still producing successful lyrics for Phillips as late as 1962, he still felt bitter about the negative side of their relationship. In 1968, when Jimmy Phillips's secretary tried to get them together socially, he wrote to tell her:

I appreciated very much indeed your effort to bring me and Mr. Phillips together the other day, and I was, and am, sorry that it wasn't possible. I'm sure you don't understand how long the differences between us exist. It goes back to the *Isle of Capri*. And that is 34 years. So it's gone deep. And nobody but me can realize how many times I have been deeply hurt but didn't show it!

He has always, admittedly, given me the build-up as a lyric writer. But he has also always belittled my music just because I wasn't a pianist.

To give you a petty example: the artist who did the cover for *Red Sails*, credited the music to H. Williams (a pen-name for Will Grosz) who only did the first eight bars (but played beautiful piano) and a correction was promised in the next edition. But though many editions have been printed since, it has never been put right. This is the sort of petty obstinacy that I have found terribly irritating.

And only on Tuesday when we were in a sort-of-conversation, the first thing Mr. Phillips said: 'Didn't I put you on the map again?'!! Well, for the information of all concerned, I've never been 'off' the map...'

Kennedy aired his views on publishers once in a John Bowman Radio Telefís Eireann (RTE) Radio 1 programme: 'They liked to keep writers under their thumb – they were supposed to know their place. Publishers did not want writers to get too important because they would be too difficult to deal with. They were interested only in getting productivity out of writers and that is why you nearly always found they wanted two writers working together. That, they reasoned, made them compete with each other and that led to more songs – on the basis of "anything you can do, I can do better!"' But a songwriter could never break free completely because publishers held the major percentage of the copyrights and therefore had more control. So writers were to a large extent yoked to their publishers for the duration of copyrights on their own material even when working for other publishers or for themselves.

Towards the end of 1934, shortly after *The Isle of Capri* ended its three month reign as the UK No 1. song, Jimmy Kennedy wrote the words and music for his first western success, *Roll Along Covered Wagon*. Cowboy-style songs – albeit fake – were very much in vogue at the time, spurred on by the increasing output of western films and novels. My father was an avid reader of this type of fiction, especially the books of Zane Gray. He told me that he got the idea for *Roll Along Covered Wagon* after reading a novel by Emerson Hough called *The Covered Wagon*, a book which had inspired one of the first great western films of the same name and had been a box office smash several years before. Its story was well-known: an epic journey of families in two covered wagons who head out west, overcoming all kinds of hazards along the way – desert heat, mountain snow, hunger, thirst, and attacks by Indians. There is also a love story subplot. Adapting the familiar title for the song gave it immediate resonance with the public. *Roll Along Covered Wagon* was an instant success on both sides of the Atlantic, so much so that Jimmy Phillips was able to sell it to Hollywood where the rights were acquired for another film, *The Arizonian* (1935), starring Richard Dix (The song was sung by Margot Grahame in the film). The best known British recording was by Harry Roy and his orchestra. His was the version featured in the courtroom scene in Dennis Potter's award-winning television drama, *Pennies from Heaven* (1978) starring Bob Hoskins as sheet music salesman Arthur Parker. *Pennies from Heaven* also included two other Jimmy Kennedy songs, a pot-boiler called *On the Other Side of the Hill* and the very successful *Serenade in the Night*. Roy Fox, Sydney Lipton, Debroy Somers, and The Hillbillies did popular versions of *Roll Along Covered Wagon* and it is still a standard.

> *Roll along covered wagon, roll along,*
> *To the turn of your wheels I sing a song,*
> *City ladies may be fine,*
> *But give me that girl of mine,*
> *Roll along covered wagon, roll along...*

In October 1935, with *Roll Along Covered Wagon* being played by bands up and down the country, Italian Fascist dictator Benito Mussolini invaded Abyssinia (Ethiopia) to try to establish an Italian East African empire. His powerful modern army quickly overcame the poverty-stricken Abyssinians, whose only firepower came from antiquated World War I rifles. There was widespread public revulsion at this unfair invasion and sympathy for the Abyssinians. Public opinion resonated even in school playgrounds where British schoolchildren made their views clear using their own words to the Jimmy Kennedy tune: *Roll along Mussolini, roll along/Oh! you won't be in Abyssinia very long/You'll be sitting on a plane/ With a bullet in your brain/Roll along, Mussolini, roll along!* A second version went: *Will you come to Abyssinia, will you come?/ Bring your own ammunition and your gun./ Mussolini will be there shooting peanuts in the air/ Will you come to Abyssinia, will you come?* A ruder version has *You'll be sitting on the grass, / with a bullet up your arse,* and, doubtless, there must have been many other versions. (These verses were recorded by Iona and Peter Opie in their fascinating book, *The Lore and Language of Schoolchildren*, Clarendon Press, 1959).

*Roll Along Covered Wagon* continued to be popular down the years. My father even received a letter from Jimmy Phillips in 1962 asking him to verify that he had written it. Apparently a Belgian record company had published it as a South African folk song. Mindful of Peter Maurice's royalties, Jimmy Phillips told the Belgians that Jimmy Kennedy had physically composed the song in his firm's offices. But they still insisted that the writer verify how and where it was composed. Wagons – albeit pulled by oxen – were part of South African history, so it is easy to understand the mistake.

The success of *Isle of Capri* and *Roll Along Covered Wagon* meant that Jimmy Kennedy was able to sign a new contract with Peter Maurice, more than doubling his basic salary. Much of his output – especially the lyrics and musical adaptations for continental tunes – was written in the office, rather like a nine-to-five copywriter in an advertising agency. 'I suppose I used to turn out an average of two or three songs a week,' he once said. 'But if someone wanted a batch of songs for a film, then, usually working with Carr, we would up the production rate to 10 or more a week – writing them in buses, trains, or taxis, if need be. Occasionally, I would write at home at Walton-on-Thames – especially after a pleasant Sunday lunch! I did not mind doing that because, disagreements with publishers aside, writing lyrics was a hobby, a compulsion. I loved doing it, and I was lucky enough to be making a living out of it.'

Though Jimmy Kennedy was primarily employed as a writer and lyric editor at Peter Maurice, he used to get involved in other aspects of the business – just as he had at Feldman's – including helping in the exploitation of all Peter Maurice songs through promotion and publicity, liaising with artists, band leaders, record producers and people from the entertainment industry. As a successful songwriter in his own right, there were guest appearances on radio, films and variety shows. On one occasion, it must have been late in 1934 or early in 1935, he and the great band leader Bert Ambrose went down to East Ham Town Hall in the East End of London to interview some young singers for a recording they had in mind: 'Eventually a young girl – she could not have been more than 17 at the time – came on stage dressed head-to-toe in fawn: fawn hair, fawn dress, and fawn shoes. She sang a couple of songs very professionally but, at the end of her audition, we turned to each other and said in unison: "She'll never make it!" How wrong could we be: it was Vera Lynn!' Soon after her 'failed' audition, she joined a rival band and, in a nice touch of irony, helped to make the next song by Kennedy and Grosz, *Red Sails in the Sunset*, the biggest hit of 1935. Later, she became perhaps my father's favourite female performer, singing, he said, 'with wonderful heart, diction and delivery.' Vera Lynn worked as a vocalist with numerous bands– including, Charlie Kunz, Billy Cotton and, later on, Bert Ambrose himself – before going solo. As everybody knows she was voted the 'Forces Sweetheart' during the War and became perhaps the most popular female singer of all time in Britain.

# 10: *Red Sails in the Sunset*

The great American songwriter, showman and wit, Sammy Cahn, was often asked, 'What comes first, the music or the lyric?' His answer? 'The telephone call!' Jimmy Kennedy used to say his answer to the question would have been 'The bank manager!', joking that whether he wrote with Michael Carr or with Will Grosz depended on who needed money the most – and that was usually Carr. However, before he wrote anything with Carr, Jimmy Kennedy had more very successful songs with Will Grosz, including possibly his most famous ballad, *Red Sails in the Sunset*.

*Red Sails in the Sunset* sold more copies than any other UK song in 1935, with notable recordings by Lew Stone, Ambrose, Joe Loss and virtually all the other orchestras. Top vocalists included Vera Lynn, Gracie Fields, Al Bowlly and Greta Keller. In America it was voted the No. 2 song of the year by NBC's new and influential radio network show, *Your Hit Parade*, a kind of Top of The Pops radio programme which used to proclaim rankings based on its own surveys: in fact the show was popularly referred to as 'The Hit Parade'. The ballad's success was reflected in numerous contemporary American recordings made, for example, by Bing Crosby and Guy Lombardo (both had records of it at No. 1 in America in 1935), Mantovani (No. 2), Jack Johnson (No. 13), Louis Armstrong (No. 15 in 1936), Les Brown, and many others. As the years went by, it continued to be covered by a host of stars, including Nat King Cole (No. 21 in 1951), Perry Como, Dean Martin, Pat Boone, Fats Domino (a rock version entered the American charts in 1963), Tab Hunter, Dinah Washington, Englebert Humperdink, The Platters (it reached the US Top 10 in

1958), and probably more than two hundred others. Even The Beatles sang it at a gig in Hamburg in 1962. More unconventionally, the British comedienne Suzette Tarri, who became well known on the BBC's ITMA radio shows during World War II, adopted it as her signature tune.

Seventy years after *Red Sails in the Sunset* was written, many recordings of it are commercially available in compilations of different sorts through record shops and the internet. There are several versions on YouTube. Despite the failed 'fawn dress' audition, *Red Sails in the Sunset* was the first song that Vera Lynn broadcast professionally. She was just 18 when she sang it with Joe Loss and his band from the Casani Club in London's Regent Street. She later recorded it with him on the Octacros label and it was also one of the very first records she cut as a solo artist, on a label called Crown – a record that could be bought for six old pence.

*Red Sails in the Sunset* has been very popular in Northern Ireland because the lyric was inspired by the beautiful seascape of Portstewart, County Antrim. My father told me he could trace the germ of the idea for the lyric right back to when he was only six years old and his mother Anna gave him a book that contained a poem he liked: *A little ship was on the sea/It was a pretty sight/ It sailed along so merrily/And all was calm and bright.* On the opposite page was a coloured picture of the ship with a white sail. As a small child he used to look at the picture and draw funny faces over it. That was all but forgotten until the image unexpectedly came back to him one evening in 1933. He had gone to Portstewart to visit his mother, father, and two sisters, Nell and Nina. Their house was in Strand Road which then had an uninterrupted view of the sea. When the weather was warm the family would sit in the garden and watch the sunset. Often at about that time a small fishing boat with white sails would cross the sea in the direction of Inishowen Head in County Donegal, a peninsular to the north-west – a lovely sight on a nice evening. The boat was well known locally and was called *Kitty of Coleraine*, after an Irish folk song. One evening my father was with Nina watching a particularly beautiful sunset as *Kitty of Coleraine* sailed across and they noticed how its normally white sails slowly became tinged red by the rays of the setting sun. Nina, a talented artist, started to sketch the scene and, as she looked out over the water, she asked her brother what she should call the picture. It was then that his mind flashed back more than a quarter of a century to the ship with the white sail and the poem in the book he had admired as a child and it prompted him to say 'Why not call it *White Sails in the Sunset*?' Then, realising that the boat's sails were red, he corrected himself to say <u>Red</u> *Sails in the Sunset*. But Nina replied 'That would be a better title for a song!' Will Grosz had not arrived in England in 1933, but the idea and the image behind a world hit had been born.

'And there the matter rested until two years later when, back in the Peter Maurice office, Will Grosz came up with a few bars of music in a style which was unfamiliar to me, a sort of lively 6/8 tarantella, something quite unusual for Tin Pan Alley,' said my father many years later. 'Jimmy Phillips said he thought that if we slowed it down it had the makings of a good tune and suggested that I do a musical adaptation. Though the tarantella was a fast whirling dance to ward off the spider's supposedly fatal bite, he suggested the tune could be adapted to make a good lullaby and I should write the words accordingly. Later I found out his wife was pregnant at the time. Leaving aside the inconsistency of the tarantella and a child's song, I could see no commercial prospects for a lullaby and thought he must be joking. Fifty years before, perhaps!'

But what would be the best style to commercialize the music and what kind of lyric would suit it? Many years later when we lived in Somerset, I saw my father's creative process in action. There, you would see him in the drawing room gazing out of the French windows towards the Blackdown Hills, quietly humming a melody to himself as he worked out the words to fit. Occasionally he would pick out a tune on the rosewood grand. Then, perhaps days later, when everything had 'clicked', he would sit down in a favourite armchair and write out the completed lyric and top line of the melody directly onto a piece of manuscript paper.

I am sure he did the same thing with the Will Grosz tune at his home in Walton-on-Thames in 1935, searching for an idea, something brand new or something old with a new twist, an idea that would turn the music into a song that would capture the imagination of the public. That is when he must once again have remembered how two years before, he and Nina had come up with *Red Sails in the Sunset* as a wonderful title for a song. And he would have also realised that the six syllables of that title fitted the 6/8 time signature of the tune. Then he would have sat down at the piano and hummed his way to the *Red Sails in the Sunset* that everybody now knows, by slowing down the tempo of the music, revising and completing the melody into a more conventional 4/4 but keeping the triplets for each phrase of the chorus '... sails-in-the'... 'out-on-the'... 'safely-to'... and so on, to fit. Everything would then have fallen neatly into place:

*Red Sails in the Sunset*
*Way out on the sea*
*Oh, carry my lov'd one home safely to me...*

*Swift wings you must borrow*
*Make straight for the shore*
*We marry tomorrow*
*And he goes sailing no more.*

*Red Sails in the Sunset*
*'Way out on the sea*
*Oh, carry my lov'd one home safely to me...*

*A huge best-seller in Britain and America in 1935,*
*Red Sails in the Sunset went on to become one of*
*Kennedy and Grosz's (writing as 'Hugh Williams')*
*most enduring world standards.*

Will Grosz, who used the pen name 'Hugh Williams' for this composition, would have made some further compositional improvements when Kennedy brought his editorial efforts back to the office and would then have been content. Jimmy Phillips was not. He had the band and orchestral arrangements distributed in the normal way but would not promote the song, probably because Kennedy had not followed up his suggestion of writing a lullaby. Fortunately, the dance bands and recording companies fell in love with it and within a matter of weeks recordings reached double figures, all on the A side. And it stayed on the A side from then on, with one exception: it was on the flipside of the young film star Tab Hunter's first record, *Young Love*. But, as *Young Love* sold over a million records, so did *Red Sails in the Sunset*!

Jimmy Kennedy heard the first broadcast, by Greta Keller, when he visited his wife Peggy on the same day his first child, Derek, was born on 9 August 1935. His comment years later after it had become a standard? 'Perhaps there was something in the lullaby idea, after all. Certainly it was a family song – it has helped keep me and my family in comfort ever since!'

Henry Hall took an arrangement across to America where it was taken up by Fred Waring and his Pennsylvanians and also by Ray Noble and his orchestra on New York radio. Ray Noble was English but had left England in 1934 to lead one of the best bands in America at the time – a band that included Glenn Miller on trombone. Noble's output included memorable numbers such as *The Very Thought of You* and *Love is the Sweetest Thing*. A big band success had been his 1934 arrangement of *Isle of Capri*. With Noble and others playing it in America, *Red Sails in the Sunset* was selling 50,000 copies a week less than a month after its first broadcast, among the fastest sheet music best-sellers of all time up to then. It went on to sell over 600,000 copies in America that year and over one and a quarter million worldwide. Since then, these figures have multiplied many times as the song became a world standard. Ray Noble's version with a vocal by Al Bowlly together with several other recordings, including the Casani Club orchestra, are all on the internet.

People were curious about the origins of the 'picture' evoked by the song and used to ask Jimmy Kennedy about it and why he thought everybody loved it. He used to say that a key reason was its simplicity. It has a memorable romantic theme, easy-to-remember words and the idea of the boat sailing across the sea is an easy image to transfer to a place you know. For example, the song was very popular on the west coast of America where it is still thought of as Hawaiian, and there are many Hawaiian-style recordings of it. On the East Coast, it is considered to be a New England song. He was always running into people who liked to guess where it was written – from the west coast of Ireland, to Norfolk, Brittany, the Adriatic, Japan, and Australia.

The biggest social event of 1935 provided the impulse for Kennedy's next composition, *Let us Sing unto Their Majesties*. Everybody in England was excited about the Jubilee of King George V and Queen Mary in May 1935 and major celebrations took place all over the country, with commemorative issues in newspapers and magazines, special radio broadcasts, the manufacture of all kinds of memorabilia and a big procession in London. Jimmy Kennedy seized the moment to write a 'state occasion' song. It suffered many of the faults you might expect – rather like the efforts of poets laureate to write poems for major royal events, which repeatedly seem to fall flat. But it turned out to be a success at the time. This is how *The Morning Post* described it:

Just after the King has broadcast on Accession Day, Jack Payne and his band will be on the air. The first tune they will play will be *Let us Sing unto Their Majesties*, which seems as if it will be the theme song of the Jubilee. You will hear it at the Cup Final on Saturday week; it will be played in regimental messes; sung by schoolchildren; plugged in the Gaumont British Jubilee film – in fact there will be no escaping it.

Fortunately it is a very good song. Over a drink with Jimmy Kennedy, who did the words, and 'Peter Maurice', who did the music, I listened to the first record of *Let us Sing*. It struck me as exactly the kind of stirring, swinging tune to meet the occasion. 'Peter Maurice' who is very well known in Mayfair by his real name of Peter Maurice Koch de Gooreynd, cuts an unusual figure in Tin Pan Alley, where the tone is brisk, American and go-getting. By contrast, he is urbane, Mayfairish and pleasantly casual. He drifted into music-publishing four years ago 'as a joke'. Then, he began in one room. Now, his offices fill an entire building, and few people outside America do bigger business in songs.

Possibly his biggest publishing hit so far is *Isle of Capri*. And I learned just how big a song can be when he told me that 1,200,000 copies of *Capri* have been sold in Europe and America. Jimmy Kennedy, a slim dark and unobtrusive young man, wrote the lyric for that, too.

Jimmy Kennedy was by now an established Tin Pan Alley song writing star but had yet to collaborate officially with Michael Carr who had been building a successful song writing career independently since he had first met Jimmy Kennedy at Lareine's. He had worked with several well known writers including Leo Towers and Harry Leon, though his biggest hit up to that time, *Ole Faithful*, had in fact been written with Jimmy's younger brother, Hamilton Kennedy. *Ole Faithful* was an in vogue cowboy song and had been a smash on both sides of the Atlantic, selling two million records and over a million copies of sheet music. Another success for Carr had been a comedy number called *Fonso, My hot Spanish (K)night*, which Gracie Fields made famous. And, around that time, in 1935, he wrote *Dinner for One Please, James*, later a best seller for Nat King Cole. Now brought in to Peter Maurice by Jimmy Phillips he was poised to be even more successful working with Jimmy Kennedy. His career was about to take off into the big time.

# 11: Kennedy and Carr

*Michael Carr (left) and Jimmy Kennedy, pictured in 1936, hated each other, but formed the most productive and successful British song writing partnership during the second half of the 1930s.*

Jimmy Kennedy was a diligent individual who took his work at Peter Maurice seriously. He regarded song writing as a creative profession which could be compared with being an author, a *Times* journalist, a serious painter – even a lawyer or doctor. And he dressed the part in sober suits and TCD University Association tie. Carr was the opposite in nearly every way. He was tremendously talented, a good pianist, could write words or music, was a (useful) slick salesman, an eternal optimist. On the other hand he was what the Irish would call a chancer, hoping to get as much as possible for nothing. He was, said my father, never around when you wanted him. Song plugger Eddie Rogers, in his book *Tin Pan Alley* (Robert Hale, 1964), said not only could he charm the birds from the trees, he could talk them into singing his songs: 'Carr,' he added, 'didn't just kiss the Blarney Stone, he had an affair with it!' My father had strong views about him. Here's an example:

Although Michael Carr was talented, he was crazy and difficult. We would start a song and then he would disappear. Then Jimmy Phillips would ask to see what we had produced and I would have to finish it myself. That would lead to a row for all kinds of obvious reasons, not least the fact that he would still get his share of the royalties, regardless of how little effort he put into it. Our professional relationship was quite different from the one I had with Will Grosz in that Grosz was first and foremost a musician but Carr and I both wrote words as well as music. Carr always wanted to produce the big line and so did I. Then he would want to get the tune right and I would find myself correcting it. So there was an endless battle going on. I think a fundamental reason why we were so successful was because our characters were so opposed, it made us determined to prove we were better than the other – and that spurred us on to better and better ideas.

There was an apocryphal Tin Pan Alley story told to me by Bill Cotton Jnr about Kennedy and Carr which gives another insight into the latter's character. It went like this: Carr is down on his luck and living in a bed-sit. He is also supposedly ill. Kennedy hears about it and pays a visit. 'I'm feeling terrible' Carr says. 'I am in this awful place with no money for food or medicines.'

Kennedy feels sorry for him and gives him a £5 note. Carr thanks him with tears of gratitude. The next day at work a colleague says he met Carr the previous evening. Kennedy says: 'But that can't be true! He was seriously ill in bed when I went to see him yesterday afternoon. He seemed so ill that I thought he might have to go to hospital. I gave him a fiver to buy some things he needed!' 'Well, when I met him he was in The Royal George downing a large glass of Jameson's whiskey!'

My father said that the only real reason he wrote with Michael Carr was because they were both under contract to the same publisher: 'I had ructions with Carr because of his unreliability. He would come up with dream stuff; he was a very fanciful chap. He used to think up all kinds of things related to films he had seen and he frequently did not make a lot of sense. He was always full of himself but sometimes remarkably touchy, insecure even. I remember one day he came into the office and struck an attitude and said: "Mr Kennedy (he always called me 'Mr Kennedy'), I've got an idea: I am the greatest!" So I said: "Since Ananias!" Then he turned on his heel and I didn't see him for a week!'

Eddie Rogers, who wrote his book at the beginning of the 1960s just before the groups had begun to totally dominate the British music scene, claimed the Kennedy and Carr partnership was the most successful professional song writing team that British popular music had produced since Gilbert and Sullivan – who also used to squabble. That was an exaggeration but they were certainly the most successful and prolific partnership in British popular music for the second half of the 1930s, achieving an output of over 90 successful songs during their five years together. Practically everything they wrote would have got into the charts if they had had official charts then. Their partnership culminated in *South of the Border Down Mexico Way*, their most successful No. 1, and *We're Going to Hang out the Washing on the Siegfried Line*, which was so popular during the early years of World War II. They also contributed songs for three London Palladium shows for the Crazy Gang – *O-Kay For Sound* (1936), *London Rhapsody* (1937) and *The Little Dog Laughed* (1939), plus an estimated 20 low-budget British films.

Their first collaboration, in 1935, was *Why Did She Fall for the Leader of the Band?*, the music hall-style number Jimmy Kennedy had had originally written in 1922 while still a student. Carr added a few finishing touches to give it a more professional, comic, finish. It became a huge success for band leader Jack Hylton in a film *She Shall Have Music*, a version that can still be listened to on the internet. Gracie Fields and the Big Ben Banjo Band also made recordings at the time.

Kennedy and Carr were jacks of all the popular music trades, turning their hands not only to songs to reach the very top of the best seller lists but to many smaller projects to generate publicity for the Peter Maurice brand or simply keep up a profitable flow of sheet music sales. They wrote words and music for a *Sunday Express* children's strip cartoon series called *Rusty and Dusty*, for example. The *Sunday Express* was still a broadsheet and the strip took up half a page – including the picture story, the lyrics and the all-important and very-simple-to-play music, which you could play directly from the newspaper by propping it up on your piano. The series attracted an enthusiastic following, so much so that someone on the newspaper had the idea that circulation would be boosted if they could get Henry Hall's BBC Dance orchestra to broadcast it. When the features editor of the *Sunday Express* rang up the bandleader to ask him if he would do a tie-up, Hall said: 'That depends on the lyrics, the tune and all that goes with it. Why not prepare three for me? If we like them, we'll do them. If they're good, we'll do six. If they're very good, we'll do 12.' They did 12. And then they did more.

The very first *Rusty and Dusty* strip appeared in *The Sunday Express* on 20 December 1936 and was all about how the two heroes had performed a dance act to make enough money to buy all their friends Christmas presents. That was on page 10. On page 13, there was another story headlined 'The worst thief of all – he even took a baby's toy.' And who were the thieves stealing from?

Like thousands of other men, Mr Jimmy Kennedy, of Walton-on-Thames, went Christmas shopping with his wife in London, yesterday.

From 10 am they went from shop to shop and by 4 pm, when they decided to go home, parcels were piled up to the roof inside Mr Kennedy's car. At Bayswater Road, they went together into the post office to make a telephone call and to buy stamps.

When they returned, the car was empty. All the parcels, containing expensive gifts for more than a dozen people, had been stolen.

Sympathy turns to irony, because Mr Kennedy is one of the team who tells of the joyous adventures of *Rusty and Dusty* in our new feature on Page 10. The thing that annoys him most is that a toy train for his 18-month old boy Derek was stolen. He says: 'A man who steals a baby's toy...'

One-off songs for periodicals, newspapers and advertisements were reproduced in full, so that they could be played on the piano at home, just like the *Rusty and Dusty* series. Kennedy wrote a song for the *Women's Home Journal* called *Room for You*. Will Grosz did an unintentionally amusing lullaby to fit in with an advertisement for a company called W. Woodward: 'All over the world,' the introduction read, 'mothers are singing and crooning to their babies...and so Woodward's are giving Mothers and all lovers of music, the loveliest Lullaby of the century...sing it to your baby.' The facing page read, 'All over the world, Woodward's are known as makers of Gripe Water for babies… 50,000,000 babies have found comfort from it in the small digestive disturbances – such as "wind" – which come to every baby.'

Jimmy Kennedy had more successes with Carr in 1936, including a popular Scottish ballad, *Misty Islands of the Highlands,* and a children's song recorded by Elsie Carlisle called *The General's Fast Asleep.* But before their partnership really got going, Kennedy followed up *Red Sails in the Sunset* with two more best sellers with Will Grosz, *At the Café Continental* and *Poor Little Angeline.*

*At the Café Continental a popular tango with a story, a hit in 1936.*

With escapism still all the rage, Viennese café society was considered particularly glamorous, an image reinforced by the romantic films of the era. Jimmy Kennedy told how he and Will Grosz got the idea for a tango which became very popular at the time, *At the Café Continental.*

In 1935, I visited Budapest with Will Grosz because there was to be a show featuring our songs in one of the biggest theatres there. Budapest must be high on the list of the fairest cities in Europe and the rival of Vienna for gaiety and beautiful women. After we had finished the rehearsals, we went for a walk along the principal boulevard and, seeing a nice café, we went in, sat down and watched the passers-by. At a table near to us there was a good-looking man who seemed rather bored until a pretty girl came in. As she passed the young man's table, she dropped a glove and he quickly picked it up.

After a brief conversation, she sat down and joined him. Obviously the young man was very much taken with her beauty and was clearly disappointed when she got up to go a few moments later. We got the impression, though, that she had promised to return because the young man continued to watch the entrance expectantly.

We decided to leave, however, and moved on to sample another café only to see the whole scene re-enacted. In came the same girl. As she passed the table of another young man, she dropped a glove. He picked it up. They had a brief conversation and she sat down with him "in close collaboration", as we songwriters say.

'Can you beat that!' I said to Grosz, 'She's dropped her glove again!' And that remark became the punch-line of the song. Out came the pencil and paper and we got to work there and then. We worked on it for two hours, forgetting our first night show, but we finished *At the Café Continental* and if you read the story in the lyrics, you will sense they ring true. Well, they were founded on fact!'

*Picture a café down where the lights are gleaming,*
*Picture a stranger lonely and idly dreaming,*
*Picture a meeting two dark eyes softly smiling,*
*Now hear his story how romance passed him by.*

*At the Café Continental, like a fool I fell in love,*
*It was all so accidental, picking up a lady's glove,*
*I had eyes but for her only, as we sipped a glass of wine,*
*And I told her I was lonely, as she slipped her hand in mine.*

*She arranged to meet me later but we've never met since then*
*Maybe in some other café she dropp'd her glove again...*

Their next collaboration, *Poor Little Angeline*, was a folk-based narrative or 'story' song. Numerous big band recordings of it were made by, among others, Roy Fox, the New Mayfair orchestra and Victor Sylvester. More recently there was a country version by Slim Whitman. *Angeline* has been parodied, especially by rugby teams, but the original words are:

*She was sweet sixteen, little Angeline,*
*Always dancing on the village green,*
*As the boys pass'd by, you would hear them cry*
*'Poor little Angeline.'*

*Oh! her eyes were brown and her hair hung down,*
*Ladder'd stockings and an old blue gown.*
*But she dream'd, we're told, of a lover bold.*
*'Poor little Angeline...*

*Poor Little Angeline* did not fit into any of the conventional dance routines of the time and unintentionally started a new dance craze. When it was first featured at the Glasgow Palais, the dancers weren't quite certain what steps were supposed to accompany it. The music had a 'different' rhythm, unlike the quicksteps, foxtrots and tangos they were used to. So, almost instinctively, they linked arms and danced up and down the floor, slid to a halt and then turned round and did the same thing again. Great fun! A new dance was born—the Palais Glide!

Though Kennedy, Carr and other professional songwriters were ready to undertake any assignment, they targeted their material carefully to make it interesting for a range of performers. As Kennedy said in a BBC Ulster documentary in 1975:

You had to channel everything you wrote towards a particular medium and the bands were the most important. Even if you wrote a song for Gracie Fields, you had to bear in mind that it had to be suitable for Ambrose or Lew Stone or one of the other major orchestras. The arrangers were the kings of the whole thing, because they were the men behind the bands, so you also had to make your song sufficiently interesting for the arrangers to work on. Everything had to be according to the dictates of the day. Usually arrangers, to save themselves a lot of bother, wanted the AABA (eight bar chorus, repeat, middle eight, chorus) musical structure, making altogether 32 bars, the basis of most songs written here and in America. When there was a verse, that would be extra but it would also have eight bars, which would then be repeated. That kept things nice and simple for the bands and their arrangers, and they were paramount in the whole thing. In actual fact, the eight-bar phrase was also commonly used by many of the great classical composers, so we were in good company!

Though a few band leaders, such as Ray Noble, wrote some very big hits, most of the arrangements they played, broadcast on the radio or were danced to in the local palais, came from songs originally dreamt up by Tin Pan Alley professionals. These would be promoted by the publishers' exploitation departments - through publicity, special band arrangements, plugging and deals for retailers, for example. If the publicity was successful and there was sufficient interest from bands and record companies, there could be as many as a dozen recordings of a new song. After that, the record companies themselves would continue promoting the numbers. It was a very different situation from the modern music scene where in most cases the production, not the song, comes first. The AABA structure of the time was a considerable constraint and meant songwriters had to work hard to come up with new and completely original musical and lyrical ideas within this limiting framework. It was an extraordinary achievement that Jimmy Kennedy, either on his own or with a partner, managed to have three or four international songs, many still world standards, high in the bestsellers list every year for so many years, sticking faithfully to AABA. They were songs which were made into first-class band arrangements and were sung and danced to by millions. They were the cream of thousands of other Tin Pan Alley efforts, many good, most mediocre. Unfortunately, these latter are frequently featured by many broadcasting organizations as background music for dramas and other programmes set in the 1920s, 30s and 40s and this does little for the reputation of the golden age or the quality of the output of the time. It is a bit like covering the 1960s without including a song by the Beatles. It is a shame because it is easy to portray the period as full of empty-headed upper-class people fox-trotting to vacuous music, but this is a very superficial and untrue representation.

While Kennedy was collaborating with Carr and Grosz, Continental melodies continued to arrive on his desk in a steady stream and he would write lyrics to order. Among them, in 1936, was a tango which he called *Serenade in the Night*. 'I adapted this from an Italian *Violino Tzigano* tune by C.A. Bixio and B. Cherubini, which had Italian words that were almost the same as my English lyric for *Play*

*To Me, Gypsy*', my father once told me. 'I couldn't repeat that, so I changed it to something more like a Romeo and Juliet setting with the young Romeo serenading his lady love beneath her window, writing new music to double the length from 16 to 32 bars.'

> *There's a melody that plays upon my heart-strings,*
> *When the splendour of the setting sun is fading,*
> *And tonight it comes a-stealing once again.*
> *Just a melody that comes but to remind me,*
> *That one night I sang a love song all in vain....*
>
> *Serenade in the night*
> *'neath a fair lady's window*
> *Just the same serenade that I tenderly played*
> *on a night long ago,*
>
> *There were stars in the sky*
> *As I sang 'neath the roses,*
> *But she gave not a sign that she'd ever been mine,*
> *and my love story closes...*

Primo Scala's Accordion Band version was a huge success in 1937. Ambrose, Billy Cotton, Roy Fox, Geraldo, Joe Loss, Mantovani, Lew Stone, Tino Rossi and Vic Damone also recorded it, making this a best seller at the time and it has been a standard across the world ever since.

Early in 1937 Kennedy and Carr got together to write *Did Your Mother Come from Ireland?* Songs about Ireland were popular in the 1930s, especially in American cities like Boston and New York which had large Irish populations. Michael Carr came up with the original idea. He was heading home on the boat train to Dublin for Christmas and found himself sitting next to a pretty girl and was trying to think of a suitable chat-up line when another man in the compartment beat him to it by saying to her, 'Is your mother Irish?' What a good title that would make, thought Carr and he spent the rest of the journey working out some words and music. When he got back from Ireland after the holiday, he tried the idea out on Kennedy, who changed the words and gave it a different title, *Did Your Mother Come From Ireland*. It went on to be a hit. In a radio programme towards the end of his career Bing Crosby said: 'I recall one of Jimmy's songs with particular gratitude: it was Irish, something I love and was called *Did Your Mother Come From Ireland?* A beautiful song really – nice melody.' Bing used to say that *Did Your Mother Come From Ireland?* and *Galway Bay* were his two favourite Irish songs.

> *Did your mother come from Ireland?*
> *'Cos there's something in you Irish,*
> *Will you tell me where you get those Irish eyes?*
>
> *And before she left Killarney*
> *Did your mother kiss the blarney?*
> *'Cos your little touch of brogue you can't disguise...*
>
> *Did your mother come from Ireland?*
> *'Cos there's something in you Irish,*
> *And that bit of Irish steals my heart away.*

'Ireland' and 'the Irish' were common themes for popular songs in those days. So, too, were 'mothers'. Edwin Sefton, a well-known entertainment journalist of the day, explained the thinking of the time in a newspaper column:

Geraldo, in his fortnightly broadcasts, tells you what the best-sellers of the moment are going to be. But I can give you 'inside information' about what's coming direct from the publishers because they open their hearts and books and tell me exactly which songs they are going to spend their money on. Take notice and you will see that the songs I talk about each week get there eventually. Whether you like it or not, you will hum the tunes the publishers' decree you will.

We have not had any of the 'mother' variety for some time. So recently the idea and instructions were given to Harry Leon and Leo Towers to produce one immediately. They set to work and have given us *When My Mother Says Her Prayers For Me*. Simplicity is the keynote and already it has had several broadcasts.

Here is another song I want you to watch closely – also about 'Mother'. It is *Did Your Mother Come From Ireland?* It was recently introduced by Henry Hall. The writers, Jimmy Kennedy and Michael Carr, who are perhaps the greatest of our present-day popular songwriters, are both Irish so they should be able to get the correct atmosphere. They are to be the guest artists in Henry Hall's Hour tonight at 10.30. Jimmy's other arrangement, *Serenade in the Night*, is creeping up into the position of best seller.

As Jimmy Kennedy became better known in showbiz circles, he was the subject of many newspaper articles. A particularly flattering entry appeared in the *Glasgow Evening News* on 30 January 1937. It was headed 'Potted Personalities, Jimmy Kennedy, Songwriter.' Under a head and shoulders photo, it read:

Age 34. Married with a son 17 months old. Born Omagh. Educated Trinity College, Dublin. After brilliant scholastic career, graduated B.A. in 1925. Became School Master but in 1929 resigned to enter music world as a freelance songwriter – most hazardous of professions. Wrote first songs at age of 15 for charity concerts.

In unique position at the moment because he is cornerstone of two world-famous teams, Kennedy & Grosz, responsible for *Isle of Capri*, *Red Sails*, *Poor Little Angeline* etc, and Kennedy & Carr, of *Misty Islands*, *Leader* of the Band, *There's a New World*, *Did Your Mother Come from Ireland?* etc. Has a flair for adapting foreign imports such as *Play to me, Gipsy*, *Oh! Donna Clara* and *Serenade in the Night.*

One of few writers without temperament. Can write a song under any conditions and at any time. Prefers country life – with ambition to be farmer in the colonies. Seldom goes to any amusement houses – not even to hear his own latest success.

Is easy going, modest, generous, but not foolish with his money – unspoilt by success, and friends say has yet to write biggest hit. Admits in song writing, idea is nearly everything – writing just workmanship and the rest, luck!

Hobbies – gardening, stamp collecting and motoring. Hates – nothing and nobody.

Signature tune should be *Ah! Lucky Jim.*

1937 was the year of the coronation of George VI and Queen Elizabeth and my father, who was a fan of the royal family, wrote *The Coronation Waltz* for the occasion. He took its composition very seriously. He described how he went about writing it in a contemporary article in *Melody Maker*:

There has always been a tradition of producing songs to celebrate great occasions such as a Coronation, going back to the beginning of history. The last Coronation had been that of George V in 1910 and everybody was singing a rousing six-eight grand march called *On Coronation Day*. The chorus finished with the following words:

*We'll be merry, drinking whisky, wine and sherry,*
*We'll be merry on Coronation Day.*

Bearing in mind the little local difficulty I had with the BBC when they banned *The Barmaid's Song* for encouraging people to drink, I would have to think of something different! Anyway, by 1937, we had moved away from the pre-War, almost Edwardian, era and needed something more in tune with the 1930s. I remember thinking at the time that we needed something to celebrate the Coronation that everybody would sing during the festivities and at the same time would have a personal appeal in pretty much the same way as the average love song.

I wondered what other writers like Irving Berlin would have done. I even thought about Johann Strauss. I would not compare myself with him, of course, but he gave me the clue. He had composed many of his greatest melodies in the form of waltzes for his orchestra to play on special occasions such as state or court balls in Vienna. Why not take a hint from such a master and write a waltz for the Coronation? Naturally my composition would have to be completely different from Strauss in style and conception, as the technique of popular waltz composition has changed since those days. Instead of a straight orchestral waltz, it would have to be a modern-style ballroom waltz. So I wrote:

*Bells are ringing,*
*Crowds are singing,*
*Orchestras play and the music charms.*
*Dreams enfold you,*
*While I hold you –*
*For this waltz you must be in my arms.*

*This is the Coronation Waltz,*
*Let us sway on our way to romance.*
*This is the Coronation Waltz,*
*We can dream to its theme while we dance.*
*Every chime that's ringing, our love story tells*
*In imagination they're our Wedding Bells.*
*After the Coronation Waltz,*
*You'll be Queen in my heart, always.*

The tune came with the words, and the whole thing was completed in less than an hour. *The Coronation Waltz* came out in time for the big event, with a superb recording by Ambrose. Peter Maurice gave it big support and copies were sent off to Australia and South Africa by air and to Canada and America by boat. They printed off 250,000 copies which were all sold. There was a spate of Coronation-inspired songs but mine was the only one played at the Coronation Ball.

Kennedy was particularly proud of this song, which Gracie Fields also recorded. He thought it one of his best. On the day of the Coronation, he went and stood in the crowd outside Buckingham Palace, knowing that his waltz was being played and that all the crowned heads of Europe would be dancing to it.

# 12: A country pub inspires a ballad

Successful ideas for songs in Tin Pan Alley often went in cycles during the 1930s (something that is often the case today). If a song about South Sea islands or cowboys or Broadway or Vienna caught on, writers would try to follow it up with something similar in the hope it would also be a best seller. With this in mind, Kennedy and Grosz tried hard to work out a follow-up to *Red Sails in the Sunset*. They were not alone in this. Another writer came up with *White Sails in the Moonlight*, for example but it never caught on. But, try as they might, the star writers from Peter Maurice could not come up with a good enough idea. Then, one dark evening Kennedy got lost in unfamiliar surroundings and paid an unintended visit to a pub. There he saw something which gave him the inspiration for the follow-up which had been eluding them for months:

I had had a few ideas for a *Red Sails* follow-up, but nothing had really worked. In the end it happened quite by chance. I had just been to Portsmouth where I had seen off my mother and sister Nell on a trip to New York and was driving home in the dark when by mistake I turned left at the top of Portsdown Hill towards Fareham instead of going right towards Weybridge, where I lived. Luckily, the car headlights soon picked out a pub sign, The Harbour Lights, so I was able to turn the car round in its car park. As I did so, I saw the pub's name again on the car park sign and suddenly realised its association with the sea could make it a perfect title for a song, maybe even the follow-up we were looking for. As I drove back, I worked on the idea in my head so that by the time I was home, the lyric was half done. The next day, I showed it to Will Grosz, who came up with a beautiful and romantic melody – one of his best, I think. There was no need for any adaptation to suit commercial taste and within weeks we had another smash on our hands – and one of the very few romantic ballads to be named after a pub!'

*I saw the Harbour Lights,*
*They only told me we were parting,*
*The same old Harbour Lights,*
*That once brought you to me.*

*I watch'd the Harbour Lights,*
*How could I help if tears were starting?*
*Goodbye to tender nights,*
*Beside the silvr'y sea.*

*I long to hold you near and kiss you just once more*
*But you were on the ship and I was on the shore…*

A contemporary newspaper came up with an amusing and highly original version of how the ballad was written. It reported that Jimmy Kennedy and Hugh Williams (Grosz used this pen name again) were in Southampton seeing off some friends who were going to Hollywood. Along with the party were a young Englishman and his charming fiancée, an American actress, who were parting for the first time. Up to the moment of sailing, the lovers were whispering last fond farewells – he from the quay and she from the ship's rails. And the fact that they obviously wanted to say good-bye again, said the report, gave the romantic Jimmy, the lines: *I long to hold you near and kiss you just once more/But you were on the ship and I was on the shore…* 'That evening', continued the article, 'the songwriters were missing and when some of the party found them, they were in the smoke room of the hotel, where there was an old piano and the song they had just completed was *Harbour Lights* – a number that rings true because it was inspired by a true-life lovers' parting.' Kennedy agreed: 'That is what it means to most people,' he said. 'It means parting.'

*Harbour Lights* sold well over a million copies of sheet music in 1937 and there were numerous English recordings: by Ambrose, Roy Fox, Charlie Kunz, Mantovani, Harry Roy and many others. In America, Frances Langford took *Harbour Lights* to No. 6 in the US, Claude Thornhill had a recording at No. 7, and there was also a popular Rudy Vallée recording in the same year.

*Harbour Lights was the top British sheet music best seller in 1937, a US record No.1 in 1950, and The Platters took it into the US Top 10 for a third time in 1960.*

How well songs were selling in those days was still unofficial with various measures coming from publishers, radio stations, retailers etc and the very influential radio show, *Your Hit Parade.* Billboard was also beginning to get a more composite rankings system together at around this time. But it was all very rudimentary by today's standards. Whatever measure was used, it tended to reflect the composition itself – not the sales of records. *Harbour Lights* featured on *Your Hit Parade* for ten weeks. It also has quite a claim to fame in that it was one of the six most frequently played songs during the 20 plus years the programme was broadcast in the pre-pop era. (The others were *White Christmas, People Will Say We're in Love, I'll be seeing You, You'll Never Know* and *Too Young*). In 1950, *Harbour Lights* again reached No. 1 in the US with a Sammy Kaye recording. And it was in the Top 10 for a third time in 1960, thanks to a recording by The Platters.

Though the Kennedy & Grosz ballads like *Harbour Lights* topped the best seller lists, Kennedy and Carr turned their hands to a steady stream of successful songs of many other genres. They did not usually reach the same heights of popular appeal as Kennedy-Grosz, but they made up for that in the sheer volume of their output. For example, they produced any number of songs to order for British films at Pinewood and Beaconsfield and for other enterprises that Jimmy Phillips and his exploitation department dreamed up. They also co-wrote *The Tin Pan Alley Symphony* and a series of BBC radio shows called *Songs You Might Never Have Heard,* where the listeners voted on which song they wanted most to be recorded. Then, in 1936 they began their first collaboration as the leading writers for the sell-out London Palladium variety shows of The Crazy Gang – the most popular British comedy act of the 1930s in the nation's biggest and most famous theatre. The Gang consisted of three comedy double acts: Nervo and Knox were acrobats who did 'slow-motion' walking and spoof ballet. Naughton and Gold were slapstick comedians with a background in pantomime and Bud Flanagan and Chesney Allen, who were the stars, were long-standing comedians and singers who had worked with music hall artists like Florrie Forde way back in the 1920s. Flanagan and Allen made many well loved recordings including *Underneath the Arches*, by Bud Flanagan and Reg Connelly, *Strollin'*, by Ralph Reader, and two Kennedy and Carr contributions, *Hometown* and *The Washing on the Siegfried Line*. Another of the songs they were associated with, *Run Rabbit, Run*, is often credited to Jimmy Kennedy but it was actually written by Noel Gay and Ralph Butler.

Kennedy and Carr wrote numbers for their first London Palladium Crazy Gang show, *O-Kay for Sound*, in September 1936. The show was later made into a film and was, according to contemporary accounts, 'a riot of wisecracks, circus acrobatics, slapstick, farce and sentimentality'. The film version of the Gang singing one of the show's best sellers, *Free,* is on YouTube. But three other songs were very popular at the time, an Ambrose favourite called *There's a New World,* the opening number, *O-Kay for Sound,* and *The Spice of Life*, a hit for Geraldo's orchestra, which was later chosen as the signature tune to John Sharman's *Music Hall* – for many years the peak entertainment on the BBC's Saturday night programmes.

A second show, *London Rhapsody*, had its first performance a year later in October 1937, and included *Hometown*, still a standard, and four other songs – *Waltz of the Gypsies, Youth Goes Marching On, Along the River with You*, and *Sing a Song of London*. Jimmy Kennedy used to say he thought *Hometown* must have been the quickest chart success he and Michael Carr ever wrote. The two had had the general idea and title for *Hometown* in mind as a typical folksy Crazy Gang sketch for some time and they had told George Black, the impresario and producer of *London Rhapsody* they were working on it. But somehow it would not come right. They had only come up with the first six bars when they were summoned to the Palladium to play it to the Gang. 'We were at panic stations. All we could do was to hope we could finish it off in the taxi in the 15 minutes it took to get from our offices in Denmark Street to the theatre. It was the only time I remember praying for a traffic jam! I don't know whether it was desperation or inspiration, but the lines that had been eluding our concentrated efforts for days just arrived out of the blue. While Carr hummed the tune, I jotted down a final lyric punctuated by the jolts of the cab and we finished it just as we drew up to the theatre.' The verdict? Mr Black was delighted and Flanagan and Allen insisted that they would sing it themselves.

*Hometown – want to wander down your back streets,*
*See you tumble down old shack streets,*
*I'd love to walk in on those country cousins of mine.*

*Hometown – where the dove's are softly cooin',*
*Where there's always nothing doin',*
*I'd get a welcome from those corny*
*country cousins of mine.*

*There's an old schoolhouse door we used to*
*tumble thro' at four*
*And a small candy store where I could*
*go a dozen lollipops and ask for more...*

Kennedy said he thought that the reason why *Hometown* was such a big hit was because of the ....*corny country cousins of mine* idea with its *da da da tumty tumty tumty tumty tumty <u>tum</u> <u>tum</u>* rhythm. 'It gave the song a lift where it was needed,' he said. 'And it stopped the show on the opening night.'

*London Rhapsody* was considered at the time to be among the most spectacular shows ever presented at the London Palladium. A contemporary critic wrote: 'It is interesting that whereas Mr Ivor Novello has put Drury Lane back on the map by altering the standard of production there to a point far removed from the theatre's traditions, Mr George Black has achieved the same results at the Palladium by a different process. The Palladium reviews have been going one better every time. *London Rhapsody* is the best yet.'

The third and last Crazy Gang show involving Kennedy and Carr was *The Little Dog Laughed*, which opened at the London Palladium in September 1939 during the first few months of World War II. The show ran for 461 performances and introduced *The Washing on the Siegfried Line*. Two other Kennedy/Carr inclusions were *My Secret Love* and *There's Danger in the Waltz.*

Though Kennedy used to say that he would love to have collaborated on a musical, the three Crazy Gang shows the two writers were involved with were the nearest they ever got to doing so. The opportunity never arose again. As it was, the style of the Palladium shows was very different from the American musical, much closer to Variety, with topical sketches, jokes and songs and these had a relatively short shelf life. The shows had no plots as such and were very dependent on the popularity of the Crazy Gang and the supporting acts which performed with them. The Gang's popularity continued, incidentally, well into the television age with peak-time programmes on television in the 1950s. It was not until 1962, after a long run at the Victoria Palace Theatre in London, that the curtain finally came down on their long careers.

When not busy at the Palladium, the Kennedy and Carr partnership contributed songs for something like 20

British films. While they were writing material for *London Rhapsody*, they were also working on seven numbers for *Let's Make a Night of It*, an Associated British musical filmed at Elstree Studios, which came out in early 1938. The film was billed as having the biggest gathering of famous British jazz players ever seen, yet was filmed over one weekend! At the time, it was more customary for films to be centred on one band but in this case there were seven. The film's climax takes place in a night club setting with a medley of tunes by Kennedy and Carr featuring all seven bands – Jack Jackson, Sydney Lipton, Jack Harris, Eddie Carroll, Joe Loss and Rudy Starita, plus Elstree's own band. Carr got an acting part. Much to the amusement of Kennedy, the film's director, Walter Mycroft, took one look at him and cast him as a gangster! Band leader Jack Jackson commented: 'Michael certainly fits the part with his broken nose and sandy hair.'

Edwin Sefton, writing in the Glasgow Evening News, said:

'The tunes will not be heard until the New Year, but they spell big money. All this is in addition to the winners they now have running in this country and America. You want to know what Kennedy and Carr are making in hard cash? Well. I'll whisper it very softly – £60 a week each. Not so bad for giving us something to sing – eh? But please don't think it is easy and you can all do it, for only about one in a million makes real big money from song writing and, believe me, there's no room for any more!'

Another film from this period was *Songwriters on Parade*, a British Lion film made at Beaconsfield and directed by Herbert Smith, a follow-up to stage and radio presentations of the same name. The film was based on the rise to fame of the top writers from Tin Pan Alley and both Kennedy and Carr had speaking parts as well as singing their famous numbers and contributing new material. They were joined by Tin Pan Alley 'founder' Lawrence Wright and other well-known songwriters, including the trio of Box, Cox and Roberts, Ralph Butler, and Bruce Sievier. The press hand-out accompanying the film said: 'No more fascinating or romantic career than song writing exists. The film will take you behind the scenes to reveal the secrets of the song writing business.' The well-known actor, Jack Hobbs also took part, together with several variety artists. Maurice Winnick and his orchestra played the music. The publicity people at the film studios got someone to suggest to *The Sunday Graphic* that Kennedy and Carr were doing a special arrangement for a striptease act for the film – something unheard of for this kind of film – and completely untrue. The paper thought it a great piece of scandal and wrote up the story prominently. That gave Kennedy and Carr an opportunity to write to the paper to 'demand' an apology which was duly published: '*Songwriters on Parade* does not contain an act of this style nor has the inclusion of such an act ever been considered.' All good publicity!

The pair again wrote seven new songs for their next film, *Kicking the Moon Around,* a Vogue Films production shot at Pinewood Studios, directed by Walter Forde and released in 1938. Florence Desmond and singer Evelyn Dall were the stars, backed by Ambrose and his orchestra. Four songs from the score were *Mayfair Merry-go-round, It's the rhythm in Me, Two Bouquets* and *You're What's the Matter with Me.* Ambrose is quoted as saying that he was delighted to at last be making a film that he believed would be a challenge to the Americans 'since it is seldom one finds a strong story mingled with a series of original and catchy tunes'. Its producers billed it as the most ambitious musical production yet attempted by the British film industry – with a budget of £80,000! Incidentally, the publicity flysheet that went out with the film not only mentioned the running time, 78 minutes, but how many reels, nine, and the length, 7,038 feet.

Meanwhile Kennedy and Carr continued writing for other forms of entertainment. On one occasion the 'Street Singer', Arthur Tracey, an American vocalist who was immensely popular in the 1930s, needed a song in a hurry for a show he was doing at the Grand Theatre, Wolverhampton, so Kennedy and Carr had to drive 125 pre-motorway miles from London to see him personally to find out what he wanted. Then they rushed back to London at one o'clock in the morning, with Carr jotting down their ideas on the back of an old AA road map by torchlight as they drove along. By the time they were home, they had somehow contrived to finish the song. The next morning they had a hand-written copy ready and put it on an express train to Wolverhampton (they used to run on time!), so that Tracey had it soon after lunch. The whole thing was so quick that Tracey thought he had been fobbed off with an old song, something which would have been unacceptable to a top-line performer, so he rang them up to complain: 'I asked you for a new song, not an old one!' Once the pair had reassured him they actually *had* written a new song overnight to suit his requirements, he was full of praise. That night it went down so well with the audience, he decided to include it with other Kennedy and Carr numbers in his 1938 film, *Follow Your Star,* a musical romance based on his life set, fictitiously, in England.

Kennedy and Carr contributed song scores to many other films in those years. *Soft Lights and Sweet Music* (1936), for example, was a typical British musical featuring Ambrose and his orchestra and several variety acts. Another similar musical film was called *Around the Town,* starring comedian and scratchy violin player, Vic Oliver. Kennedy and Carr also penned the theme song for a British Lion production directed by Herbert Smith, *It's a Grand Old World,* starring Yorkshire comedian Sandy Powell, a national figure at the time. Then there was *Melody and Romance* for Hughie Green and his gang, starring Margaret Lockwood, a British Lion film made at Beaconsfield, directed by Maurice Elvey and they followed that up with a British International Pictures production called *Radio Parade of 1937* which co-starred bandleader Buddy Rogers and June Clyde. *Jericho* was their last film. It featured a song called *My Way*, which was sung in the film and later recorded by the great American bass baritone, Paul Robeson. There is usually no copyright in the title of a song – or a book – and in most cases anyone can reuse a title: The *My Way*, made famous by Frank Sinatra, is a completely different song and came out nearly thirty years later, in 1968. It was based on the French Francois and Thibaut *chanson, Comme d'Habitude*, which came out the year before but had been substantially rewritten by Paul Anka.

With so much work involved in writing potential million sellers, potboilers for shows, films, and other ad hoc occasions, £60 a week, the income quoted by Edwin Sefton for a successful songwriter, might not seem very much (though it works out at well over £100,000 a year in today's money). It was certainly nothing compared to what the bandleaders were reputed to earn. Jack Hylton, it was said, picked up £1,600 a week when he was doing shows at the London Palladium – presumably that included the wages for the band! Sefton's music business arithmetic nevertheless makes for interesting reading. Why was there such a disparity in earnings between writers and performers? Because the BBC paid out such small royalties on the music it broadcast, said Sefton. Although about 70 per cent of the programmes broadcast were music, only £100,000 of the £3.5 million public licence fees found its way to the composers, lyric writers and publishers. Since the publishers took most of that revenue, there was little left over for the creative writers. Thanks to the efforts of the Performing Right Society, things improved somewhat in 1937 when it negotiated better terms from the BBC so that another £250,000 a year was made available. However, the royalties paid were still a disproportionately small amount. In effect, popular music was subsidising the rest of the BBC's output. Looking at other sources of income from songs, Sefton said that sheet music for individual popular songs, the most important source of revenue for songwriters, usually retailed at around six old pence a copy. 25 per cent of this sum was supposed to go to the writer or writers. In practice, thanks to the spurious contracts that many had signed, or the involvement of foreign writers or publishers, things were rarely that simple and writers often earned far less than 25 per cent. Even smaller percentage royalties were earned from records: publishers and writers shared only 6.25 per cent of the selling price, with writers getting only 2 per cent to split between them. A fourth but very small source of income came from the few pennies earned for public performances at a dance or theatre. Where did the magic £60 a week come from? Edward Sefton went on to suggest that if a song sold 50,000 copies of sheet music and 10,000 records, the publishers would get around £600 and the writers would split about £125 between them, i.e. about £62 each. Most of Kennedy and Carr's songs sold far more copies than 50,000, so they and other top writers picked up higher royalties. But what a contrast with today, when songwriters – most of whom are also performers – can earn millions!

Films and shows and the glamorous social scene – mixing with other writers, artists and broadcasters – must have made for a very satisfying life for Kennedy and Carr. But they still had to contend with Peter Maurice's hard-headed boss, Jimmy Phillips. One Friday evening he asked Kennedy to write a song based on some musical ideas that Will Grosz had drafted and to have it ready by the following Tuesday for an Ambrose recording session. 'For once, probably because I was annoyed at having my weekend interrupted, I couldn't think of anything sufficiently distinctive to turn the raw music into something special,' my father recalled. 'But early on Monday morning, with the deadline only a day away, I walked out onto the lawn seeking inspiration and there coming down the road was a party of about ten schoolgirls – sixth formers, and very attractive – including a redhead. I had my title immediately: *Ten Pretty Girls*! After that the lyric was done in a matter of minutes. Naturally, I included the line, "And one was a saucy little redhead" . . .'

> *There were ten pretty girls at the village school.*
> *Picture ten pretty girls at the village school!*
> *They were sweet, small and tall*
> *And the boy loved them all*
> *But you can't marry ten pretty girls...*
> *Now, five were blondes and four brunettes*
> *And one was a saucy little redhead.*
> *The girls grew up and the boy left school*
> *And at 21 he wedded the saucy little red-head...*

The Ambrose recording, with a Sam Browne vocal, sent the English 'quaintie' very nearly to the top in America. Sadly, however, it was the last important song Jimmy Kennedy wrote with Will Grosz, who had decided to relocate to New York. He was a man of real talent and it is ironic that he probably made more money out of his popular compositions than he did out of his more classical music. He wrote to Kennedy in May 1939 saying that he had had good receptions from every publisher he had met in New York. Judging from his letters, Grosz seems to have liked America and he was very optimistic about the future: 'They all seem to like my music very much indeed – and, Jimmy, if we both could work over here we could make really a lot of hits.'

I think my father was tempted. He certainly had always intended to go over to the United States at some time –

preferably when he had a No. 1. But he still had a young family and war was becoming a near certainty. He wrote back that he would come over but the time was not yet right. Grosz had approached Shapiro, Bernstein & Co. in New York because of the firm's links with Peter Maurice but it seems that initially he did not get an enthusiastic response from Louis Bernstein, the senior partner in the firm: 'It looks like he is afraid to do business with me because of P.M. [Peter Maurice],' he wrote. In a later letter, in June 1939, Grosz told Kennedy that he had managed to place some of their work with other publishers, but nothing had come of it. But his talent was recognized because Louis Bernstein then asked him to collaborate with Billy Hill, a well-known American songwriter who had the words and music for two big hits behind him, *The Last Round-up* (1933) and *The Glory of Love* (1936). But he did not like Hill: 'I have never hoped to write with Billy Hill after the first time I saw him – drinking!' Writing to his friend later in the same year, he said, 'I wish you could spare the time to come over....Glad to hear that *South of the Border* [Kennedy and Carr wrote this in 1939] is No.1!

With the political situation getting ever worse in Europe, Will Grosz was very naturally worried about his family. In the same letter he added a postscript: 'Jimmy – something very important. Would you be so nice and extend the guarantee for my aunt, also for my uncle, because they need it – otherwise they never can come out of Austria. As you know, it is only a pro-forma thing and they have money in England and hope to get soon to the USA. Please, Jimmy, do me that favour and ring up my mother at home. She will be able to tell you all about it – she is terribly worried about her sister that the Nazis put her into a concentration camp. Please phone her at my home (MAI 6575) as soon as you get my letter and talk this over with her – Thanks!' My father provided the necessary guarantees and, as far as I am aware, the family also later moved to New York.

Who knows what would have happened if the Kennedy-Grosz partnership had continued. Unfortunately, it was not to be. Will Grosz had a heart attack and died on 10 December 1939 in New York, aged only 45.

# 13: Britain's first one-two in the American charts

Although Jimmy Kennedy wrote almost exclusively with Michael Carr during the last two years of the 1930s he also co-wrote a very popular novelty dance, *The Chestnut Tree*, with Tommie Connor and his younger brother Hamilton. It became the dance sensation of 1938. Hamilton had followed in his brother's footsteps, going up to Trinity College, Dublin and then coming to London in 1931 where he taught for a period while he waited for his own chance to break into the music business. He lived for a time with Jimmy in Ladbroke Grove and then, helped by contacts made through him, began to get known for performing and writing songs, especially hillbillies, either on his own or in collaboration with writers such as Michael Carr, with whom he wrote, *Ole Faithful*, a million-seller 'fake' cowboy best seller which was a favourite of Will Rogers, the top-paid American movie star of the 1930s. Hamilton, however, never made song writing his full time career despite considerable success over the years. Instead, thanks in part to his performing talent, he joined the light entertainment side of the BBC, becoming well-known for his long-running show, 'Call of the West'.

C. L. Heimann, the Danish head of Mecca, owner of Britain's biggest dance circuit, the Locarno, sparked off the idea of a new dance. Mecca controlled 300 dance bands in its 2000 establishments so was among the most influential organizations in the British dance scene. *The Lambeth Walk* had taken his dance halls by storm in early 1938 and he wanted something just as successful to follow it, commissioning Jimmy Phillips to see what his writers could come up with.

*Jimmy Kennedy's younger brother, Hamilton,*
*had a successful career as a songwriter,*
*performer and BBC producer.*

Conceiving a guaranteed dance sensation out of the blue was a tall order and Kennedy, Connor and Kennedy struggled to find ideas for several days. In the end inspiration came from a photograph the elder Kennedy had puzzled over in the newspaper a few months earlier. It had shown a youthful King George VI at a Boy Scout jamboree and it was an unusual picture because the King and the scouts around him all had a hand on their heads. When he asked his wife Peggy what they were doing, she said she thought it was probably a Boy Scout game. Back at the office, Kennedy showed the picture to Tommie Connor, who remembered it as the Scouts doing their version of *The Village Blacksmith*. The Longfellow poem was well known to every schoolchild and began '*Under a spreading chestnut tree, the village smithy stands...*' It was a long shot but could they turn the game into a dance?

*A youthful King George VI unwittingly inspired The Chestnut Tree.*

A 1939 article shows the three songwriters in the Peter Maurice offices, smoking furiously, collars and ties loosened, laughing their heads off as they tried to brainstorm a lyric based on the Longfellow poem with the dance steps to go with it: 'We wanted something that was fun, that anyone could do – a dance for the non-dancer, if you like,' said Jimmy Kennedy at the time. Eventually they came up with a jointly composed tune and some rudimentary steps, inviting Adele England, who had choreographed *The Lambeth Walk*, to make them more professional. She knew how to invent movements to fit in with the Heinmann philosophy of creating actions that were so simple and fun that anyone could do them straight away.

The result was a hilarious dance performance. Phillips was against it at first but came round to the idea when Heimann said he liked it and mobilised his vast publicity resources to promote it – he even got Jimmy Kennedy, not the best of actors, to do a stunt newspaper photo call 'teaching' a chimpanzee how to do the dance. Two weeks later, *The Chestnut Tree* sheet music was on sale in the shops, complete with all the steps and hand actions and with the strict warning that 'this dance must not be performed until the evening of Tuesday, 15 November 1938'. That was the day the bands would have their parts and the dance could be rolled out simultaneously across the country. Adele England coached the Locarno dance instructors so they could show customers the steps when the tune was played for the first time, and she was also up with the band, leading dancers at the first performance in Streatham.

Soon *The Chestnut Tree* was selling over 10,000 copies a day – taking the British dancing public by storm. It was recorded by Ambrose and all the other bands – including Jack Hylton, Joe Loss, Oscar Rabin, Harry Leader and Victor Silvester. American band leader Hal Kemp gave it a boost in the US where it reached No.12, adding it to his repertoire at the Waldorf Astoria in New York, and making it an instant hit with the smart set there. Later it was taken up by dance halls all over America. Glenn

Miller's big band version was later featured in the film classic, *Memphis Belle* (1990).

The words became so well-known that they are almost themselves part of folk music:

*Underneath the Spreading Chestnut Tree*
*I loved her and she loved me*
*There she used to sit upon my knee*
*'Neath the spreading chestnut tree.*

*There beneath the boughs we used to meet,*
*All her kisses were so sweet*
*All the little birds went tweet, tweet, tweet,*
*'Neath the spreading chestnut tree.*

*I said, 'I love you, and there ain't no ifs or buts'*
*She said, 'I love you.' And the Blacksmith shouted, Chestnuts!'*
*Underneath the Spreading Chestnut Tree*
*There she said she'd marry me*
*Now you ought to see our family*
*'Neath the Spreading Chestnut Tree.*

The popularity of the action song inspired numerous rhyming parodies, especially among children, just like *Roll Along Covered Wagon* a few years before. Again, they were recorded by Iona and Peter Opie in *The Language and Lore of Schoolchildren*. In their book, they identified the four main social events of the 1930s as being Amy Johnson's 1930 record-breaking solo flight to Australia; Mussolini's invasion of Abyssinia in 1935; the abdication of Edward VIII in 1936; and, in the run-up to the War, air-raid precautions, or 'ARP'. These events, together with murders and other notorious news stories, figured in the topical rhymes that children sang in the playgrounds when they played games or when they got together with school friends at home. Most of these rhymes were sung to the tunes of the Tin Pan Alley songs of the day and could spread round the country from playground to playground like wildfire – frequently in a matter of 24 hours or less after a radio broadcast.

One early *Chestnut Tree* rhyme took up the air raid precaution/ ARP theme: *Underneath the spreading chestnut tree / Mr Chamberlain said to me / If you want to get your gas mask free / join the blinking ARP* According to the Opies, this same rhyme was still being used 14 years later in 1952 in Aberdeen, where schoolgirls who had not even been born when the Munich Pact was signed in 1938, used it to count the bounces when 'playing balls'. During the War, many other versions of the dance circulated among youngsters. *Underneath the churchyard six feet deep / There lies Hitler fast asleep/ All the little micey tickle his feet / 'Neath the churchyard six feet deep.* This was collected in 1954 in Stockton-on-Tees. Another, which was very similar, from Tunstall in Staffordshire, went *Underneath the water six feet deep / There lies Hitler fast asleep / All the little tadpoles tickle his feet / 'Neath the water six feet deep.*

A few years earlier the words of *Red Sails in the Sunset* had been changed out of all recognition by schoolchildren: *Red stains on the carpet, Red stains on your knife / Oh Dr. Buck Ruxton, you murdered your wife / The nursemaid saw you, and threatened to tell / Oh Dr Buck Ruxton, you killed her as well.* The grisly new lyric referred to a famous murder case in 1935 when Dr Buck Ruxton, an Indian-born doctor (he had changed his name by deed poll from Hakim Buktyar Rustomji Ratanji) working in Lancaster, was hanged for murder. He had killed his wife and nursemaid in a jealous rage, dismembered their bodies, and dumped them in a ravine in Dumfriesshire. Apart from the gruesome nature of the murder, the case was interesting at the time as one of the first to be solved using fingerprints.

Following *The Chestnut Tree*, Kennedy and Carr got together to write a 1938 waltz intended for a pantomime called *Cinderella (Stay in my Arms)*. It was very popular on both sides of the Atlantic thanks to US recordings by Glenn Miller and Kenny Baker; and UK recordings by Joe Loss with a Chick Henderson vocal, Ambrose with a Vera Lynn vocal, and Victor Silvester, in strict tempo. After the War, Val Doonican sang it with the Frank Chacksfield orchestra in his first radio programme. But *Cinderella* was nothing like as big as the song which followed it, *South of the Border (Down Mexico Way)* which, so my father told me, started in a 'funny sort of way':

Michael Carr came into the office one day and sat down at the piano and said, 'I've got a great opening for a western, Mr Kennedy. When he played the first few bars, I thought...western? I'm not so sure. It's got more colour than a western. I thought it perhaps sounded more Spanish.

As he played, I remembered that my sister Nell, who was teaching in California at the time, had sent me a postcard a few days before from Tijuana in Mexico, with the words 'Today we've gone Mexican - we're south of the border...' What about *South of the Border* as a title? I said to Carr, who quick as a flash added, '...*Down Mexico Way*!'. We both instantly realised that this would fit the music perfectly. I wrote the lyric for the chorus and added a middle - words and music - that afternoon.'

*South of the Border down Mexico way*
*That's where I fell in love, when stars above came out to play*
*And now as I wander my thoughts ever stray*
*South of the Border down Mexico way.*

*She was a picture in old Spanish lace*
*Just for a tender while I kissed the smile upon her face*
*For it was 'Fiesta' and we were so gay*
*South of the Border, down Mexico way...*

*Ay! Ay! Ay! Ay*
*Ay! Ay! Ay! Ay! ....etc*

139

Although both writers thought the song could go right to the top, Jimmy Phillips was not enthusiastic about it and refused to promote it and so it disappeared into a desk drawer, the graveyard of many other creative dreams. A few months later, however, Phillips decided to promote an Eric Maschwitz number called *The Same Old Story*. Peter Maurice used to have a sheet music service called the Orchestral Club, through which two arrangements were released back to back each month and sent off to club members, most of whom were provincial bandleaders – a cheap way for them to get professional arrangements. The Maschwitz song was to be the lead – 'the next big hit' – and Phillips asked Jimmy Kennedy to write something to accompany it. He refused. 'Why write something else when you've already got *South of the Border*?' he asked. He added: 'If you do not promote it, I will never write for you again.' Fearing he might carry out his threat, Phillips reluctantly agreed to include it and sent out an arrangement along with the Maschwitz song, but still as the 'B side'. However, when the arrangements reached the bands, they preferred *South of the Border* and it was soon on its way to the top of the best seller lists.

In Britain, *South of the Border* was played by all the contemporary bands, with leading recordings by Ambrose, Joe Loss, and a vocal version by Al Bowlly. In America, *Your Hit Parade* listeners voted it the No. 1 song of the year and it was also the No.1 sheet music seller there. A recording by Shep Fields and his orchestra topped the Billboard charts. Other contemporary recordings were by Guy Lombardo, Tony Martin, Gene Autry (who sang it in a film of the same name) and Ambrose (with a vocal by Denny Dennis) which reached No. 8 in 1940. They were followed at the time and down the years by hundreds of others in America, including Sammy Kaye, Kenny Baker, Benny Goodman, Tommy Dorsey, Perry Como, Tony Bennett, The Mills Brothers, Patti Page, The Stargazers, Horace Heidt, Gail Storm and many others.

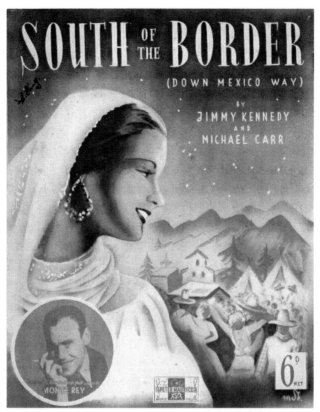

*South of the Border (Down Mexico Way) was voted top song of 1939 in America and remains a world standard.*

The song got a new lease of life with a recording by Frank Sinatra which reached No. 2 in the US charts in February 1954. Sinatra was followed by Bing Crosby singing the song in the 1960 Oscar nominated film *Pepe*, which starred the Mexican, idol, Cantinflas. Later Dean Martin sang it (with *Red Sails in the Sunset)*, in the film *The Silencers.* There was a stylish up-tempo version by Mel Tormé and a million-plus instrumental album version by Herb Alpert's appropriately named Tijuana Brass, which reached No. 6 in America in 1964. *South of the Border* has developed into a favourite for American country and western singers. Patsy Cline's 1961 version has been a steady seller for years and Connie Francis also recorded it. Many of the recordings are now available on the internet, including one by crooner Chris Isaacs, which can be heard on YouTube, where there are many other versions, including Patsy Cline's. Though the song never hit the peaks in the UK compared with America, it was still a colossal best seller and was recorded and played by all the main cotemporary UK bands and vocalists, and there were several later recordings, too, including The Shadows in 1962, part of their album *Out of the Shadows*. By then it had sold over 6 million records and over a million copies of sheet music. It was what Jimmy Kennedy called, 'a songwriter's dream'. Back in 1939, the original wrangle between Phillips and Kennedy had delayed its publication and this produced a surprising victim – Michael Carr. He had been rather hard up and thinking the song would end up in the archives never to be seen again, sold his writer's share and so lost out on years of royalties which must eventually have cost him tens of thousands of pounds. When asked what he did with the money from the sale of his rights, he came out with a typically flamboyant excuse: 'I decided to use it to play the stock market' – with World War II only months away!

While *South of the Border* was on its way to the top, Jimmy Kennedy was facing a challenge of a different kind: how to turn a long and soulful composition by the French salon violinist and composer, Georges Boulanger, into something more commercial. The melody of the composition had the unpromising title *Avant de Mourir*, which means 'Before Dying'. It was the kind of quaint nostalgic melody that musicians would play late at night in Parisian cafés. But the structure of the piece was not suitable for Tin Pan Alley arrangers and it had unusual minor chord sequences which seemed too complicated for a commercial popular song. Another problem was that the melody covered two octaves, a wide range for most singers. This is how he got over the problem:

I am not a trained musician and could not do the necessary major surgery to turn the music into something that would be commercial so I turned to Wally Ridley, the professional manager at Peter Maurice, who was a very talented piano player and arranger. With his technical help, I cut the 12-bar main theme of the piece to eight, with more understandable chords. Then I composed words and music for an introductory verse – "*When the twilight is gone/And no songbirds are singing*" etc – and added a new middle section. Finally we worked out a stronger finale. We kept the classical music instructions: *Andante Serenade* for the verse and *Con Sentimento* for the chorus. I had been somewhat stuck for an idea as to what to call it, until my wife Peggy came to my rescue. Why not call it *My Prayer*, she suggested. With that idea, I was able to finish the lyric relatively easily.

*When the twilight is gone*
*And no songbird is singing,*
*When the twilight is gone*
*You come into my heart,*
*And here in my heart you will stay*
*While I pray.*

*My Prayer is to linger with you*
*At the end of the day in a dream that's divine.*
*My Prayer is a rapture in blue*
*With the world far away and your lips close to mine...*

Glenn Miller's recording reached No. 2 in the US at exactly the same time that Shep Fields's version of *South of the Border* was No. 1, something no other British songwriter had done before – I understand a one-two in the American hit parade was not achieved again until The Beatles did it in the 1960s. *My Prayer* was featured on *Your Hit Parade* for 14 weeks. In addition to the Glenn Miller recording, The Ink Spots did a version which reached No. 3, one of the group's first big hits (Others included *Whispering Grass* and *Do I Worry?*). Jimmy Dorsey's version with a Frank Sinatra vocal was also popular at the time. Subsequent best-selling recording artists have included Joe Loss, Jack Hylton, Bert Kaempfert, Vera Lynn, Mantovani, Louis Armstrong, Roy Orbison, The Righteous Brothers and Tom Jones. But the list is almost endless. Perhaps the definitive version is the The Platters American No. 1 version of 1956/57.

*My Prayer* closed the chapter on the most successful decade of Jimmy Kennedy's professional career. He had risen from obscurity as a fresh-faced song writing hopeful from Ireland to a Tin Pan Alley star with worldwide hits to his name. But as the War became more and more inevitable, he decided to sacrifice his career, to join up in the common fight against Hitler. In the months leading up to the Declaration of War, he enlisted in the Territorial Army (TA), and shortly after that he swapped his tailor-made suits for the khaki serge of a bombardier in the Royal Artillery.

# 14: *Have you any dirty washing, mother dear?*

Jimmy Kennedy joined the TA as a trainee soldier in the spring of 1939 along with thousands of other people, including his brother. But Hamilton was not to see out the War in the forces. He was discharged on grounds of ill health, returning to his job as a BBC producer. Despite his army duties, Jimmy managed to write several best-sellers during the War, continuing his agreement with Peter Maurice as best he could until 1942 and then switching to Campbell, Connelly & Co.

It was while he was learning the soldier's trade that he teamed up with Michael Carr to write one of the most popular songs of the early part of the War, *The Washing on the Siegfried Line.* This was the period in late 1939 known as the 'phoney War', a time when people began to get increasingly nervous about what was going to happen, particularly the frightening prospect of air raids. Thousands of people had been killed in air raids in World War I and there were predictions that there could be as many as 65,000 casualties a week when, as was expected, Hitler started to bomb Britain a second time. Gas masks were handed out, artificial shelters devised, blackouts were introduced and plans for evacuation from cities were drawn up, all part of the air-raid precautions. *The Washing on the Siegfried Line* was a comedy song in the music hall tradition which helped lift the public mood by poking fun at the Germans.

There is an amusing story behind the writing of *The Siegfried Line.* The Territorial Army was not full-time, so Jimmy Kennedy and other volunteers were allowed to stay where they liked at this early stage of their training.

He frequently based himself at the up-market Mitre Hotel near Hampton Court, in south west London.

*One of many 1939 cartoons mocking the German's 'impregnable' Siegfried Line.*

One morning *The Daily Express* carried a cartoon drawn by St. John Cooper showing a young soldier writing home to his mother saying, 'I'm sending you the Siegfried Line to hang your washing on'. The Siegfried Line was a 630 kilometre long concrete fortification peppered with tunnels, forts and tank traps that had been built by the Germans along the country's western flank opposite the French Maginot Line and was supposedly Hitler's most impregnable line of defence. Naturally the Germans took it very seriously but the idea of hanging washing from it brought a chuckle to many Daily Express readers and, as he read it over breakfast, Kennedy thought he might be able to write something comic based on the cartoon. The next time he was in London he joked about it with Jimmy Phillips and back in the TA army mess he followed up the idea by writing some words and music for a *Siegfried Line* chorus to amuse his fellow soldiers and they sang it around an old piano, doubtless in riotous fashion after a few beers:

*We're gonna hang out the washing on the Siegfried Line,*
*Have you any dirty washing, mother dear?*
*We're gonna hang out the washing on the Siegfried Line*
*'Cos the washing day is here*
*Whether the weather may be wet or fine*
*We'll just rub along without a care.*
*We're gonna hang out the washing on the Siegfried Line*
*If the Siegfried Line's still there.*

At around the same time, the BBC rang up Jimmy Phillips urgently needing a comedy song for a Tommy Handley radio show going out the next night from its Bristol studios. Tommy Handley was the biggest star on radio, so it was a terrific song plugging opportunity and Phillips was keen to oblige. Remembering the conversation about the Daily Express cartoon, he dispatched Michael Carr to find Kennedy with orders to turn the idea into a song that day so that it could be hand-delivered to the BBC's Bristol studios in time for the show the same evening. Carr hoped to find his colleague at The Mitre where they could write something over a pint. But he was not there so Carr had to go down to the Territorial Army unit HQ to find out where he was and to request permission to see him on 'urgent business'. There he was informed that Bombardier Kennedy was patrolling a local reservoir at Sunbury and the duty sergeant emphasised that under no circumstances should he be disturbed. Carr was not fussed about army regulations. The song was much more important. So he sneaked up to the reservoir to find his co-writer and see if they could cobble up something *al fresco* just as they had done so many times before.

My father recalled the rest of the story some years later:

I knew nothing of this because I had been away from the hotel on duty all morning. But then, as I was patrolling the reservoir, I spotted Carr's familiar figure waving at me from behind a bush and I thought to myself, whatever he is up to this time! When I got to him, he told me all about the BBC request and how we had to write something there and then. With such a short deadline, all I could do was to sing him the chorus I'd already done. But he still wanted me to help him finish the whole thing off by writing lyrics for the verses. There was nothing for it but to make them up as I marched round the reservoir, whispering them to Carr after each circuit. The first lap produced:

*Mother dear, I'm writing you from somewhere in France,*
*Hoping this finds you well.*
*Sergeant says I'm doing fine 'A soldier and a half'.*
*Here's the song that we'll all sing*
*It'll make you laugh!*

The second circuit produced:

*Ev'rybody's mucking in and doing their job*
*Wearing a great big smile.*
*Ev'rybody's got to keep their spirits up today.*
*If you want to keep in swing*
*Here's the song to sing.*

As I went round, Carr tidied everything up and at the end sang it right the way through. Amazingly, it was OK. We had another hit on our hands. Written on patrol!'

With the scribbled ditty in his pocket, Carr rushed off to meet Phillips in London and the two of them caught a train to Bristol to make sure personally the BBC got it on time. It was broadcast that evening on the Tommy Handley show and was an instant success. The next day, Jimmy Phillips promoted it by stringing washing across Tin Pan Alley. This was strictly illegal and the police came to tell him to take it down, but it made for a good story and generated plenty of publicity, with pictures in all the newspapers. Phillips continued working very hard on promotion, updating his star writer in a letter of 29 September 1939 to say: 'I am sending out 1,500 records to every cinema of note in the country. This is the Billy Cotton record sung by Alan Breeze and it is a smasher. I have sent out about 200 slides and taken half a page in *Era* and *Stage* and the front page of *Performer* and have sent professional copies to every name on the files, which includes about 10,000 people. *Military and Brass* goes out next week and I am sending it to the army bands with thousands of small leaflets, about 100,000, with the words for the boys to sing.'

In addition to Billy Cotton all the other bands featured the song with recordings by Ambrose, Joe Loss, Sydney Lipton and Harry Roy. And it was a natural for leading comedians and entertainers such as Arthur Askey, Tommy Trinder, Evelyn Laye, Lupino Lane, Bebe Daniels and Ben Lyon and The Crazy Gang stars Flanagan and Allen, who featured it, along with other Kennedy and Carr songs, in the London Palladium show, *The Little Dog Laughed*, in late 1939.

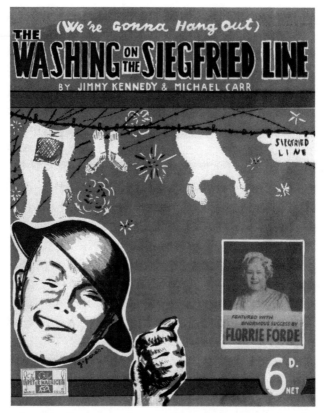

*The Washing on the Siegfried Line, the best-selling morale-booster of the early part of World War II.*

Michael Carr, who was still a civilian, had been going round the country being introduced as the man who had thought up the *Siegfried Line,* which annoyed Kennedy, who *had* joined up and had written most of it. Knowing the friction between the two men, I think this probably amused Jimmy Phillips. He refers to it in his letter: 'I know your nose is out of joint regarding Mike but I can assure you he has not been grabbing the space at your expense. One or two write-ups have come out where he has been on the spot on the stage singing it and reporters naturally made a fuss of him but I have got the publicity book in the office at Farnham and you can see all the publicity yourself. You can see that the major part of it covers you and refers to you owing to the fact that you are in the army, and they have picked up this point first. In fact that has been one of my main points in the campaign, that you wrote the song in snatches off duty and so forth.'

Phillips then goes on to talk about sales. Jimmy Kennedy was not the only person to think up the idea of writing a song based on the cartoon. Ross Parker and Hughie Charles (later to write the big wartime standard, *There'll Always be an England*) wrote a version as well and it was published by Irwin Dash. Phillips goes on to say: 'Now, regarding sales. I am pleased to tell you that we have smashed the Dash song. Yesterday we did 3,000 copies and today we look like doing 6,000 and we have got rid of the best part of 15,000 copies in a week. I think this is remarkable as we only had sales copies out a week.'

There follows a revealing paragraph about dealings with the BBC and the difficulty of getting the all-important plugs:

Regarding the BBC angle, this is particularly stringy. The only plugs that have been available up to now have been the BBC's new productions and these are just like the productions they used to run and are just as awkward and difficult to get a popular song in. You know the old snag, the producer writes a script and sticks in a lot of manuscript material (i.e. unpublished music) so that they can collect the royalties and get the fees? Well, it is just the same at [BBC] Bristol. There are about eight to ten shows going over every week and the producers have their own ideas as to what they ought to use as far as published songs are concerned. There are 20 representatives down there from the publishers and you can imagine each producer is pestered to death by these 20 fellows including our own and it is a nightmare for them as well as the boys, but we are getting a little daylight now. They are putting on bands once a fortnight. Hylton is on for a fortnight and Billy Cotton follows him and then Jack Payne and then Geraldo and so forth. So we are going to line up the bands and make sure we get three or four smashing plugs from the bands that are working.

We had the song on in the *Sing Song* last Monday and it was on the records last Wednesday. It was on last night in *At the Billet-Doux* and it is on Saturday night in *Gentlemen you may smoke*. That isn't a bad average, Jimmy, three shows a week. Billy Ternent, who is running Hylton's band, is going to play it also and we are trying to move heaven and earth to get Jack Hulbert to sing it on Saturday night.

Well, I think that's all the news for the moment, Jimmy. I would like to see you but only got back from Bristol myself yesterday and have been up to my neck in work at the office since and I am going to Bognor over the weekend to see the Missus and the kiddies, but will be back on Monday and then onwards, and in the evenings at Farnham Royal until the end of the week anyway, so get in touch with me and let us have a chat on the 'phone, or better still, let's try and fix a time so that we can get together.

In case Kennedy had forgotten that he was still under contract he added: 'I hope you got the top lines that I sent you OK and hope you are working on them.'

It was not just the bands and the BBC that performed *The Siegfried Line*. The Ministry of Information liked it so much that it was smuggled to neutral countries in Diplomatic Bags. In a matter of days, Allied countries and the Dominions cabled for rights and the lyric was translated into many languages. However, despite the fact that it was the most popular song of the first phase of the War, it was banned by some American radio stations because the United States was neutral at that time.

When the Germans heard it broadcast by the BBC in 1939, they were furious that the British should mock their supposedly impregnable defensive wall. German radio said it could not understand how a song like that could be produced by the 'men of a British anti-aircraft unit' because 'soldiers do not brag'. And, the broadcast went on, since it could not have been written by soldiers, the 'Jewish scribes' of the BBC must have been responsible. Lord Haw Haw, the American-born Irish-educated Nazi radio propagandist William Joyce, made wild attacks in his German radio broadcasts every few nights, calling it 'A low ditty in disgusting taste for the debauched British soldiery'. 'Haw Haw said as soon as the German army got to London, they would put the writers and the publishers into a concentration camp!' said my father. 'It was a terrific laugh because everybody knew they would never ever make it to London! Even better, after every broadcast we sold another 50,000 copies!'

But Dunkirk stopped the song in its tracks. The evacuation of the British Expeditionary Force in May 1940 signalled the end of the phoney phase of the War and the song, with its cheeky, optimistic words was taken off the air – though the troops still kept singing it. Then the Germans started to get their own back. With the Allies temporarily on the back foot, the Germans used it against them by playing parody versions in all the countries they occupied. Lord Haw Haw sent out mocking broadcasts and Goebbels used the song in a propaganda film. Jimmy Kennedy was furious: 'He did it in a minor key, like a dirge, with a lot of rat-a-tat-a-tat, saying "…and that is the British hanging out the washing. Ha! Ha! Ha!"' Kennedy was also upset by a book called *All Our Tomorrows* (1942) by a well-respected author and journalist, Douglas Reed, who knew nothing about the amusing background to *The Siegfried Line.* He wrote that the Nazi propaganda based on the song could not have been more damaging to the Allied cause at the time: 'The German films made at the German campaign in Belgium, France and Holland, and distributed throughout the neutral world, begin with a long picture of British soldiers trudging to the tune of *We're Gonna Hang out the Washing on the Siegfried Line.* These unfortunate men, many of them today prisoners in Germany, were the dupes of the BBC's "Sing 'em to sleep" policy which played so great a part in the process of mass delusion leading to the War. How many times a day was that lunatic tune dinned into the ears of a hopelessly unready people?' A year or two before he wrote the book, Reed had resigned as central Europe correspondent of *The Times* over Chamberlain's appeasement strategy and his words carried a lot of weight (though a few years later his apparently anti-Semitic views led to him being discredited by many).

Kennedy reacted by saying that he certainly did not consider himself as part of any propaganda machine: 'Nor was I deluding the public. I thought Reed took a very defeatist line. *The Washing on the Siegfried Line* was a song of hope, with the battlefield and the family as its backdrop.' As a response, he wrote a love song based on the title of Reed's book with a lyric that was also optimistic, if somewhat romantic, even though victory in the War was still by no means assured when it was eventually published, in 1943:

> *Today, we wonder much about tomorrow*
> *Will we be together or apart?*
> *Here's a little song for each tomorrow.*
> *Keep it in the corner of your heart.*
>
> *All Our Tomorrows will be sunny days.*
> *In so many ways, I'll make you happy.*
> *All Our Tomorrows will be one sweet song.*
> *How can we go wrong with so much love?*

He sent *All Our Tomorrows* to Reed but never got a reply. However, it soared to the top of the wartime best-seller list thanks to recordings by Joe Loss, Jimmy Miller and the Royal Air Force Dance orchestra, and Wilfred Pickles.

At the end of the War, Jimmy Kennedy found out first hand that *The Washing on the Siegfried Line* really had been a song of hope, not despair. As a staff officer during the final phase of the War in Europe, he was invited to a concert in 1945 to celebrate the liberation of Brussels and the return of the famous Brussels Metropole orchestra, which had not played in public since the Germans occupied the city. The concert programme started with the Belgian national anthem, then the *Marseillaise, God Save the King, The Stars and Stripes* – all the Allies' national anthems, finishing with a second rendition of the Belgian national anthem. The event took an hour or more, with pauses in between each anthem as everyone cheered. Jimmy Kennedy takes up the story: 'And then the concert ended, or so I thought. We were all about to get up and leave when suddenly the band struck up a chord. And what did they play? Quite unexpectedly it was *The Washing on the Siegfried Line*! I was astonished. And I was there! It was really a dramatic thing – in fact I was almost in tears. After everything that had gone before, I at last felt justified. It really was a tremendous thing.' Apparently the song had achieved cult status in Belgium. It had been taught to children studying English right through the German occupation. In defiance of the Gestapo – any adult found singing it would have been shot – even the youngest child delighted in learning the words in secret so they would be able to sing them to '*Les Anglais*' when they arrived to liberate them.

Then, in the spring of 1945, Kennedy was with a Second Army HQ convoy moving into Germany and its route crossed the Reichwald Forest, through which the Siegfried Line had run. The sector was in Canadian Army territory and the Canadians had clearly sign-posted the route. As the convoy approached a gigantic fortification captured by the Canadians, there was a very large sign in enormous letters bearing the legend 'THIS IS THE SIEGFRIED LINE'. A few hundred yards further was a wire slung across the road between two massive forts with an incredible collection of nylons, socks and so on hanging from it. Above was an even bigger sign saying, 'AND THIS IS THE WASHING!'

*The Washing on the Siegfried Line* was the last important song Kennedy and Carr wrote together. Carr went on to write some more hits, including a wartime favourite called *Somewhere in France with You* and eventually joined the army on special entertainment duties, where he was given the rank of sergeant. Typically, he used his 'promotion' to write *How Did You Ever Become a Sergeant?* After the War, like most other older professional songwriters, Carr found it difficult to adjust to the new pop scene as it moved down the generations to a progressively younger audience. He had few successes during the 1950s, but achieved some good UK best-sellers in the early 1960s, notably with The Shadows, who recorded *Man of Mystery* (1960), the theme for the Edgar Wallace TV series, which reached No. 2, and *Kon-Tiki* (1961), which got to the top of the British charts. He died in 1968.

In 1940, just before Dunkirk, Jimmy Kennedy had an important but short-lived chart success with *There's a Boy Coming Home on Leave,* which was popularised by Flanagan and Allen and also recorded by Ambrose (vocal Jack Cooper), and Maurice Winnick (vocal Al Bowlly). The idea came when my father was on leave, travelling on a London bus. He overheard two women talking to each other, one of whom said: 'She's very happy. Her boy's coming home on leave!' Although the song was an instant hit, it quickly met the same fate as *The Siegfried Line* and had to be taken off the air by the BBC. After the Dunkirk disaster, too many soldiers were not coming home.

Soon after, in July 1940, the Battle of Britain started in earnest and, as the German and British air forces locked horns for mastery of the skies, hundreds of thousands of children were evacuated away from vulnerable towns and cities to stay with families in the safer countryside. With bombs dropping and talk of an invasion by the Germans, Jimmy Kennedy decided that his own family also needed protection. After much thought, he decided to send them off to America while it was still possible to leave the country. His relationship with Peggy had been rocky for some time. She was sulky and bad tempered, given to throwing plates around and, moreover, did not treat their children well but he decided her attitude might improve if she left the tensions of the marriage and the bombings in England behind her. He was earning sizeable royalties in America so she could draw on these and if anything happened to him, the family would be safe until the end of the War. So, in August 1940, he said good-bye to Peggy and their two children, five-year-old Derek and three-year-old Janet. They sailed from Southampton to New York and a very different life in America. Seven months later, in March 1941, she gave birth in New York to an unexpected second son, James, the author of this book.

With his family now settled far away from the bombing, Jimmy Kennedy continued a small but steady output from a succession of army camps – the War did not stop the flow of ideas. *St Mary's in the Twilight*, which he wrote in 1941, the No. 1 best seller for several weeks, is an interesting example in that it evoked strongly the mood of the period. He wrote it when he heard about the bombing of a famous church designed by Sir Christopher Wren, in London's East End. The bombing had a sequel. After the War, the residents of Fulton, Missouri had the ruins of the church transported to the United States and it was rebuilt stone by stone in their town as a memorial to Sir Winston Churchill. *St Mary's in the Twilight* was recorded by Vera Lynn and by Anne Shelton.

*Only four walls and an altar stand,*
*All that is left is a shrine.*
*Tho' it is old, those walls still hold many mem'ries divine.*
*St Mary's in the twilight*
*With ivy clinging*
*Two lovers often wander*
*Where once a choir was singing.*
*With so much to remember.*
*St Mary's in the twilight*
*Just as it used to be.*

Though Kennedy continued to write new material, his 1930s standards were played extensively. Jimmy Phillips repackaged *South of the Border* during the War, taking the picture of the alluring *señorita* off the pre-War sheet music cover and substituting a squad of kilted Scottish soldiers on the march. He then gave it a subtitle, *The Tommie's Theme Song*, raised the cover price from sixpence to a shilling, and it became one of the most popular songs of the War years.

Soldiers at the front frequently put their own (often very rude) words to popular songs to suit their own circumstances – their homes, girl friends, regiments, battles, campaigns – singing these versions at concert parties or simply when they were on the march. For example, there are many troop song versions of *South of the Border*. Many versions – *South of Colombo, South of the Sango* and *South of Meiktila, for example* – can be found in Roy Palmer's fascinating book, *What a Lovely War!* (Michael Joseph, 1990). As their names imply, these were places where troops were involved in heavy jungle fighting and the lyrics reflect this. *The Chestnut Tree* was also a popular template for some very interesting and unorthodox lyrics.

As might be expected, the entertainment industry slowed down as the War went on. Blackout regulations were universal, affecting not just the lighting in homes and factories but even car headlamps. Many theatres and cinemas struggled on despite the difficulties – but radio became the paramount source of entertainment and information led by people like disc jockey Christopher Stone, whose article on Gracie Fields had given Jimmy Kennedy the idea for *Isle of Capri*, and cinema theatre organist Sandy Macpherson. Other light music programmes such as *Music While You Work* and *Workers' Playtime* were very popular and there were numerous special shows for the armed forces featuring stars such as Vera Lynn, the 'Forces Sweetheart'. She had her own show, *Sincerely Yours*, as did singer Anne Shelton with *Calling Malta*. And Henry Hall, who had made the famous *Teddy Bears' Picnic* recording, had a programme called *Guest Night*. Variety shows on radio also became a key element in keeping beleaguered Britain smiling. Tommy Handley, who had introduced *The Washing on the Siegfried Line*, headed the cast in the best known of all the wartime shows, *ITMA (It's That Man Again)*. Bebe Daniels and Ben Lyon had a show called *Hi Gang*.

Men and women serving in the armed forces also put on their own entertainment, even in faraway places like the jungle in Burma, and these home-grown efforts were boosted in 1940 by a dedicated organisation called ENSA. The initials stood for 'Entertainments National Service Association', though it was popularly called 'Every Night Something Awful'. Despite what people called it, ENSA was considered to be very successful and is credited with playing a big part in keeping up morale in the services. It was based at Drury Lane and headed by a well-known impresario of the time, Basil Dean. ENSA was responsible for sending out thousands of entertainers at home, in service centres, clubs, tube stations, air raid shelters and factories, and abroad, wherever troops were serving

159

in the various theatres of war. All the top performers – and legions of lesser-known artists – did their bit for ENSA, often travelling under very dangerous conditions. George Formby was reputedly one of the first to go out to new war zones and Gracie Fields gave the first concert in France. But there were countless others, including Vera Lynn, who travelled extensively in the Far East, as did nearly all the bands. Allied Forces also supplied entertainment for the troops and this led to one of the most tragic casualties, Glenn Miller, who was killed in an air crash in 1944.

In June 1940, Jimmy Kennedy was sent to the Officer Cadet Training Unit at Shrivenham, Wiltshire, and on completing his training in September, was commissioned as a Second Lieutenant in the Royal Artillery. Because of his song writing background, he was given a welfare remit to help boost morale on the entertainment side, though he had other staff duties, too, and was trained to fight just like a regular soldier (so he said!). For a time, he was stationed at the Bishop's Palace, Llandaff, Cardiff, with the 9th Anti-Aircraft division. There everybody knew his songs, so it was difficult for him to avoid the limelight. But there were some things he did not know. For example, a few years ago after I was a guest on a BBC radio programme talking about his career, a lady wrote in to say that she and some other female civilians had been stationed in an office on the driveway up to the Palace in Cardiff and... 'Every time Lieutenant Kennedy passed our windows we would quietly strike up *Red Sails in the Sunset* la-la...and everybody would say "Ah!" He was always referred to as 'Red Sails'. I remember then he had dark wavy hair and was smart and slim.' If only he had known he had those secret admirers!

The rigours of wartime army life must have meant it was hard to remain aloof to the charms of the opposite sex and the young Lieutenant did fall very hard some 18 months later for a young lady called Kitty, a redhead he met on a train when he was going on weekend leave. According to a later girlfriend, Kitty was the love of his life. But the relationship never developed. She was posted somewhere else and they lost touch. All that is left of the brief affair is a silver-plated tankard that she gave him for his fortieth birthday inscribed with the words:

'To Jims from Kit. July 20 1942. Life beJims at 40!'

# 15: Denis Thatcher – an unlikely friendship

While he was in Cardiff, Kennedy helped to script comedy entertainments for the forces (sometimes produced by his brother, Hamilton), many of which were broadcast by the BBC with titles which were 'in' at the time like '*ACK-ACK, BEER-BEER*', '*She Was a Smart Girl*' and '*The Gag Song*'. And it was there, too, that he began a life-long friendship with Denis Thatcher. Lieutenant Kennedy was allocated a desk in the office of Staff Captain Thatcher. At first, the more serious minded Thatcher was not too pleased about having the entertainments officer so close but they soon got on very well. In a radio programme almost 50 years later, Denis was asked what kind of soldier my father was: 'Soldier?' he replied, 'He was never a soldier! I first met him when I was a staff captain in the Royal Artillery in Cardiff. He came into my office, gave me the sloppiest salute I had ever seen, and said he had been allocated a desk there. But we got on famously. He was a lovely, lovely person. He was such a generous-hearted man. That made him an exception. He was one of the most generous-hearted men I have ever met in my life. And he was always charming. And his sense of humour! He would start telling stories and I would say, "Jim, for God's sake get out of here – I've got work to do!" He was absolutely super and everybody loved him. He was also a good businessman but, strangely enough, despite obviously being a good musician having written all those songs, he did not play the piano very well.' For good measure, Denis also remembered something that Kennedy often used to say: that the important thing about a song was the idea, but it was no good repeating the idea too closely, or it would not work. Many years later, in the 1980s, Denis Thatcher made some additional and revealing comments about him in a letter to broadcaster Steve Race, who was at the time compiling an entry about Jimmy Kennedy in the National Dictionary of Biography:

Jim had all the charm and kindness of the Irish and the Irishman's temper on occasion. His own father's experiences during the 'troubles' of 1921/22 had a great influence on Jim, who was old enough by that time to realise what was going on. From his father and his father's profession, Jim had an enormous feel for people of all ages and conditions and this was reflected in his work. He was a wonderful friend to those who *were* his friends BUT he disliked the insincere and the pompous and showed it.

In those years and immediately after, Jim's hobby was women. A hobby he pursued with enthusiasm and determination. He could charm them witless from 16 to 60, sending 'em weak at the knees in three minutes flat!

I wonder if Denis knew that Jimmy Kennedy's favourite present for his lady friends was a very nice cuddly teddy bear!

Jimmy Kennedy had an important influence on Denis Thatcher's life in those middle years of the War. Denis, who was ten or so years younger, was unmarried when they first got to know each other and, with Peggy in America, Jimmy was on his own, too. The two men liked to go up to London when they had short periods of leave. Jimmy knew London well so he would lead the way, taking Denis to a show or to a club to socialise and hear the latest hot numbers played by the top bands. In fact, it was he who introduced Denis to his first wife, Margaret Kempson, at one of the war-time tea dances held at the Grosvenor House Hotel in Park Lane. The two must have got on well very quickly because he proposed to her soon after that introduction. They were married in March 1942, with Kennedy as best man. I think it reasonable to assume that Margaret and Jimmy had been good friends before the introduction. Certainly, when Denis had to leave on a trip not long after their wedding, he asked his friend to ensure Margaret was looked after. Many years later, Jimmy told his closest female friend that on one occasion when he was invited to dinner *à deux* with Margaret, she disappeared upstairs while he was mixing the cocktails. A few minutes later, she called out to him from the landing and when he looked up, she was leaning over the banisters with a come hither look, stark naked.

Unhappily, the marriage between Margaret and Denis did not survive the War and, along with thousands of other couples, they were divorced in 1948. Margaret Kempson went on to marry a diplomat and Denis went on to marry Margaret Roberts, so starting on a path that would eventually lead to him becoming the consort of Britain's first lady Prime Minister. Denis and Jimmy Kennedy temporarily lost touch in 1943 when Denis was promoted and went overseas and after the War, Kennedy spent several years in America so they rarely met up again until the 1960s when they started to have occasional sociable lunches – less frequently after Denis went to live at Number 10, Downing Street following the 1979 general election. As a result of his association with Denis, Kennedy also occasionally met the second Margaret. Again, he was always very discreet about such social activity but I do remember him telling me after a reception at Number 10 during the early 1980s that she laughed uproariously at his rendition of the story of the elephant and the mouse – the one where the she elephant rewards a mouse who has pulled a thorn out of its foot with any wish it wants......and ends with the punch line of the amorous mouse saying to the elephant, 'Am I hurting you darling?'

# 16: How he did the *Cokey Cokey*

*Kennedy adapted a Canadian folk song to create the famous party dance after a night out with Canadian troops while on leave in London in 1942.*

In 1942, at the height of the War, Jimmy Kennedy left Peter Maurice and joined publisher Campbell, Connelly & Co, which was still owned and managed by its two songwriter founders and was by now one of the leading popular music publishing houses. As part of the informal arrangement with them he created his own Kennedy Music Co under a Campbell, Connelly umbrella and, free of Jimmy Phillips, was able to write whatever he wanted whenever he wanted to, no strings attached.

Soon after, in 1942, he wrote his most famous dance lyric, an adaptation of a Canadian folk song, the *Cokey Cokey* (Kennedy always insisted on calling it *Cokey Cokey* not *Hokey Cokey*). 'Writing it was an accident,' he once told me. 'It was late 1942 and I was on leave in London staying at The Dorchester, which used to give me a special room rate during the War, and went to see an old friend of mine, Al Tabor. Al had a band in a Soho dance haunt called Murray's Club and some Canadian officers were there having a party. They were having a hilarious time, singing and playing games, one of which they said was a Canadian children's game called the *Cokey Cokey*, in which they moved their arms and legs in and out to an old Canadian tune. I thought to myself, wouldn't it be fun if I could turn all those seemingly random movements into a dance to cheer people up! When I got back to the hotel, I wrote a chorus based on the feet and hand movements the Canadians had used, with a few adaptations. Later, when I returned to my unit in Cardiff, I wrote additional lyrics but kept the title. Campbell, Connelly, published it and as everybody knows, it became a big hit and is danced everywhere at the end of just about every party.'

*Way out West where there ain't no swing,*
*Old time Ragtime's still the thing,*
*They've a little song they like to dance and sing*
*It's called the 'Cokey Cokey!'*

*Ev'rybody on their toes,*
*This is the way it goes.*

*You put your Left arm out, Left arm in,*
*Left arm out and shake it all about,*
*You do the Cokey Cokey and turn around*
*That's what it's all about. SEE?*
*It's called the Cokey Cokey*
*It's corny but it's O.K.*
*Cokey Cokey Okey Dokey*
*Next time Right arm out. SEE?*

*You put your Right arm out, Right arm in etc....*

Many versions have been recorded over the years and many claim to have been the first to write the modern words to the dance, including, so I have read, Al Tabor himself. Lou Preager and his orchestra did what Jimmy Kennedy called an 'outstanding' version in America and, in Britain, it was featured and broadcast by Joe Loss, Billy Cotton (vocal by Alan Breeze), Josephine Bradley (who led a ballroom orchestra) and Russ Morgan and his orchestra. But it is still most popular as a party dance. There have been all sorts of guesses about the origin of the name and the unusual movements associated with the dance. A priest in West Yorkshire claimed in a letter to *The Daily Telegraph* that its origins were connected with the Latin mass. He said the words 'Hokey Pokey' were a parody of the phrase used in the mass, *Hoc est enim corpus meum* (This is my body), the phrase that had given rise to *hocus pocus*, words used by magicians when casting spells. But, according to Jimmy Kennedy, there was another reason, drugs. He explained the movements of the dance and its origins on the back of the *Cokey Cokey* sheet music like this:

This is one of the simplest dances ever. You hold your partner in the normal way and while the verse is being played you may fox-trot using any steps you like. When the chorus starts, that is, on the words, 'Left arm out', you put your left arm in line with your shoulder, continuing on the words 'Left arm in' by bending the left arm in and touching your shoulder. Then 'left arm out' as before. 'Shake it all about' explains itself – you simply shake your hand and arm with a circular motion.

On the next line, 'You do the *Cokey Cokey* and you [usually] turn around', the appropriate action is to place the forefinger of the right hand pointing downward on top of your head and do a complete turn around. 'That's what it's all about' ends the actions and you take hold of your partner in the normal way and continue dancing for the next eight-bar interlude. Then the chorus starts over again with the right arm, then the left foot and then the right foot etc. It should not be taken too fast. And don't forget the 'SEE' at the end of each chorus!

The dance, since its introduction here by the Canadian forces, has caught on like wildfire and bids fair to out-rival some of the most sensational dance successes of the past. It is founded on a traditional action song long ago known in the mining camps and the saloons of the Canadian West. The word 'Cokey' means a dope-fiend! – but what this has got to do with the dance is not at all clear!

The Cokey Cokey goes on being part of popular culture. A tongue-in-cheek (London) *Sunday Times* leader (November 2010) suggested it should be taken up by the England rugby team as its equivalent of the New Zealand haka: 'At the very least, we should have a proper British haka,' said the article's writer. 'Crouching low, we could slap our thighs and roar out the haka-cokey …It would be a good ten minutes before the New Zealand team regained their composure.' Though the dance, either as the *Cokey Cokey, Hokey Cokey* or *Hokey Pokey* has been played by bands all over the world, especially in the UK and in America, Kennedy can lay claim to being the man who popularized it and his version is copyrighted and still the most commonly played.

The Campbell, Connelly tie-up, though a friendly relationship, did not lead to any more world standards during the War but Kennedy's three songs, *St Mary's in the Twilight* (1941), *All Our Tomorrows* (1943) and *An Hour Never Passes* (1944) were recorded by leading artists including Vera Lynn and Jo Loss and each topped the war-time best sellers. Though he was no longer under contract to Peter Maurice, the indefatigable Jimmy Phillips had not forgotten Jimmy Kennedy's lyric-writing abilities. One evening in a local pub he met a senior officer who told him about a German song called *Lili Marlene* which was popular with the troops in North Africa. It had an interesting history in that it had originally been published as a German poem about a girl called Lili Marlene, though with a different title, way back in 1915. Lale Anderson had recorded a popular song version, *The Girl under the Lantern,* in 1939 but it got nowhere. Then in 1943 it was 'rediscovered' by a disc jockey among a pile of records used by Radio Belgrade, the German forces station broadcasting to troops fighting in North Africa. He rechristened it *Lili Marlene* and played it a lot and it caught on. German troops started to sing it on the battlefield and then it was picked up by Allied forces - who also tried to copy the German words, much to the annoyance of their officers. On hearing the story, Phillips realised that all that was needed to make the song a hit were English words and, even though Kennedy was no longer under contract, he wrote to him with all the details and asked him to write a lyric. However, before he had time to consider the request Phillips over-eagerly sent him a follow-up telegram: 'Urgently required lyrics for Lili Marlene tune sent some days ago'. The peremptory nature of the cable annoyed Kennedy who retaliated by firing off a cable in response: 'Impossible for serving officer to collaborate with the enemy'! Undeterred, Phillips then turned to another top lyricist, Tommie Connor, who agreed to do English words. No one knows if it is true that Connor wrote it sheltering under his grand piano during an air raid! But *Lili Marlene* was a huge success, possibly the biggest of the War. Marlene Dietrich covered it in 1945 and her recording has become the best-known version.

Jimmy Kennedy continued his morale-boosting duties for most of the War. Generally speaking, and surprisingly, he seemed to think that the army was a good thing for personal development. Perhaps this was a subconscious attempt to emulate his policeman father. He also used to say that his army duties helped him overcome his shyness: although he entertained millions through his songs, he did not personally much like the limelight, preferring small group or one-to-one situations. Another skill he acquired in the army stopped him from getting promoted: 'I used to get invitations of all sorts because of my song writing background and was on the "list". I would be around when we gathered in the officers' mess to discuss the progress of the War, telling stories and socializing generally. It so happened that some time around 1943, there was a move by the higher authorities to send off my regiment, me included, on active service to North Africa. But the camp commander wouldn't hear of it, "We can't let Kennedy go," he said, "Where else will we find someone who can mix martinis like he does!"

By 1945, Jimmy Kennedy had become a staff captain attached to Montgomery's 2nd Army Group which invaded Normandy in May of that year. I do not know if he ever met Montgomery, but he admired him tremendously. Monty was frequently in the news during and after the War as much for his controversial right wing views as for his record as a great general. (Interestingly, Monty's family, like the Baskins, came from County Donegal and his father was a bishop!). The Normandy landings were Jimmy Kennedy's first direct experience of the unpleasantness of war on the ground in Europe, something that he never forgot. However, he tried to find some humour in the situation and could not resist telling amusing stories about it. I remember him telling me a probably apocryphal tale about what happened in northern France when his unit spent a night in a château recently captured from the retreating Germans. It so happened that they had all picked up a severe dose of the 'runs'. Latrines had been dug in the remoter regions of the château grounds but most members of the unit were on their way back to the latrines almost as soon as they had left them. Meanwhile various wine bottles had been found in the cellar, so it was decided to sample them. I expect a few glasses of red were a pleasant change from boiled water and helped wash down their army rations of dry biscuit and bully beef nicely. After the wine, they noticed some other bottles, this time brandy and liqueurs – which my father rarely drank. They were ceremonially opened and a few loyal toasts were made, stories told…and, the next day they woke up with horrible hangovers and raging thirsts. And the 'runs'? They were gone – cured by the medicinal properties of alcoholic dehydration.

During the campaign from Normandy to the Baltic, Kennedy saw with concern the distress of millions of displaced persons. On the table of his bedroom at the family house he was later to buy in the 1950s, near Taunton, Somerset, he used to keep the original 1945 warrant saying that he had been 'dusted' and was authorized to go into Belsen concentration camp. It was a daily reminder of the unspeakable horrors he had witnessed there. From the moment he visited the camp, he would have nothing to do with the Germans and never knowingly bought anything German, not even a gramophone. Indeed, long after the War was over, when I was briefly articled to a firm of solicitors in the 1960s, he even threatened to stop my allowance (trainee lawyers were not paid a living wage at the time: they were dependent on their parents) because I had a German girlfriend.

As the War drew to a close, Jimmy Kennedy met a musical comedy actress called Constance Carpenter. Everybody called her Connie. He had almost certainly seen her on the stage in the 1930s when she performed in many of the famous revues staged by André Charlot in London. These revues, which also took place with huge success in New York, produced stars like Beatrice Lillie, Gertrude Lawrence and Jack Buchanan. I do not know if my father personally knew Connie then but he certainly got to know her later when she worked for ENSA and the Red Cross, entertaining troops in Europe, and the Middle and Far East. He mentioned that she once performed for troops in France in August 1944 dressed in a rather unusual shark-skin tropical outfit. She would sing accompanied by pianists such as songwriter Ronnie Bridges, who later worked at the Tin Pan Alley publishers Box & Cox and who, with Kennedy, later became a member of the Council of BASCA, the British Academy of Songwriters, Composers and Authors.

I don't think my father would have been too keen on the shark skin suit – he was old-fashioned when it came to dress. But he fell for Connie nevertheless. She was not only an attractive blonde, she was witty, sophisticated, liked a cocktail and could tell a joke, the kind of outgoing, amusing and demonstrative lady that he liked. By 1945, she was 41 to his 43. Meanwhile, his wife Peggy was still in America and I think my father's attitude to her is best summed up by the words of the Hoagy Carmichael song, 'I get along without you very well...' And it seems from her letters to him that she felt the same. She had embraced the American way of life and, more important, now had an American lover. It was this knowledge, coupled with his blossoming friendship with Connie that gave my father the decisive push he needed to make a final break with Peggy and obtain a divorce. This he did as soon as was possible after he was demobbed in 1946, joining countless other returning servicemen including his friend Denis Thatcher. However, he and Connie did not get married immediately. They waited a year whilst they thought through their respective careers. He had also to decide what to do about his three children, still with their mother in America. Should he leave them in America or bring them back? Connie had a major influence on his final decision. She was childless and thought it would be wonderful to have a ready-made family to look after.

*Actress Constance Carpenter, who starred opposite Yul Brynner in The King and I, was Jimmy Kennedy's second wife.*

Jimmy Kennedy always used to say that after five years of war, and especially after seeing first-hand the horrors of Belsen, the thought of rhyming 'arms with charms' and 'blue with true' seemed trivial and banal, impossible to take seriously. So, soon after he was demobbed, he decided to put the music business on ice and try to earn a completely different living by buying and selling houses, something that did not involve a publisher breathing down his neck. Connie encouraged the idea. She had a theatrical flair for interior design, with a penchant for the ornate styles of the various French kings from Louis XIV onwards. For that style to succeed, big rooms and big houses were needed. The couple first bought a multi-storied house in London's Herbert Crescent, just behind Harrods and used that as a base. Then they sold it and bought Vale Lodge, a mansion near Leatherhead, Surrey. My father even toyed with the idea of buying Selwyn House, an enormous baronial pile near St James's Palace, overlooking Green Park. It was later to become the London headquarters of Pilkington, the glass firm. But their amateurish real estate efforts did not and could not make any money so soon after the War. It was the right idea, perhaps, but definitely the wrong time. Years later, the house in Herbert Crescent alone was worth as much or more than all the Jimmy Kennedy songs put together.

Real estate was perhaps almost a piece of bravado, a gesture of independence from the music publishers of the world. Though Jimmy Kennedy had more freedom from them than before because he was no longer employed by Peter Maurice, it was nearly impossible for him to break entirely free, whether he liked it or not. The royalties from his established standards, for example, had to be monitored and promoted. He had to keep up his contacts, to meet fellow writers, publishers and other people in the business. Indeed, he was a founder member of the Songwriters Guild, set up at around that time (1947) to protect and advance British song writing. He still had his arrangement for publishing with Campbell,

Connelly. And Jimmy Phillips kept writing to him trying to persuade him to pen lyrics for more new hits for Peter Maurice.

As the months went by during 1946, he found himself thinking that the best thing to do would be to try for the best of both worlds by combining his property dealings with a return to song writing. But, could he pick up where he had left off in 1939 and write as a freelance in London? He thought about this a lot but had his doubts. Although outwardly business in Denmark Street continued much as it used to, with producers, performers and band leaders coming to the publishers to listen and cosily rehearse the latest songs on the spot just as they had always done, underneath the surface the cash-strapped UK music business was beginning to acquire an ever sharper commercial edge as it tried to find its feet again in a blitzed-out London. A new generation was coming into the music business. Change was in the air. The record industry was beginning to flex its muscles – singles and LPs were only months away from being introduced and they were about to change the face of popular music. I expect Jimmy Kennedy was well aware of what was going on and uncertain of his place as this new scene developed, so it is not really surprising that he began to turn his attention towards America, which he knew was a much larger market for his type of song than Britain. The American economy was starting to boom, nowhere more so than at the world centre of the popular music business – New York. He had talked about going to America when the time was right. He decided that time was now.

# 17: New York sparks off a hit revival

Jimmy Kennedy must have been astonished at what he saw when he arrived in New York for the first time in December 1946. Hardly a year out of his army quarters, he was suddenly confronted by an insomniac city awash with money, optimism and opportunity. The noise of progress was almost deafening. Above the manic traffic and the people-packed sidewalks, skyscrapers, apartment buildings and department stores were shooting upwards everywhere as frantic attempts were made to satisfy the appetite of a population suddenly released from the constraints of war. You could buy what you wanted almost whenever you wanted it. And that included entertainment. What a contrast with bombed-out London which was just pulling itself together, knitting its own comforts, where money was tight and purchasing power limited by the ration book, with shortages of just about everything.

Mid-town Manhattan, the original Tin Pan Alley, was still the centre of the American popular music business, with most of the leading record companies, recording studios and publishers located there. The good news for Jimmy Kennedy was that although this immediate post-war period was ushering in a period of major cultural change in art, literature and music, much of it radical, America remained basically conservative in its taste for popular music. This meant that there were chances for his type of song in the biggest, wealthiest and most diverse entertainment market in the world. Making the most of his opportunities, he had two songs in the charts within two months, both in collaboration with American composer, Nat Simon, *And Mimi* and *An Apple Blossom*

*Wedding.* Both made the US Top 20 at the same time, in the late spring of 1947. Though not quite as impressive as having *South of the Border* and *My Prayer* occupying the top two hit parade places in 1939, Jimmy Kennedy must have felt he was continuing where he had left off.

My father once told me the story of the day he first went to meet composer Nat Simon. It was early in 1947, a perfect spring morning, he said, with the blossom on the trees bursting out in response to the warm spring sunshine. He had dressed for the occasion in one of his favourite grey hand-stitched Savile Row suits, Royal Artillery tie, brown felt Trilby hat, a flower in his buttonhole, reckoning that a morning's work would be followed by a convivial lunch. As he walked down to his publisher, he thought, what a perfect day for a lovely romantic song! Once there, he was introduced to Nat Simon and soon they were discussing ideas for their first collaboration. His mood enlivened by the lovely sunshine, Jimmy said to Nat: 'It's such a wonderful day, let's write something really spring-like. How about something in the title like...mimosa!' (the first flower that came into his head). Nat replied: 'Yeah, I like that. By the way, where is Mimosa?' Amused, my father decided to ignore the response, smiled, and instead steered the conversation to other possible ideas before they both went off to lunch. A couple of days later he joked about Nat's reaction to the 'mimosa' idea with a publisher friend who said: 'Well, you know, Jimmy, I studied geography at school but if you asked me where 'mimosa' was right now, I couldn't tell you either!' My father was even more amused by this response so he told the story to another friend, the publisher Lou Levy (who ran Leeds Music and was married to one of the Andrews Sisters) because he knew Levy had travelled the world and would get the joke. 'It's really funny, isn't it!' he said. Levy roared with laughter: 'You're damned right it is. Fancy those two not knowing where 'mimosa' is!'

When Jimmy Kennedy and Nat Simon got down to writing their first song a few weeks later, they kept the flower idea but replaced 'mimosa' with 'apple blossom'. Before spring was out, *An Apple Blossom Wedding* was riding high in the American charts with numerous recordings, including Sammy Kaye and his orchestra (vocal by Don Cornell), No. 5 in the US charts, Eddie Howard with his orchestra (No. 9) and Buddy Clark with Mitchell Ayre's orchestra (No. 14). It was also covered by Bing Crosby, Ginny Simms, and Russ Morgan and his orchestra (vocal by Kenny Baker). *An Apple Blossom Wedding* not only did very well in America but it reached No. 1 in Britain, coinciding with the big event of the year, the wedding of Princess Elizabeth and the Duke of Edinburgh. That took place in November 1947 and both writers were laughing that the song made it to the top in the British winter when the blossom was long gone and the only apples left were windfalls. It remained a best seller for 18 weeks right through the very cold winter. Kennedy and Simon followed up their *Apple Blossom* success almost immediately with *And Mimi* which Art Lund took to No. 14, Dick Haymes to No. 15, and Frankie Clarke to No. 24 in the US best-seller list, with other covers by major stars including Al Jolson, Mel Tormé and Jean Caval.

Although Jimmy Kennedy was on the threshold of a second successful career in America, Jimmy Phillips fired off a series of letters trying to persuade him to return to write for Peter Maurice, offering various inducements including generous advance royalties. ...'and it's up to us both to try and dig out some big hits so that you get back to your old earning stride as in the past....Well, drop me a line, Jimmy, and let me know what's what, so that we can get cracking.' But Kennedy was still not keen to renew the relationship. 'Forget me writing new material, why don't you promote the songs you've already got?' he wrote to Phillips, 'For example, what about *Flamingos*?'

Phillips responded by promoting the song, writing to say: 'Currently we are bashing *Flamingos* as hard as we can. We've had it on air about thirty times in the top spots and we've got records released by Anne Shelton on Decca, Georges Guetary on Columbia and we're also getting the Ink Spots record released. Now, to be perfectly frank with you Jim, it's not showing a sign and we are dead scared about it. Usually, you get sales of 3/400 copies a day, but we are not getting a tumble at all, but we are still hoping that everybody is wrong.'

Phillips also referred in one letter to a song written by Connie, 'I was very pleased to hear that Connie has such a good number in *Amelia Cordelia Mc Who* [recorded by Danny Kaye and The Andrews Sisters, but got nowhere] ...Can you do lyrics for any of the melodies that I've got over here? ....No kidding, Jim, I think you still write the heads off any of them when you get down to it.... Give my best regards to Connie and look after yourself and keeping banging away with confidence. I will do everything I can with *Flamingos,* but if it's a dog, well we won't be able to help it. I am trying to get it up there because of the American angle – the Ink Spots record etc.'

'Banging away' was an apt description of what Jimmy Kennedy continued to do. After his first two early chart successes, he had little luck for a couple of years but he kept on producing a barrage of complete songs or lyrics to other tunes – just as he had done when he started out in London's Tin Pan Alley 20 years earlier. Although he had many more big chart successes – some of which were revivals - as the 1950s progressed, he still continued to work on new ideas, some of which he tried (and occasionally succeeded) to promote through his established contacts and others which never got beyond the manuscript phase. But the titles make interesting reading: *Last Night's Kisses, You and Love, The Old Irish Church, Little Cockney Cowboy, The Angels are Lighting God's Little Candles, My Love For You, Blue Grotto, All*

*Roads Lead to London, Faithful, Where Water Lilies Dream, Olwen, Dreambound, If I wasn't in Love With You, Autumn Leaves* (written in the 1930s, not the famous standard), *C'est Paris, If My Heart was a Ship, I'll Cry, Roger de Coverley, Moon Above Malaya* (which crept into the charts in the UK, in 1952), *Write to Me from Naples* ( recorded by Dean Martin), *I'm Writing a Letter to the Lord, Listening to the Green Grass Grow* (which also charted in the UK) and countless others. They reflected his work philosophy that if you keep on producing songs, eventually one of them will be a hit.

Away from the music business, his family life was still unsettled. Having divorced Peggy in 1946, he married Connie in 1947. Then, as his career began to take off again, he had to decide what to do about his three children, then aged 12, nine and six. Since Connie had promised to take on the maternal role and look after the children, and he had always wanted them to be educated in England rather than America, he decided all three should be brought back to England. So early in 1947 he came to Clearwater, Florida where Peggy lived, to arrange things. It must have been quite a shock to him when he got there. He had not seen his first two children, Derek and Janet, for the seven years since they had left England, aged five and two, in 1940. And he had never seen the youngest, James, at all. I imagine he would have been confronted by three lively Americans kids with Florida accents, crew cuts, jeans and T-shirts, who knew *The Stars and Stripes* but not the British or Irish national anthems, who knew all about baseball, but thought 'cricket' was a kind of grasshopper that sang in trees. It was probably an emotional experience for him. I naturally thought my mother's live-in lover, who was called Marvin, was 'Dad'. So when my *real* father was introduced to me, I replied scornfully, 'You're not *my* Daddy!' I do not remember his reply but he probably laughed wryly. The upshot of his negotiations with Peggy was that the three of us left her and Florida for good just a few months later. In August 1947 we were put on a train and travelled the 1300 miles north to a humid summertime New York where we were greeted by step-mother Connie and my father and put up in a grand hotel.

None of us had ever been on a train, so the journey to New York was a very exciting adventure – the 'parp-parp' sound of the horn, sleeping in our own cabins, the uniformed attendants bringing food and Pepsi on trolleys, and, through the windows, America hurtling by. Then, in New York, we saw real skyscrapers for the first time. We went up the Empire State Building and Connie indulged us like mad. She immediately fell in love with us, so she said. After a few days seeing the sights of New York, we sailed for England on *The Queen Mary* on 5 August 1947. Connie told me many years later that on board ship I was kissed by the reclusive film star Greta Garbo, which may possibly make me unique. We arrived to a warm and incredibly green England five days later and travelled up to London where we stayed briefly at Herbert Crescent, followed by a short visit to Rottingdean, near Brighton, and then on to Hove, where Connie's sister, Mabel looked after us for a few weeks. From now on corn muffins, iced tea, hummingbirds, the home help who always seemed to have tooth ache, and the huge sun slipping down the sky at sunset became memories. The accents around us changed, we had to put up with Coca-Cola instead of Pepsi, we could not have a banana when we wanted one – everything was rationed – and we seemed to spend a lot of time visiting zoos as various grown-ups tried to think of what to do with us.

Despite her talk of taking on the role of mother of the family, Connie was in reality much more interested in resuming her theatre career and she showed less and less interest in her second-hand brood of children. Meanwhile, her songwriter husband needed to get back to work to justify his royalty advances, so we were packed off in the freezing winter of 1947/48 to separate boys' and girls' private boarding schools in Leamington Spa. The school that Derek and I went to, Ardmore, moved after only one term to a beautiful old mansion, The Hendre, near Monmouth, formerly the home of Charles Stewart Rolls, joint founder of Rolls Royce. There, our American accents and habits made us targets for unruly British barbarians and, on a crash survival course, we learnt the King's English in record time. The school was full of semi-wild children, whose parents, like ours, were picking up the pieces after the War. It's funny how you can remember incidents from the remote past. I can recall vividly one boy slightly older than me being scragged by several short-trousered savages and as he struggled on the floor to escape, he called out, 'Mercy! Mercy!' as an assailant joked, 'Ha! Ha! Merci! means Thank you! in French!' And the assault went on. Despite its beautiful surroundings, Ardmore was not a pleasant place to be, even by the standards of the 1940s. The authorities closed it a year or so later at the end of the 1949 summer term. The head went to prison.

Badly advised, my father was unaware of what the school was like, and, believing his three children to be comfortably settled, continued to spend considerable periods of time in America staying either in Florida or New York and keeping up his prolific output. He wrote a Christmas song, *The Mistletoe Kiss*, which was interesting because it was a first for him in that for once he did not write the lyrics – Connie did. The best recording was by Primo Scala (Decca). In 1947, Jimmy also wrote a fake western with Kenneth Leslie-Smith called *Down the Old Spanish Trail* based on the story of a famous historic trading route dating back to the early 1700s which crossed Texas well before cowboys were invented. The Spanish trail originally linked the French in Louisiana with the Spanish in northern Mexico and over time it developed into the main route across Texas from Mexico to Louisiana. Now it is a modern highway:

*Let me tell you a tale, of the Old Spanish Trail;*
*She and I used to ride, side by side, down the Old Spanish Trail.*
*Desert stars high above, seem'd to say 'Fall in love',*
*So we talked of a June honeymoon on the Old Spanish Trail.*

A professor of history at Texas University said in a note which accompanied some versions of the song: 'Up and down the trail, the forces of empire have flowed and ebbed, Spanish, French, Mexican and Anglo-American. The story of the old Spanish trail is the story of America.' The music library at the university listed *Down the Old Spanish Trail*, as 'an important contribution to the musical saga of the State' – though it is hard to see why from the lyric. It was basically another of Jimmy Kennedy's 'story' songs which he had excelled at writing during his 10 years in London's Tin Pan Alley before the War. As such, it cantered into the charts with recordings by, among others, Eddy Howard and his orchestra, Art Lund and Andy Russell. It was also covered by cowboy star Roy Rogers, Monte Rey and Issy Bonn. Cowboy songs were still very popular at the end of the 1940s and 1950s. Films starring Roy Rogers, Gene Autrey, Tom Mix, The Lone Ranger et al were possibly the most watched of all, certainly by the younger generation. They were the entertainment mainstay of Saturday mornings. *Down the Old Spanish Trail* reached No. 4 in the UK and stayed in the charts there for 15 weeks.

During his first few years in America, Jimmy Kennedy used to spend time in Florida, living at Star Island, an exclusive man-made residential development just off the coast of Miami. Later residents included Madonna, Gloria Estefan and Sylvester Stallone. Connie liked it there. It was a wonderful place to be when she was 'resting' between performances, even when there weren't any. Thanks to Connie's musical comedy background, the two of them had a lot of fun thinking up ideas for songs, though few were published. Kennedy also used to write there with other collaborators, especially Nat Simon. When he travelled back to New York, a journey of well over a thousand miles, he would often take his car. He was a careful driver, claiming that if he travelled at no more than 60 miles an hour he would get to his destination just as fast as people racing along at 80 mph. He had a small model St Christopher (the patron saint of travelers) attached to the dashboard and liked to point out to people that if he went over the speed limit it would say 'This is St Christopher calling, you're on your own now!' But he used to hate stopping. When he had to, to buy petrol or eat, he claimed he would pour a can of Coca-Cola over the windscreen to clean it. He swore it was the most effective cleaning fluid you could buy for dissolving all the grease and rubber that accumulated on the windscreen, frequently quoting the old wives tale that if you left a tooth overnight in a glass of Coca Cola, it would be gone the next morning. Maybe that was a story! He drove a Dodge, a green tank of a car which he grew to love so much that he still had it 20 years later by which time the milometer had been round the clock twice and he had retired to Switzerland. When he visited Europe, he would usually go by air but the car would be transported across the Atlantic on a liner such as *The Queen Mary*. If he was not intending to be in Europe for long, he would have it garaged in New York for 50 dollars a week. The car did not reach the end of the road until the 1970s by which time it must have had more loving care – and money – lavished on it than any Dodge ...ever.

The year that his three children came to England, 1947, his youngest sister, Nina – who had sat next to him in the garden in Portstewart's Strand Road when they thought up the title for *Red Sails in the Sunset* – died unexpectedly of Hodgkin's disease, a form of cancer, while still in her thirties. Hodgkin's disease is frequently curable these days, but at that time the doctors were unable to diagnose it correctly in time to save her. She had been living in Vancouver, Canada, where her husband was captain of a ship in the Royal Canadian Merchant Navy, and left a daughter of six, Deirdre. Deirdre's father could not easily look after her because he was away at sea for most of the time and she needed a mother figure. So elder sister Nell arranged for her to come to live for the time being in Rostrevor, County Down, Northern Ireland, a village on the shores of Carlingford Lough with views to the Mountains of Mourne, mountains made famous by Percy French's eponymous song. Nell was already living there with Anna, by then in her seventies and honoured with the title 'granny'. I remember staying with my brother and sister for Christmas in 1948. One event stands out. It was cold and we had those ceramic hot water bottles that had to be covered with a pillow case because they were too hot to touch directly but you could just reach the warm spots near them with your toes if you snuggled down to the bottom of the bed. As I tried to locate mine, my foot instead felt something wet and cold. Alarmed, I threw back the bed clothes and there was the wind pipe of the Christmas goose. Granny, who had gutted the bird earlier in the day, had been going round the house blowing through it to make a honking noise to amuse everybody. Later, she put it in my bed as a joke. Black Donegal humour.

With the addition of Deirdre, there were now four young children in the family without live-in parents or a permanent home. For a couple of school holidays, we were all billeted with Uncle Hamilton and his intemperate gin-soaked wife, Auntie Margaret, in Bristol. I also remember spending one August with my sister Janet, it must have been the summer of 1948, in Holyhead, Anglesea, with the aged mother of the soon-to-be-disgraced headmaster of Ardmore, the Monmouth school to which Derek and

I had been sent. It never stopped raining and the house overlooked a graveyard. The single high spot holiday came a year later, in the summer of 1949, when Derek and I camped with my father in an enormous dark-green ex-army ridge tent in the spacious grounds of Vale Lodge, the still unsold and unlived-in real estate investment my father had bought in Surrey in 1947. August 1949 was very hot and I remember him going up to London and returning with a beautiful on-the-bone Wiltshire ham from Fortnum's. It was delicious for supper that evening but, said my father, it would last for days if we put it in cool water out of the direct rays of the sun. So we carefully wrapped it and placed it in cold water in a bright shiny new metal bin at the 'kitchen end' of the tent. Three days later we thought it would be nice to have some more and as Derek and I buttered the bread for a picnic lunch, my father took the lid off the bin and then put it back again, fast. His scientific premise that the ham would stay cool was wrong. Inside, the ham had gone: all that remained were a few thousand half-drowned but well-fed maggots! We spent most of the holiday using billhooks to try to clear the vast shrubberies in the Vale Lodge gardens. When I embedded the sharp end of one of these tools in the fleshy part of my eight-year-old thigh, my father's cure was straight from the battlefield: boiling water to clean and sterilize it, then neat iodine. Ouch! I still have the scar! The best part of the holiday was the excitement of watching as a wing of the house was blown up to bring the place down to a more manageable size.

Meanwhile, a solution was being sought as to where to settle the family. After what I imagine must have been considerable debate, Nell agreed to take on the difficult role of looking after all four children plus granny, who by then was not only ageing but supposedly dying of pernicious anaemia and had to have an injection from one of those old glass phials every day. But where would we all live? Vale Lodge was deemed to be unsuitable, so it was decided to try to find somewhere else in the English countryside. My father wanted a house he could reach easily when he was in London, one near to good schools. There was much scouring of the property pages of *The Daily Telegraph* and *Country Life* before they found what they were looking for. In late 1949, Staplegrove Elm, a draughty unfurnished 8-bedroomed Georgian-style mansion with a three-and-a half acre garden, was found for rent (at £5 a week) in Somerset. It was set in attractive countryside near a village called Staplegrove, just outside Taunton and only two and quarter hours by express train from Paddington. Staplegrove Elm had all the space you could want but was cold and damp – there was no central heating. We all arrived in the autumn and the grass on the croquet lawn was three feet high. My father and Derek ceremonially cut the first square yard of grass with a pair of kitchen scissors. Later we had a man in to scythe it, leaving us with a mouse-ridden haystack next to the house for at least two years, great for playing in. During cold weather, my brother Derek lit fires every morning in the living rooms, stoked the solid-fuel Aga in the kitchen and the Beeston hot-water boiler in the back-kitchen every morning before cycling seven miles to school. In the evening the process was repeated. I was sent to a preparatory boarding school in Crewkerne, Somerset, taking over the domestic chores from my brother in the holidays, inheriting them full-time when he went on to the Royal Agricultural College, Cirencester.

So, like the youngest members of many families in large houses, I spent a lot of my youth emptying ashes and filling coal hods and hot-water bottles and mowing the lawn and the surrounding paddock – four and a half miles, I calculated, each time. The unconscious physical training the garden provided was probably the reason I became captain of the school athletics team! Nell was a rather inhibited, reserved lady, not a natural mother, but she was very conscientious and had a strong sense of duty.

*Staplegrove Elm, near Taunton, Somerset, for 20 years the Kennedy family home*

She had a sentimental attraction to animals – she had three Maltese terriers, Princess, Pixie and Pepper—during our time at Staplegrove, plus a collie and loved animals in general, including farm animals. So she got quite a shock the first time she went to hang out some washing in the stable yard and was presented with a row of dead hens hanging by their feet on the clothesline, dripping blood onto the cobbles. Before we arrived, the house had been empty for some time, and it seems the entrepreneurial gardener had taken to running a little organic chicken farm on the side to earn some spare cash. But wringing the necks of chickens like that was just too much for Nell and the blood-thirsty gardener was replaced by a new one, Potter, who was more horticulturally inclined and used to amuse me by calling carnations, 'coronations'. Managing Staplegrove and looking after an increasingly infirm granny plus four children was certainly a brave undertaking for Nell, who herself was well into her forties. She had broken her back before she came over to England from Ireland so had to wear a supporting corset and was always on a diet – frequently boiled fish – because of a 'delicate' stomach.

Practically everything normal people really wanted to eat – meat, eggs, oranges, bananas, butter, cake, tea – was still rationed in the early 1950s. All four children used to jealously guard their two-ounces of butter, lining up individual weekly portions in the huge American-style fridge. We photographed the weekly meat ration – a pound and a half piece of beef looking bizarrely isolated surrounded by white porcelain in the centre of a large plate. Luckily for us, Nell was a good cook and made the most of what little was there. She also used to make a wonderful selection of Irish breads, cakes, jams and other preserves, using the fresh produce from the huge garden. This was sometimes supplemented by produce from relatives back home in Northern Ireland. I always remember the big goose – feathers, feet, guts and all – which used to arrive in time for New Year's Day, sent from a cousin called Willie Sloan who lived in Moneymore. He sent the goose by parcel post tied with string and wrapped in nothing more than brown paper! When my father came for Christmas, he would arrive laden with goodies from Fortnums including ham, cheeses and tins of all kinds of exotic foods, most of which were squirreled away by Nell 'just in case'. Granny, whom I am afraid we impishly called Granny Grunt because she had put on weight and breathed rather heavily, was also a good country cook, though she had a habit of blowing her nose into her apron in the kitchen, something I found unsettling even at the tender age of eight. It is easy to assume that people living in big houses are rich, but that is rarely the case. Hard cash was a very scarce commodity at Staplegrove. Nell was on a tight budget and constantly complained about the coal bill, the cost of repairs for the roof, clothes, school fees, the wages of the domestic staff and so on. I sometimes think our absentee parent did not realize just how hard and expensive it was to run such an enormous house. In reality, he had cause to be very grateful to Nell's instinctive thrift. She had taken over the wider family responsibilities dutifully so that Connie's rejection of the maternal role was no longer such a big issue and he was able to get back to his bread-winning role as a songwriter.

Meanwhile, life in New York at the beginning of the 1950s was a far cry from the austerity of Staplegrove. Jimmy Kennedy lived in the heart of Manhattan in an apartment on Park Avenue (a former occupant was, reputedly, Nat King Cole), frequently weekending in Florida. He worked hard developing his professional contacts (and, hence, his royalty earnings), getting to know key people on the business and technical side of the profession – publishers, record producers, song pluggers and so on. At the same time he began to mix with many of the famous songwriters that he had only read about when he had worked in London's Tin Pan Alley. It was a genuine thrill for him to meet people he had tried to emulate down the years – people like Richard Rodgers and Oscar Hammerstein II, Cole Porter, Irving Berlin, Hoagy Carmichael, Sammy Cahn and Harry Warren. I think he found it a great stimulus to meet writers of this calibre for the first time and to talk to them about songs and songwriting. He said that Irving Berlin might have been the greatest songwriter of all time, but he found him very 'conceited'. He greatly admired Richard Rodgers. And he told me, despite all his wonderful standards (which included *Stardust* and *Georgia on My Mind*) even Hoagy Carmichael had difficulties getting his style of songs published as the 1950s progressed because the music business was changing so much. Hoagy told him that if he had been starting out again and had tried to get any of his most successful songs published in the mid-1950s, he doubted he would have got through a publisher's front door.

Of all the writers Jimmy Kennedy met at that time, the one he admired most was Cole Porter. He lived in a suite at the Waldorf Astoria Hotel, where he had been since 1939, and his white grand piano was still in the lobby when I was last there in the 1990s. *Kiss Me Kate* was a masterpiece, he once told me, because it merged Shakespeare's *The Taming of the Shrew* with the modern world of musical comedy in such a sophisticated way: 'I thought Cole Porter's musical score of *Kiss Me Kate* was one of the most fantastic things that has ever taken place in our business because he had, previous to writing it, fallen off his horse and the horse had rolled over breaking both his legs, crushing him completely. He wrote the score while he was suffering absolute agonies with all those broken bones. It was a wonderful achievement. He was a man with a wonderful spirit that overcame much illness yet he put so much humour into his songs and such witty sophistication.'

Around 1950, on a visit to Europe, Jimmy Kennedy passed up a great opportunity for his speciality of writing the English lyrics for continental tunes when he was offered the opportunity to write the English lyrics for a song called *Les Feuilles Mortes* (Autumn Leaves). Perhaps there had been a deal of some sort involving Jimmy Phillips, though my father never mentioned this. At the time the French publisher had English lyrics for two other French songs, *Sous les Ponts de Paris* (*Under the bridges of Paris*), which had been originally composed in 1931, and *La Seine*, written in 1949. But for once Kennedy misjudged things. He thought *Les Feuilles Mortes* had too mournful a tune and title to be successful commercially and said he would only do the lyric if he could rewrite the two others. He even produced a sample lyric for *Under the Bridges of Paris*. But the French publisher could not go back on the agreement with the other writers.

The English lyric for *Autumn Leaves* was instead penned by the great Johnny Mercer (who wrote the chorus) and British lyricist Geoffrey Parsons (who added a verse) and became a huge international standard, one, like *Lili Marlene*, that would have made Kennedy a lot more popular with his bank manager. The English language versions of *Under the Bridges of Paris* and *La Seine* have now also become popular standards. But, way back in 1950, what was the unpublished lyric Jimmy Kennedy drafted for *Sous les Ponts de Paris*? He called the song *Love Me For Evermore* and the lyric went like this:

> *Love me for evermore,*
> *Never been loved before,*
> *Don't keep your kisses and don't save your sighs...and...*
> *Don't let the starlight get out of your eyes.*
> *I'm in a dream in blue,*
> *Madly in love with you,*
> *Love is the key that will open the door,*
> *Love me for evermore!*
>
> *Love me for evermore,*
> *Open the golden door,*
> *Give me your heart and forget to be wise...and...*
> *Don't let the starlight get out of your eyes.*
> *I'm in a dream in blue,*
> *Madly in love with you,*
> *I've never loved anybody before,*
> *Love me for evermore!*
> *© Bow Bells Music Ltd*

Whether or not this is the finished lyric, I am not certain, but he liked it enough to keep it among his private papers.

1950 was the start of the Korean War where British and American forces fought together. Jimmy Kennedy co-wrote a song with Bickley Reichner called *The Red*

*We Want is the Red we've Got (in the old Red, White and Blue)* which captured the patriotic mood of the time in America and sold a million records for Hugo Winterhalter and Eddie Fisher. It was a commercial decision to write it so I think my father was quite astonished - and proud – to be awarded a Freedom Foundation Gold Award for it a couple of years later presented by the American war hero General Omar Bradley at Valley Forge, Gettysberg, the shrine of American Independence. The citation thanked him for 'a valuable contribution to the American way of life'.

Another song from the period was *My Bolero*, written with Nat Simon, which was recorded by Vic Damone, with Glenn Osser's orchestra. In Britain he also had a success with *The French Can-Can Polka* (1950) where he rearranged Offenbach's famous dance and put amusing lyrics to it. It was recorded by Michel Legrand, Billy Cotton, Ethel Smith (organ), and Lou Preager among others and reached No. 6 in the UK, remaining there for 15 weeks.

*The fun of the folies in a Jimmy Kennedy lyric of 1950.*

*I can-can and you can-can, so why should not we two can-can?*
*Who can-can like you can-can?*
*Who can do can-can like you can?*
*To the tune they can-can to, we'll polka while we 'parlez voo'.*
*Few can-can like you can-can,*
*In the can-can polka!*

But his outstanding song of 1950 was *Harbour Lights*, a revival from 1937. Sammy Kaye's recording reached No. 1, the version by Guy Lombardo and his orchestra got to No. 2, and recordings by Ray Anthony, Ralph Flanagan,

Bing Crosby, Ken Griffiths, and Jerry Byrd and Jerry Murad's Harmonicists all crowded into the hit parade at slightly lesser positions. Thanks to the huge scale of the American market it was even more successful this time than it had been 13 years before. It was also later covered by many more artists, including Elvis Presley at his first-ever Sun Studios recordings in the autumn of 1955. The 19-year-old chose it because it was his mother's favourite. In 1960 The Platters brought it near the top of the American charts yet again.

The background to these successes was, however, one of change in the music business. A key technical development came in 1948 when the first 33 rpm LP was released in the United States and 45 rpm singles also came out at around the same time. Both formats were made of vinyl and were lighter, stronger and cheaper than the shellac 78 rpm records they replaced. The two new formats dramatically expanded the market for music. From 1950 or so, record sales, rather than sheet music and air play, came to be the yardstick by which the popularity of songs was measured and chart ratings started to apply to individual records, so that the recordings and the performers who made them became more important than the song itself. Radio disc jockeys were also a major new force. They exerted a huge influence on which records sold best, effectively plugging the records they liked most. Their audience of listeners would follow their lead and go out and buy their recommendations. The market songs were aimed at also changed, moving increasingly towards a younger audience and away from the more general and usually more adult audience of the professionally written popular song of former years.

Against this background, Jimmy Kennedy maintained his prolific output, holding his own remarkably well, considering his style was so different from what was then in vogue. After the *Harbour Lights* revival, he had two

newly-minted best sellers, *April in Portugal* and *Istanbul*.
These were followed by more revivals from Frank Sinatra
and The Platters. Many lesser songs he wrote in the early
1950s were also recorded by top performers – including
Gene Autry, Vaughan Monroe, Guy Mitchell and Rosemary
Clooney. Among these was a Tin Pan Alley-style country
song, *Down the Trail of Achin' Hearts* (co-written with Nat
Simon), which entered the American charts in 1951 with
recordings by Patti Page and The Four Aces. In the UK,
Pearl Carr did well with it on Decca.

> *Down the trail of achin' hearts*
> *Where nobody's hidin' their tears,*
> *You sent me there where sadness starts,*
> *Down the trail of achin' hearts....*

The song came not long after the huge Patti Page hit,
*The Tennessee Waltz* (1950), and was a typical example of
Kennedy turning his hand to whatever genre he believed
would work commercially. He always thought he had
an affinity with country music, declaring that much of
it was based on Irish folk songs brought over by Irish
immigrants to the Appalachians in the 19th century and
then to other parts of America. A favourite example he
used to give was the *Streets of Laredo*, made famous by
Johnny Cash and other folk singers, including Joan Baez,
which he said had been based on an Irish folk ballad
called *The Bride of Armagh*.

# 18: Connie stars in *The King and I*

As Jimmy Kennedy rode the rapids of pop music change, Connie – under her stage name of Constance Carpenter – was poised to become the star of a new Rodgers and Hammerstein musical. She had been picked to understudy Gertrude Lawrence as the English governess, Anna, in the original production of *The King and I* which was to open on Broadway in 1951. Connie, was born in Bath on Primrose Day (April 19), and was just two years younger than my father. She had a superb acting and musical comedy pedigree. Her parents had been in the theatre and at the age of seven she had been taught dancing by Anna Pavlova. She made her stage debut when she was 10 and then for two years played a chorister in a hit comedy show called *Seven Days' Leave* at London's Lyceum. She then joined the chorus line in Cochran's *The Fun of the Fayre* at the London Pavilion and graduated from there to becoming a regular performer in Andre Charlot's revues in London and New York during the 1920s and 1930s. There she got to know Gertrude Lawrence well, along with other stars including Beatrice Lillie. Gertrude had sung Noël Coward's *Poor Little Rich Girl* to a youthful Connie in Charlot's *Revue of 1926* in New York. She subsequently eclipsed Connie to become one of the greatest English actresses and musical performers of the time, especially through her performances in Noël Coward productions. Connie's stage appearances in London and New York went on to include Cochran's *Revue* in 1930, *Robinson Crusoe*, *The Third Little Show*, *Music Hath Charms*, *Dirty Work* (a Ben Travers comedy, at the Aldwych*)*, *Happy Returns* (with Beatrice Lillie and Flanagan and Allen, at the Strand)

and *French Without Tears*. She also had various leading pantomime roles. A highlight of those years was when she starred with William Gaxton in the original 1927 production of Rodgers and Hart's *A Connecticut Yankee*, where she introduced *My Heart Stood Still* and *Thou Swell*. It was as a result of this role that Connie became known to the celebrated composer, perhaps the key reason why she was later asked by Rodgers and Hammerstein to stand by as understudy to Gertrude, who had remained a friend, in *The King and I*.

What was not generally known in 1951 was that Gertrude Lawrence was suffering from suspected liver cancer and her illness meant that she was frequently indisposed. Connie even took her place during the final dress rehearsals (which were attended by outsiders including the press), becoming as one theatre reviewer said at the time, 'the first understudy to star in a show before it had actually been performed'. *The King and I* opened at the St. James Theatre, New York, on 29 March 1951 with Gertrude Lawrence in the lead role. But Connie took her place opposite Yul Brynner more than 50 times in the early part of the run. When Gertrude died in September 1952, Connie took over her starring role for another 620 performances until the show closed on Broadway in March 1954, after which she went on tour with it.

However, though she was well reviewed and had a thriving fan club, Connie was by now in her early fifties and was not offered the role of Anna in the subsequent Walter Lang film of *The King and I*, released two years later. That went to a younger actress, 35-year-old Deborah Kerr, who received an Oscar nomination as Best Actress. Yul Brynner, who retained the part of the King of Siam – a role he had made his own on Broadway – won an Oscar for Best Actor. After *The King and I*, Connie never reached the same heights of stardom again, although she did get plenty of work. Broadway audiences would have seen her in a range of plays and shows, including *Third Little Show* and *Lord Pengo*. And she was much in demand on tour in plays such as *Separate Rooms, Auntie Mame* (she was reportedly superb in the leading role), *Five Finger Exercise, Toys in the Attic* and *The Canterbury Tales*, appearing opposite such notables as Charles Boyer, Sir Cedric Hardwicke, Alfred Drake and Richard Kiley. She also picked up television work. She was still active into the 1970s by which time she was in her seventies herself. Despite being a star actress – and in spite of the fact that her publicity blurb claimed she had read the Encyclopaedia Britannica in its entirety – there was one word she told me that she could not pronounce, Chevrolet! Perhaps it was the banana diet that prevented it! I was amused by her comment when I asked her once what it was like to be in the theatre: 'I am not "in" the theatre, my dear. I am "of" the theatre.'

Connie's years of fame in the early 1950s helped to make this an extremely enjoyable period for her and Jimmy Kennedy. They rented a new apartment on Fifth Avenue. Connie's income in her starring role of Anna was substantial, although, with all the trappings – clothes, jewels, daily hairdo, smart restaurants and shopping sprees – she had no problem getting through it. His earnings, too, had picked up with *Harbour Lights* and his other American chart entries. It was cabaret time for the two of them. They went to all the shows, ate regularly in the best restaurants, especially Sardi's, the American-Italian favourite of Broadway stars and well-to-do theatre-goers on 44th Street. When I was last at Sardi's in the late 1980s, Connie's photograph was still hanging on the wall with the rest of its star clientele. My father was speaking from first-hand experience when he used to say that he thought the best food in the world was not to be found in Paris, but in New York. He also learnt to enjoy the American version of gin martinis – a Beefeater, straight up, with a twist. Connie preferred the cool minty taste of iced stingers – an intoxicating mélange of brandy and crème de menthe. It was in those days, too, that they both acquired their taste for Mumms Cordon Rouge champagne.

However, despite the good times, I believe the personal relationship between the two had begun to cool down even before Connie took up her role in *The King and I.* She was great fun to be with but never stopped playing the actress and this must have been wearing for my father who, at times, could be reserved and unshowy. I do not imagine their relationship would have been helped by the fact that she was 'frigid', one reason why she had had no children during her previous marriages. He never talked about such things but Connie's closest friend and fan, and an executor of her will, assured me many years later that this was the case. I also do not think the marriage really ever quite recovered from her refusal to take on the maternal role she had promised to perform when they had first got together. She made a promise which she did not keep and that did not square with the Northern Irish tradition where if you say you are going to do something, you do it. Her decision to go back to the theatre meant not only that he had to try to be father to children living three thousand miles away but to co-opt his sister Nell, who was not only stressed out by running the house and looking after other peoples' children but had frequent illnesses. Yet she had to take on the mother role. It was all very messy. The basic flaws in the marriage were implicit in what Connie told me many years later: that they were secretly divorced in 1953, that they had remarried, also secretly, a few years later, and then divorced again in the early 1960s – so, according to her, they were married and divorced twice.

During the 1960s Connie came to London on several occasions. Once she understudied Hermione Gingold in a show at the Theatre Royal, Brighton. When I complimented her at the time on her role she remonstrated: 'Not an *understudy*, darling, stand-in-*star*.' In those years I think she hoped she could win back her former husband a third time even though he was by then living in a bachelor apartment in Lausanne, Switzerland. But it was not to be. I remember in early 1969 Connie once stayed at The Ritz in London at the same time as Judy Garland, who was doing her last ill-fated performance at The Talk of The Town. Connie had invited me to meet her at the hotel before going out to dinner but then insisted on waiting in the lobby until 'darling' Judy came down the staircase because, so she said, she wanted to introduce me. We paraded up and down for over an hour, an uncomfortable experience, while she gushed away, waiting for the star to appear. Fortunately, she did not. But, for all her faults, I was personally fond of Connie. She was a charming, amusing, talented and intelligent woman who found it hard to cope with the inevitable age-related downward slope from stardom to normality, made harder as her income declined.

Her final Broadway appearance was in the Jerome Lawrence and Robert E. Lee play, *The Incomparable Man*, in 1971, after which she effectively retired. In later years, well after her divorces from Jimmy Kennedy, she invested in New York real estate to boost her income. Unfortunately, this was no more successful than it had been in England after the War and she lost most of her money. As a result, she had to move to a fairly cheap part of Manhattan, a small apartment on East 44th Street, just a few blocks from the U.N. headquarters, where she used to complain about the bicycles at the bottom of the stairs and the constant practising of a violinist in the apartment opposite. In her declining years in the 1970s and 1980s she lavished affection on her little white dogs – all called April, after the month of her birth. As she advanced into old age and infirmity, Connie's needs which included full-time nursing, were met by her friends and fans. One of the saddest things was that she began to lose her memory in old age. That was hard for her to take and upset her greatly. A good memory is vital for an actress. She died penniless on Boxing Day 1992, aged 88. Her only recognition apart from a few press cuttings, was a memorial service at St Bartholomew's Church on New York's Park Avenue, which I attended, along with a handful of her dedicated fans and friends.

# 19: *April in Portugal* – and a secret girlfriend

As record sales began to dominate the popular music business and form the basis for chart ratings, professional songwriters increasingly aimed their material at top recording artists. Targeting performers was not new: it used to happen in the 1920s and 1930s too. But in those earlier days a good song could sometimes get up to a dozen recordings, any of which could stimulate sheet music sales and broadcasts so giving it a better chance of being successful. By the early 1950s, however, recordings were becoming one-shot affairs and, not only that, as the decade progressed into the 1960s, success had to happen fast or the song would be dropped by the record companies. These developing conditions did not suit Jimmy Kennedy's style. Not only that, New York, still the centre of the music business, was not a natural milieu for his artistic – and at times, difficult – temperament. He was offended by some of the attitudes he found. He used to say that publishers never considered the merits of a new song. All they wanted to know was: 'Will it make money?' and 'Is it legal?' I think, too, that he hated the constant noise, the round-the-clock pace of life, and the extremes of weather, especially the humidity. I came across an unpublished verse among his papers that summed up his feelings:

*How can anybody live in New York?*
*With the hustle, the bustle and the subway rattle,*
*A battle that never ceases,*
*'Twould shatter normal humans to pieces.*

However, despite the negatives and a music scene that was suiting him less and less, in 1953 he had one of his biggest and most evergreen hits, *April in Portugal.* Jimmy Kennedy used to be sensitive about being thought of as a 'geographical' writer. I remember him telling the story of Cole Porter who, when asked about how he got ideas for so many great songs, said: 'Well, I get out my atlas of the world and look up a place that sounds interesting and write a song about it.' Of course, this was not true but, being a great wit, Porter was poking gentle fun at the writers who did. And there were many like that because geographical songs were popular with the relatively untravelled audiences of those days. For ordinary people, these exotic places were dreams and publishers were only too happy to cash in on these dreams, whether their writers wanted to or not. Two Jimmy Kennedy songs of the genre, *Isle of Capri* and *South of the Border,* had been enormously successful – though they owed their success, perhaps, as much or more to their catchy tunes, their arrangements and the romantic stories in the lyrics rather than the locations they were set in. *April in Portugal* proved the point that even in the 1950s there was still a huge market for this kind of song. Its wonderful tune was based on a Portuguese folk song, or *fado,* called *Coimbra* (a city in central Portugal). It had been composed some years earlier by a Portuguese army bandmaster, Colonel Raul Ferrâo, and had been played a lot on the continent with French and Spanish lyrics. Music publishers Chappell & Co. Inc had bought the rights for America and asked Jimmy Kennedy to write an English lyric, which he did, calling it *The Whisp'ring Serenade.* This is how his original lyric went:

*The whisp'ring serenade*
*Comes softly through the night*
*And whispers of a lover*
*When the stars are bright.*

*The melody is old,*
*Temptation ever new*
*When music whispers, 'I love you!'*

*My heart had lost its wings*
*But heard the sighing strings*
*And answered like a songbird mating.*
*The moonlit patio*
*Was suddenly aglow*
*I knew that love was waiting – because –*

*The whisp'ring serenade*
*Came softly through the night...*
*I felt no more alarms,*
*Just two caressing arms*
*And lips that said so much with kisses.*
*Old ecstasy returned,*
*I lived and loved and learned*
*But then you went – and I wait until –*

*The whisp'ring serenade ...etc*

Despite some good recordings and heavy promotion in America, *The Whisp'ring Serenade* got nowhere. Then, while on holiday in Florida, Jimmy Kennedy received a surprise cable asking him to write new lyrics for the tune but with a different title, *April in Portugal*. He refused. He thought his original lyric was a good one and cabled back to suggest that *The Whisp'ring Serenade* should be promoted harder. Remembering Cole Porter's 'geography' joke, he added that he thought the new title sounded too much like *April in Paris*, the big 'Yip' Harburg / Vernon Duke song of 1932, and he didn't want people to think he had run out of ideas. He then got a further cable from the publisher saying 'We've got orders downstairs in the trade department for 50,000 copies. Are you going to write it or do we have to get someone else?' The proposition meant dollar royalties with noughts on the end. Kennedy changed his mind. Overnight he adapted his existing lyric to match the new title. To his surprise the song and its new lyric climbed to the top of the American charts in a matter of weeks. And, quite against the trend, which was towards record sales, sheet music sales topped half a million. Not only was it one of the biggest songs of the year in America, it also reached No. 4 in Britain. The new chorus went like this:

*I found my April dream, in Portugal with you*
*Where we discovered romance, like we never knew.*
*My head was in the clouds,*
*My heart went crazy too,*
*And madly, I said 'I love you.'*

The biggest-selling record of *April in Portugal* was an instrumental by Les Baxter and his orchestra, which reached No. 2 in America. Other orchestral and instrumental chart recordings were made by Richard Hayman, Freddy Martin, and Tony Martin with Lennie Hayton's orchestra. Bing Crosby also covered it, as did Louis Armstrong, Vic Damone and Eartha Kitt. In Britain, orchestral recordings included Roberto Inglez, The Melachrino Strings, Geraldo, Joe Loss, Frank Chacksfield and Mantovani. Eve Boswell, Amalia Rodrigues, Jane Morgan and Caterina Valente did solo versions. It was in the charts for 25 weeks. There were at least 40 contemporary recordings, making it perhaps the most recorded songs of the decade in Britain. It only went to prove that the old-fashioned popular song was not dead – yet!

As a US resident, Jimmy Kennedy paid American taxes during the 1950s. How he would have fared under the UK tax regime of the time I do not know. But he would have paid a lot. I remember he once showed me his royalty statement for performances, which came in a computer roll stretching from one end of the 20 foot drawing room to the other. He used to complain that to pay 97 per cent income tax on the top slice of his income was very unfair for him and for other artists with variable income because a good year heavily taxed could easily be followed by some bad years. He thought the tax should be evened out for artists over the years. A practical result of paying tax in the United States was that he was allowed to stay for only three months in Britain during the 1950s and early 1960s, so he developed a regular pattern of visits there to see his children and to maintain contact with the European end of the music business without falling foul of the tax man. He would leave New York in February or March, fly from there to the Bahamas, where he would stay at the Country Club in Nassau for a few weeks or visit other friends he made in the area and then, having achieved an enviable tan, he would fly on to England for Easter, often staying in Wicklow or Dublin en route.

Among friends he made when he visited the Caribbean were Sir Harold and Lady Mitchell, who had an estate, the Prospect Plantation, in Ocho Rios, Jamaica. Sir Harold Mitchell was a distinguished academic and writer specialising in the Caribbean and a very successful and wealthy businessman and philanthropist. During a varied career, he had been a Conservative MP and vice-chairman of the Conservative party. Among his efforts to help the local community was a school for the sons of poor Jamaicans, the Prospect Cadet Training Centre. In return for the Mitchell hospitality my father wrote a school anthem for the Centre which, dressed in their uniforms, the students would play when important visitors arrived.

After his Easter trip, which would include staying at the Kennedy family home in Somerset mixed with business and socializing in London, he would fly back to New York. A month or two later he would repeat the trip, this time going directly to England, where he would spend most of the summer. In December, he would make his third trip, staying in England for a week or two at Christmas, something he enjoyed very much. I remember him arriving at Staplegrove like Santa Claus, laden with presents and groceries from Fortnum's, Harrods or Paxton & Whitfield, looking every inch the country gentleman returning to his estate. Whatever time of year he came to stay, his sister Nell would roll out the red carpet and meals would improve markedly.

My father enjoyed his food and was no mean cook himself, introducing into our post-rationing household exotic fare such as ham and peaches, a sweet and savoury combination unheard of in rural Somerset in the early 1950s, foie gras and non-Somerset cheeses like Roquefort. His last-minute Sunday lunch gravy-making involved tipping a generous glassful of red Burgundy – Chambolle Musigny, Aloxe Corton, Volnay perhaps – into the scrapings at the bottom of the roasting pan and pouring the deglazed juices into the Georgian silver gravy boats that magically appeared when he was around. This was the prelude to a lunch peppered with his anecdotes and usually made even more pleasant because as teenagers we got to drink and appreciate some fine wines at a relatively young age. Oddly enough, despite his adventurous enthusiasm for British, French and American recipes, he couldn't bear garlic. Above all, he hated most 'over-flavoured' greasy foreign foods, especially Spanish. That is probably why he was not much impressed with my breakfast special – garlicky scrambled eggs, spiced with brandy – an occasional student hangover cure based on a recipe from an Anglo-Spanish chum of mine at Trinity College! After a good meal at home, he would retire to the drawing room. He loved to sit there in his favourite Georgian wing chair, from where he had an uninterrupted view of the Blackdown Hills through the wall-to-ceiling sash windows, writing letters and lyrics to top lines sent by publishers.

In the early 1950s we had only one telephone at Staplegrove and calls used to be made and received from the fixed black phone in the hall, which meant that you could overhear all conversations. At that time there were many calls to and from Connie in New York and this used to infuriate granny, by then in her late seventies and very much the matriarch of Staplegrove. Despite her deafness, she heard what she wanted. She had hated both her son's wives, especially Connie, and never ceased telling us so. It was bad enough that she was an actress. Even worse, she was a divorcee. One day during a particularly long telephone call, my father, slipping into actors' vernacular, said 'darling' once too often for granny's liking, and this led to a big row, ending with her taking off one of her size 11 leather-soled shoes halfway up the grand winding staircase and delivering a smart thwack to his (quite prominent) nose. Fortunately the stag's head directly above them (which came with the house) only rocked on its hook, so neither were killed or injured. We children decided to make ourselves scarce and hid in the study, hoping no wrath would be transferred to us. Knowing he had an unseen audience but failing to conceal a face of thunder, he came in to say that the altercation was nothing, concluding with the paradoxical statement, 'She almost broke my nose!' At that we all burst out laughing. He looked outraged for a minute but then saw the funny side of it himself because he left the room without saying any more and was soon heard playing the piano in the drawing room as if nothing had happened. Arguments were fairly frequent between these two strong-willed characters but were soon forgotten. However, it was noticeable that there were far fewer calls to and from New York! Connie was never invited to Staplegrove.

However, perhaps to appease granny and Nell, Connie arranged for a very special present to be sent to the house. None of us knew what to expect when we were told to assemble in the drawing room which was furnished not only with the rosewood grand piano but with antique sofas and chairs and a priceless and beautiful wall-to-wall antique Persian carpet. As we waited, there was a knock on the front door. Nell opened it and to everyone's delight a magnificent collie dog was ushered in. We were told she was called Lassie and had been groomed to star in Lassie films but never made it because she suffered from stage fright, a condition which was shortly to be revealed as chronic. Having been coaxed to the centre of the room, she took a nervous look at the expectant strangers crowding around to stroke her, cowered down and released a river which turned into a small lake right in the middle of the oriental carpet. Luckily, not being a male, the dog did not cock its leg against the silk settee. My father's face froze. Then he recovered himself and said: 'It's a present from Connie!' Nobody dared laugh!

We always called our house 'Staplegrove Elm', but its real name was The Elms. It was supposed to have got that name after the Monmouth rebellion in 1685 when Judge Jeffreys had some rebels hanged on trees at the end of the front drive after he sentenced them to death at his notorious Bloody Assizes, one of which was held in the Assembly Rooms near Taunton Castle, just two miles away. As a schoolboy I used to wonder which trees were used. But when I looked up the history books I was disappointed to find that the story could not have been true; the trees were not old enough. The rebellion had taken place almost two hundred years before the house was built. Though Staplegrove Elm with its eight bedrooms was quite large, it was part of the estate of an even larger house, Staplegrove Manor. When its owner died in 1957, my father was able to buy our house for just £5,000. It was worth far more than that, so in the end he got the property bargain that had eluded him when he was in the real estate business after he was demobbed.

In 1954, Hamilton Kennedy died as the result of an accident. He was working as a Light Entertainment producer at the BBC at the time and, aged only 48, his death came as a big shock to everyone. He had been a frequent visitor to Staplegrove and his two children, Heather and Ian, used to spend holidays in the country with us. Though Hamilton no longer had the time to write or co-write songs, his pre-War US No. 1 cowboy song *Ole Faithful, The Chestnut Tree* and *How Can You Buy Killarney?* (which was in the UK 1948 charts for 35 weeks) showed he could have been a major player in his own right in the music business. My father, who was 52 when his brother died, had black hair. Six months later, it was white. The two brothers were very close but it was an extraordinary thing.

In those days we were often visited at Staplegrove by cousin Deirdre's father, Uncle Nick. Now retired from the Canadian merchant navy, he had embarked on a new career supplying Indians living in remoter parts of the western coast of Vancouver with provisions. As he plied the creeks, the sole sailor on his boat, he often used to play his unique rendition of Schuman's Träumerei on an old violin. I am not sure what the Indians thought but there was warmth in his eccentric rubato - he would often repeat the performance at Staplegrove - which showed him to be someone with a heart, if not a musical soul. Uncle Nick was a keen amateur photographer who taught all of us a lot about photography, which in those rural pre-TV days, was one of the family's main childhood hobbies. Later he married a senior lady officer from one of the armed forces and died fairly soon after.

When my father stayed at Staplegrove during the summer, he used to take the train to London during the week, returning on Friday evenings. Normally an early riser, he had a long lie-in on Sundays when he invariably had a tray brought up to his room containing tea, toast, honey, (dietary) Flora and a copy of *The Sunday Times*. It was a nice leisurely weekend and one he perhaps needed because, as I later found out, he was not just seeing his business acquaintances and friends in London. He also had a well-kept secret – a girlfriend called Eileen Williams. After his 1953 divorce from Connie, he started a new and long-term relationship with Eileen following a chance encounter at The Cotton Club, a venue popular with show business people, not far from the famous Ivy restaurant in Soho. Eileen was behind the bar one day in 1953 when Jimmy wandered into the club for a drink. *April in Portugal* had just reached the top of the US charts, so he was on good form and in the mood for conversation. Eileen described the occasion to me many years later: 'He swept off his hat, bowed to everyone in the club, made his way to the bar and ordered a large gin and tonic. He spent the entire evening talking to me and I was to learn that however much he imbibed, he maintained his equilibrium and his faculties stayed as bright as ever, though his accent became more Irish!' As they chatted away they realised that in 1942 when he was training to be an officer at Shrivenham, she had been in the WAAF and used to go dancing at Burford Army Camp, practically next door and they must have visited the same pubs, though they never remembered meeting. Something that intrigued him was why Eileen should be employed as a barmaid? In those days jobs for women were harder to find than now, so Eileen, who was entrepreneurial by nature, told him she had taken the job at the Cotton Club with the idea of moving on to higher things in the hotel or catering business. He enjoyed talking to the attractive redhead that evening so much that he invited her to dinner the next day at The Ivy. There they discovered other things they had in common: she not only 'got' his jokes and his stories but could tell them herself. She was a good observer of people and was an amusing mimic. Her new songwriter friend flew out to New York the next day but as soon as he got there he sent her a comedy card with a picture of a lady lying on her side and a very small man tucked behind. It said: 'We fit together very well!'

A few weeks later, when he returned to London, they started their friendship in earnest. Meeting the famous songwriter, with his attractive Irish brogue and fund of amusing anecdotes, had swept her off her feet. And this, despite the fact that he was 52 and she was 33. He liked to stay at the Great Western Hotel, Paddington because it was so handy for the express train to Taunton and they could meet before he left for Somerset. Later he discovered a small hotel in Mayfair not far from Hyde Park Corner. The Headfort Place Hotel was just the place for amorous encounters, convenient and discreet. In the evenings they might go to a musical or dine out at L'Escargot in Soho, Scott's of Piccadilly, or more humbly at the Roebuck, a pub just off Haverstock Hill in Hampstead – a stone's throw from Eileen's own flat. They soon found other mutual interests including a love of good food – especially French – and the same sign of the zodiac, Cancer. And they were both avid readers, Eileen told me, 'We found we had read the same books. I remember my first present to him was *The Story of San Michele* by Axel Munthe. He had read it – it is set in the village of Anacapri on the Isle of Capri – but the copy I gave him was beautifully illustrated and he was like a dog with two tails.' She agreed with his old-fashioned values, his amusingly over-the-top views on people and events, and was discreet. She was attractive, kind, warm and understanding...a woman of the world, a good cook, and, like him, unattached. She found Jimmy 'irresistibly charming, good company and amusing'.

Eileen became Jimmy's confidential companion for 14 years, a secret that he kept from his business associates and, with the exception of his sister Nell, his family. Eileen came to know more about his life than anyone and, though in those days he was still tied to the music business in New York and had to spend a good deal of time there, when he was in Europe she joined him on trips to Ireland, Paris, the Costa Brava and, in the early 1960s, to his flat in Lausanne. When he was not with her he wrote to her every day and she replied in kind. During that time she kept her financial independence by moving into the travel business. It was a relationship between two consenting adults. Both knew this, and although thoughts of marriage certainly entered Eileen's head – she told me so – it was never on the Jimmy Kennedy agenda, regardless of the failure of his relationship with Connie. By the mid 1960s, his professional career at the top of the music business in New York and London was coming to an end and he was starting to review his life. His thoughts were turning away from London to Ireland as the best place for him to retire.

It was round that time that he decided to end his affair with Eileen. According to her, late in 1967 he took her to lunch and announced that he could no longer see her. It was all over, after 14 years. She was naturally devastated at the apparent suddenness of his decision and, indeed, it would seem that he did not handle the situation very well. She was so astonished and heart-broken that when she got back to her flat she burnt all the hundreds of letters he had sent. Relationships break down for a complex of reasons and this was no exception. Perhaps, now that he was in his sixties, he was no longer the alpha male he wanted to be. Perhaps the problems ran deeper, that the relationship was beginning to slip down the charts, anyway. On a practical level, it is hard to see how it could have gone on indefinitely. He was a wanderer. Even though his work was winding down, he was still chasing from New York to London to Paris. Moving round the world, and with a family headed by his sister and mother still based in Somerset, meant it would have been nigh on impossible to start all over again with a new wife at that phase of his life, to be tied down after so many years of freedom. Perhaps there were some more mundane reasons: possibly he could not quite bring himself to marry someone who smoked. Having previously been a twenty-a-day man himself, he now hated the habit almost more than anything. Eileen herself thought the reason was probably that she did not come from the right background. As she told me years later, 'I was an Essex girl before they became fashionable!'

*Long-term girlfriend Eileen Williams in uniform in 1942.*

But, she continued to be very fond of him. Indeed, I met her for the first time when she asked through an intermediary if she could come to his memorial service at St Giles-in-the-Fields church shortly after his death in 1984. After that, I invited her to lunch and it was then that I heard, for the first time, all about their secret love life. Over the meal she made some revealing comments about him to me: 'I loved him and would have married him, if he had asked me. I felt very close to his family because he told me all about them. I knew about all the ups and downs, how well the children had done in school, who had been naughty, who had done well. I knew as much almost as if we had been married. But it was not to be.' And she summed him up: 'Despite what people thought, Jimmy was no businessman and he failed in his marriages. His family was a dream world, really. His social life involved meeting people in a rather artificial and unreal way. At heart, he was really an Irish country lad with a sophisticated veneer and Irish charm.'

After the break-up, Elaine went into the antiques business and was successful for a time. Later she was active in church work. Even in her eighties she visited Bombay on several occasions helping to rescue homeless children. She was subsequently offered a church flat in return for cooking for the poor and needy in the East End – often for twenty or more people. She even wrote a cookery book which, among other recipes, included one for bread and butter pudding. Highly recommended!

# 20: *Istanbul,* The Platters and Sinatra

*Istanbul's tongue-in-cheek lyrics and Turkish mood
have kept it popular since it first became a hit in 1954.*

Jimmy Kennedy's friendship with Eileen took place mainly in England but meanwhile he continued to work in America, especially with Nat Simon. In 1954, right at the beginning of his relationship in London with Eileen and soon after *April in Portugal* had entered the American charts, Kennedy and Simon had their biggest hit – unintentionally, a song about yet another geographical location, this time, Istanbul. Late in 1953, the two writers were down in Florida mixing business and pleasure when, as they were amusing themselves at the piano looking for ideas, Nat came up with a musical phrase with a slightly eastern feel to it. After a martini or two they decided the mood was probably Turkish. 'It reminded me of a comic Turkish dance act by a group called Wilson, Keppel, and Betty in the days when Michael Carr and I did the London Palladium shows with the Crazy Gang. That gave me the idea to go for some amusing lyrics, to make it an entertainment,' Jimmy Kennedy said at the time, 'And both of us could see that the lyric had to have a Turkish connection. Neither of us knew much about Turkey but we did know about Istanbul and that it used to be called Constantinople. Once that had clicked, we had the title for the song, *Istanbul, not Constantinople*. Band leader Frank Chacksfield loved it: 'I adore clever lyrics. I'm sure most people do and *Istanbul* is one of my favourites. *"Why did Constantinople get the works?/That's nobody's business but the Turks!"* I think that's brilliant writing.'

*Istanbul was Constantinople!*
*Now it's Istanbul, not Constantinople.*
*Been a long time gone, Constantinople*
*Still it's Turkish delight on a moonlit night!...*
*Why did Constantinople get the works?*
*That's nobody's business but the Turks!*

*Istanbul* reached No. 10 in the American charts and No. 9 in Britain with a recording by The Four Lads, who had previously had a big hit with *Down by the Riverside*. Kennedy's favourite version was by Joe 'Fingers' Carr and his Ragtime Band. There were many other recordings

- by the Malcolm Mitchell Trio, Edmundo Ros and his orchestra, Bette Midler, Caterina Valente, Frankie Vaughan and a sultry version by Eartha Kitt. *Istanbul* has gone on to become a useful niche standard in America, France and Germany. There are wildly new versions now on the internet. College rock band, They Might Be Giants, in various guises including as Led Zeppelin, have notched up hundreds of thousands of hits.

However, despite the chart success of songs like *April in Portugal* and *Istanbul*, more revolutionary changes in American music were taking place. They were symbolized most unforgettably by the phrase, 'rock 'n' roll', a term coined in 1954 by disc jockey Alan Freed in his show, The Big Beat, to describe the fusion of country and gospel music and blues combined with his show's title, a big beat, and a completely different, far more raucous, guitar-laden sound than anything that had come before. Rock 'n' roll did not mean instant death for Jimmy Kennedy and songwriters like him, it was more like death by a thousand cuts. Along with the others, he sat out the new genre and carried on writing in his own way without, by his standards, any significant success. A song he wrote called *The Moon Grew Brighter and Brighter* went into the Disney film *Man Without a Star* and was sung and recorded by Kirk Douglas. And about this time, he had a minor chart success, *Magic Tango*, which was recorded by Hugo Winterhalter's orchestra and chorus, and Eddie Fisher. Along with these came various chart entries in England.

Then he had a big stroke of luck. 1956 was the year that Elvis Presley hit the big time, a year after his Sun recordings (which had included *Harbour Lights,* a favourite of his mother) with three No. 1 rock 'n' roll hits – *Don't be Cruel, Heartbreak Hotel* and *Love Me Tender*. It was also only a year after Bill Haley's *Rock Around the Clock*, the song that more than any signified the watershed between the old and the new styles of pop song. In the spring of

1956, with the sounds from the new galaxy of pop stars blaring from every juke box, Jimmy Kennedy lunched with Art Gallico, a good music publishing friend of his. Afterwards, as they walked back to Art's office, they ran into Buck Ram, the manager, arranger and songwriter for what was rapidly becoming one of the best vocal groups of the early rock 'n' roll era, The Platters. The group had just notched up three hits including *The Great Pretender*, which had reached No. 1.

Buck Ram was a friend of Art and as they chatted, Ram mentioned that he had a recording session the following day and needed one more number for the Extended Play (EP) record they were producing. So Art said, 'What about Jimmy's *My Prayer*?' Buck Ram knew the song and recalled that the first big recording had been by The Ink Spots, the black vocal group that was in some ways a forerunner of The Platters. So he could see that with the right treatment it might suit the group's doo-wop style. Just as Henry Hall's arranger had done for *The Teddy Bears' Picnic* 25 years earlier, he went home that evening and made an arrangement. The subsequent recording, which began with the memorable phrase, '*When the twilight is gone and no songbirds are singing...*' turned out to be among the biggest and most enduring hits that The Platters ever made, selling three million records. And it was one in the eye for rock 'n' roll because it kept Elvis Presley's *Hound Dog* off the No 1 spot for two weeks, remaining in the charts for almost three months. In Britain, the *My Prayer* revival only reached No 14, but it was in the charts for 16 weeks. Thanks to its success, The Platters went on to record two more Jimmy Kennedy standards, *Red Sails in the Sunset* in 1958 and *Harbour Lights* in 1960, both of which made the American Top 10. Their treatment of the three songs has been selling to new generations of music lovers ever since. And it was all as a result of a chance meeting on the street.

*The top line manuscript for My Prayer, Jimmy Kennedy's 1939 hit, made even bigger by The Platters in 1956 – a recording which kept Hound Dog off the American No. 1 spot for two weeks.*

At around the same time as *My Prayer* made the charts for a second time, several other Jimmy Kennedy standards were resurrected by top American recording stars. A year after *My Prayer*, Frank Sinatra recorded *Isle of Capri* and *South of the Border* on his *Come Fly with me* album, which was released in 1958 and was the No 1 album for five weeks. (Sinatra had previously recorded *South of the Border* as a single in 1954, when it reached No. 2). With Billy May arrangements, *Come Fly with me* is considered by many people to be the best of his upbeat 'swinging' concept albums. My father said that Sinatra put a lot of bounce into the song, giving it the zip that most of the other versions of the time did not: 'And I think it needed it,' he said, 'By that time *South of the Border* was beginning to linger a bit itself. Frank's up-tempo version gave it a terrific fillip and I don't think it has ever looked back since then. And it was all due to Frank.' As to *Isle of Capri*, Sinatra drove a horse and carriage through the 'ring on her finger' line, which had caused so much fuss in the 1930s. He substituted his own rather unedifying line: *'She wore a lovely meatball on her finger, 'Twas goodbye to the Villa Capri.'* The meatball reference was an in-joke referring to a famous Hollywood celebrity restaurant called Villa Capri, much frequented by Sinatra and the rest of the 'rat pack'. But Kennedy for once did not complain! He himself used to have fun with his own lyrics – admittedly not when they were being recorded. He once told me that he and the conductor Frank Chacksfield – they were close friends – used to amuse themselves over a meal by putting ridiculous words or titles to songs. *Red Sails in the Sunset* was de-romanticised to *Red Snails in the Sunset* and then, after a couple more glasses of wine, *Dead Snails in the Sunset*.

Over the next few years, Perry Como recorded *Red Sails in the Sunset* and *South of the Border*, Fats Domino rocked *Red Sails in the Sunset* into the American charts, Dinah Washington jazzed up *Harbour Lights*, Bing Crosby sang a smooth second version of *South of the Border*, and Dean Martin crooned both *South of the Border* and *Red Sails in the Sunset* in the film *The Silencers*. Later, Herb Alpert and his Tijuana Brass headlined *South of the Border* in an eponymous album which sold over five million records. That recording couldn't have been more appropriate considering the original title had come from a card posted from Tijuana by sister Nell 20 years earlier. Patsy Cline did her unique and stylish country version and so did Connie Francis, both of which are on *YouTube*, along with many others. Nat King Cole had a chart success with *Red Sails in the Sunset* and young film star Tab Hunter recorded the song on the flip side of his first record, *Young Love*. The top ten Jimmy Kennedy standards have continued to be covered ever since.

During the 1950s two pieces not intended for the charts indirectly made him as much or more money – in kind – than some of his better-known songs. He wrote a snappy TV advertising jingle lyric for the Dutch airline, KLM. But, instead of taking a fee (on which he would have had to pay tax), he negotiated two free return transatlantic flights per year until the ad series finished. The executives thought that was a good deal, since it cost them only a notional amount. The ad, however, ran for a quite a few years – so Jimmy Kennedy had several trans-Atlantic flights for nothing! He also wrote the theme song, a waltz, for a new French liner, *La France*. This was perhaps because of his connections with Alex Alstone, the French composer, with whom he often collaborated at that time. Under that deal, he had a free first class cabin, but had to pay for everything else. It sounded a good arrangement but, as he told me, 'Although a free first class passage on a wonderful ship like *La France* teaches you some interesting things – like the fact that *pâté de foie gras* should be served with a good *Sauternes* and iced vodka is better than champagne with caviar – when you count the cost of these luxuries, it's probably better to pay your own fare and go tourist.'

*J. J. Kennedy*

Popular music experts say that Jimmy Kennedy was never able to repeat his 1930s successes when he went over to the USA. I disagree. Considering his age and the way popular music was revolutionised in the 1950s – and not forgetting the twists and turns of his private life – the move turned out to be pretty shrewd. He had at least a dozen top 5 songs and three of these were No. 1 in the all important American market. Would he have had that chart success if he had not been there in person? He knew that if he did not promote his own output, no one else would. Publishers and record companies were naturally more interested in new songs and artists. He worked very hard at keeping in with the key people – he literally 'lunched' his songs back into the charts. The extra exposure he managed to achieve helped prolong the lives of several of his most important standards and did wonders for his bank balance, if not his waistline. Meanwhile, what was happening in Britain during the 1950s? Not much. Many of the UK chart entries retained a traditional almost insular British flavour and few were truly international hits. The top songs were still imported from America.

# 21: Still swinging in the Sixties

By 1960, New York's famous Madison Avenue Brill Building song factory had taken over from Tin Pan Alley as the centre of American popular music. It did not last long as the jewel in the crown – only four or five years or so – but in its heyday it housed well over 150 music businesses, publishers, arrangers, writers, managers, demo studios – virtually all that was needed to produce a song from start to finish. The style of music, led by writers like Carole King and Geoff Goffin, Barry Mann and Cynthia Weil, Jeff Barry and Ellie Greenwich, was sweet rock 'n' roll aimed at the teenage market. Artists such as Neil Sedaka (*Happy Birthday Sweet Sixteen*, *Breaking up Is Hard To Do*), Paul Anka (*Diana*, *Puppy Love*, *My Way*) and Bobby Darin (*Dream Lover*) were writing and performing just this kind of material. Some tremendous pop was produced from the Brill Building at around that time, but Jimmy Kennedy, aged nearly sixty, was no longer really in touch with this market or the new young generation rushing in to recreate pop.

Nevertheless, one of the best of the writers emerging at this time has said he was greatly influenced by Jimmy Kennedy. Hal David, who with Burt Bacharach wrote some of the most distinctive songs of the 1960s and 1970s – *What the World Needs Now is Love Sweet Love*, *Raindrops Keep Falling on my Head*, *Close to You*, and a hatful of others – recorded his admiration of the unique lyric style of Jimmy Kennedy in a contribution he made to celebrate the 100th issue of London-based music journal, MOJO magazine in 2002:

When I started out writing songs I used to go around the Brill Building and read the songs. I fell in love with the great lyric writers and decided that was part of the creation I wanted to be in. At the very beginning I was enamoured with Irving Berlin, who, when all is said and done, was probably the best lyric writer of all. He stripped away all the gingerbread, all the superfluousness, never wasting a word. It seemed so simple, so easy. Over the years Johnny Mercer became another hero.

But there's one person who's not so well known as Johnny Mercer or Irving Berlin who was very, very kind to me when I was starting out: Jimmy Kennedy, an Irishman who lived in England but spent a lot of time in the States. A very suave, elegant man. He wrote the lyrics to *Isle of Capri, Red Sails in the Sunset, South of the Border.*

I met him at his publishers in New York. I was a professional songwriter in my twenties and I'd had hits. I thought I'd like to write like him and I guess he liked it that I admired his work. He was very encouraging; a great writer, ripe for rediscovery.

At the beginning of the 1960s Jimmy Kennedy realised there was no longer any point in continuing to live in New York. His real love, Eileen, lived in England. His family was in England, too. So, he finally gave up his apartment and, for a few months, was 'homeless' as he decided where the most strategically useful place to live should be. Family apart, he could have lived just about anywhere within a few hours' distance of New York and London by air. His 'home' was the creative ferment in his mind. For a period, he continued to spend time in New York to promote his songs personally. In those days he stayed at many hotels, but I think he specially liked the Algonquin on West 44th Street, a stone's throw from Broadway. He appreciated the history of the hotel, which is famous for its literary associations. During the 1920s and 1930s its so-called Round Table was the lunching place for

American literary style-setters like Robert Benchley, Dorothy Parker and Edna Ferber. I think he may also have liked the martinis in the Oak Room (about which Dorothy Parker allegedly wrote: *I like to have a martini/ Two at the very most/Three, I'm under the table/Four, I'm under the host*). Though he tried to interest publishers and record companies in his new ideas and lyrics, he had little success. The situation was well summed up in a story he told me in 1966. He had written a lyric to an Italian tune and managed to persuade Dick Rowe, Decca's pop singles producer, to get it recorded by a girl Dick was promoting called Trudy Smith. But the recording did not turn out very well, 'Chiefly, I think,' said Dick in a letter to him, 'because your lyric is a bit sophisticated for such an artist. Do you think you could write another lyric with your sights a little lower?' That was what Jimmy Kennedy was now up against.

I remember a verse he doodled which summed up his thinking:

*My interest in song business now is so small*
*That I wonder at times if I'm in it at all.*
*I rarely get anything high in the charts*
*And I don't even know Mr Lionel Bart.*

As a freebooting breadwinner he could live where he thought best, even though the main family home continued to be Staplegrove. However, by 1960 the younger generation had practically flown the Somerset nest. Derek had left the Royal Agricultural College in Cirencester and had got his first job. Janet, who had gone to Athol Crescent, the famous domestic science college in Edinburgh, was also about to get her first job and James was studying Modern History at Trinity, Dublin, returning to Staplegrove only during the holidays. His niece Deirdre was at London's Royal Academy of Music. For most of the time the only occupants at the

Staplegrove mansion were his sister, Nell and a Northern Irish housekeeper, also called Nell, plus his mother, by now bed-ridden and needing constant care. Aged over eighty, Anna could not be moved, so Staplegrove had to be kept on.

With UK taxes still penal, Kennedy now decided to live under the more liberal financial regime of Switzerland, where he was amused to find that he was officially described as a 'leisured alien'. There he rented a small two-bed roomed apartment in Pierrefleur, with lovely views from the topmost parts of hilly Lausanne, where he could sit on his tiny terrace and look out over Lake Geneva towards the Alps. On a clear day it was just possible to see the snow-capped tip of Mont Blanc and in the evening the lights of Evian twinkled across the water from the far side of the lake. He was only a couple of hours by plane from London so could continue his annual round of visits, most frequently to Staplegrove, but, as always, to the Bahamas, London and New York, spending a little more time in Europe, especially Paris and Juan Les Pins, where he liked to stay at Scot Fitzgerald's old haunt, the art deco Hotel Belles Rives. He also began to spend longer periods in Ireland again. Although he began to give up the daily battle of writing for publishers in an increasingly unfamiliar market, he continued to enjoy the fruits of success. As one friend, Ben Nesbitt, who was head of music publishers Box and Cox, put it, 'While other writers were queuing up at Tesco's for the weekend joint, Jimmy was in Fortnum and Mason's choosing fine wine. He always used to come and visit us in Denmark Street some time in April and we used to say that heralded the start of the Spring season. He would come into my office in a beautifully cut suit, red carnation and regimental tie, hat by Fox and handmade shoes by Lobb – a very classy gentleman, a very nice gentleman, great style. He would take me in a cab and we'd go straight to *Les Ambassadeurs*, where we'd be welcomed by the *maître d'*, and he was still addressed as Captain Kennedy. Not a typical songwriter!'

Despite the many professional disagreements between Jimmy Kennedy and Jimmy Phillips over the years, the two men continued in regular contact and I am sure that though perhaps it was not in any way a warm relationship, it was professionally cordial: the grievances of Phillips's star lyricist were in the past and the only reminders were what he considered to be his smaller-than-they-should-have been royalty cheques. Phillips still rated him as the best lyric writer around and one day in 1960 when Kennedy paid him a social call, he showed him a French song, *Mon Coeur est un Violon*, suggesting he write an English lyric for it. His first reaction was to say no: 'Look, I'm sick and tired of French tunes. I've had far too many of them. I've got lovely tunes of my own, many of which are still buried in files in your offices. I don't want to start writing up any more French tunes or German tunes or Italian ones!' But when Phillips played a record of the melody, Kennedy recognized it immediately. He had heard it several times in France, but had never known where it had come from. He liked it so much that he changed his mind and agreed to do the lyrics. The music was in fact by Miarka Laparcerie and came from a 1953 Golden Globe-award winning film called *Little Boy Lost*. Jimmy Phillips already had an artist in mind to sing it, the famous comedian from Liverpool's Knotty Ash, Ken Dodd.

Ken was famous as a comedian, not a ballad singer. *Love is Like a Violin* changed all that and it was the first in a stream of hits which made him the second most recorded British artist after The Beatles during the 1960s. I met Ken at a charity do in the 1990s and he told me how Jimmy Phillips had rung him up to tell him he had a wonderful French tune that would be perfect for him and how he had wanted to turn it down, just like my father: 'I said no. I don't speak a word of French! But

Jimmy Phillips brushed that aside and told me not to worry because Britain's greatest lyric writer was sitting on top of a mountain in Switzerland at that very moment writing new words for it – in English! So I said if that's the case, I'll do it. To my delight, under its new title of *Love is Like a Violin*, it went to the top of the charts. I have always appreciated your father for that. It gave my career a vital boost just when I needed it!' Actually, Britain's 'greatest' was not up a mountain in Switzerland at that time – he hated mountains because he suffered from vertigo – but working out the words of the song in Somerset. His main idea was to change the wording of the French title from 'heart' to 'love' so that *Mon <u>coeur</u> [heart] est un violon* became <u>*Love is* Like a violon</u> – and the rest of the lyric then fell neatly into place: '*Love is like a violin/with its strings around your heart/softly sweet as dreams begin/ sadly crying when you part...*' Ken Dodd followed up *Love is Like a Violin* with even greater successes like *Tears* and *Happiness* (neither of which were by Jimmy Kennedy). But he did record one more French song with an English lyric by Kennedy, *Pianissimo*. As always, there was a story behind the tune. In the 1960s, my father would drive back from Switzerland to Somerset in the by now elderly green Dodge, staying a night or two in Paris en route. There he would invariably meet his French composer friend Alex Alstone. At about the time that *Love is Like a Violin* was riding high in the UK, he was staying at a little hotel he liked near the Champs-Élysées called the Hôtel de Sévigné and met Alstone for lunch. Alex was a superb pianist and had many French successes to his name. Over lunch he told his friend about a new tune he had just composed which he had called *Pianissimo* and which he thought would go down well in the UK. Would Jimmy like to do some English lyrics? No, said the famous songwriter. A title like that was far too old fashioned in a world by then being dominated by skiffle and rock 'n' roll! He told Alex to find someone else.

Several months later, as he worked his sociable way round his music business contacts on a visit to London, Kennedy met Jimmy Phillips, who said to him, 'Jimmy, I've got another great French tune to follow up *Love is Like a Violin.*' 'What's it called?' 'It's got a lovely title,' said Phillips, '*Pianissimo.*' 'It killed me!' recalled my father. 'This time, I felt I had to do it. But if I had not turned it down in Paris, I could have been the beneficiary of the original copyright for the lyric instead of just coming in as the writer of the English version, which cut me down to a quarter. But Ken Dodd again put it over brilliantly and it went into the UK charts, reaching about No. 5. Ruby Murray also did a recording on the Columbia label.'

Alstone frequently stayed at the Kennedy flat in Lausanne during the early 1960s, working on ideas to somehow beat the new music trends. The two became good friends, filling in spare moments with gin rummy and concluding the day with Dubonnets and a good bottle or so of red wine over dinner. Apart from buying the occasional ticket on the Irish Hospitals Sweepstake when he was in Dublin, my father never gambled, even on the Grand National, but Alex had something close to an addiction, especially to roulette and other casino games. At one time, it seems, Alex knew he would have to stop and had himself placed on a special 'gamblers anonymous' list so that if he ever felt the compulsion to go into a casino, he would be recognized and refused entry. Alex and Jimmy worked on many songs and even wrote a musical called *Janine* (or *La Petite Allouette)*, which was never published. But, despite all the talent, they never had a big hit together - tastes had changed too much for them to succeed: rebellious teenagers ruled.

However, Jimmy Kennedy never stopped writing. In 1961 he wrote a lyric for publishers Box & Cox to a well-known 1921 melody called *Salome* by Viennese operetta composer Robert Stoltz. He called it *Blue Weekend*, but Ben Nesbitt, who was head of the publishers, did not care for the idea so Kennedy came up with a completely different lyric and a new title, *Romeo*. It was put over brilliantly by Petula Clark and went to No. 3 in the 1961 UK record charts. Shortly after this success, Ben Nesbitt was amused to receive a letter from my father which, among other things, assured him that he was 'not a music publisher'. This was a high compliment indeed: 'Knowing Jimmy's dark thoughts on publishers, it's a letter I treasure,' he said.

The following year, Decca asked Jimmy Kennedy to write a straightforward song for one of their new upcoming artists, Karl Denver, as a possible entry for the UK round of an early Eurovision song contests. He came up with *Never Goodbye*, which he wrote at his Somerset home in Staplegrove after lunch on Christmas Day. 'It came 4th in the UK finals, so that was the end of it as far as my influence on the Eurovision Song Contest was concerned.' But Karl Denver's record was popular and it reached No. 3. 'So there I was,' he said, 'still at the top of the charts, 30 years after *Teddy Bears' Picnic*!'

But despite this late success, Kennedy could see the light – and it was red. He was really very much out of tune with the ever more dominant group style of material and irritated by the noise and careless diction of many of these pop stars. He used to say that there was no point in writing good lyrics 'if they won't bother to articulate!' Meanwhile, it was becoming fairly obvious that although no one was to know they were destined to become the most important group in pop music history, The Beatles phenomenon had begun to change the pop music scene for ever. December 1962 saw the first Beatles hit, *Love Me Do*, storm the charts and early in 1963 *Please, Please Me* was No. 1, followed by *From Me to You*, *She Loves You* and *I Want to Hold Your Hand* – all of which went to the top. Beatlemania was born.

But even The Beatles included a Jimmy Kennedy song in an early gig. Jimmy Kennedy would never have heard the version of *Red Sails in the Sunset* sung by the group live at the Star Club in Hamburg, Germany, in 1962. This was because, along with the other ten songs performed that night, it was released (at first unofficially) much later. Quite why The Beatles included it in their programme, I do not know. Perhaps Brian Epstein had heard that Fats Domino was going to do a rock version (it came out in 1963). Or he may have decided to try it out after perhaps hearing other US versions, such as that of Joe Turner in 1959 or Emile Ford and the Checkmates. Maybe he simply liked it! I have read that the original recording of the gig was made on a Grundig home tape recorder by someone in the audience in Hamburg, after which it disappeared. Many years later, so it is said, it was found in Liverpool by Allan Williams, the first manager of the Beatles, in a pile of old tapes. The sound quality was very poor but attempts were made to clean up the tape, leading to the production of several versions. The first 'acceptable' one, *Live at the Star Club, Vols 1 & 2*, was released by Pickwick Records in 1979. It is possibly *the* earliest recording of the full Beatles line-up with Ringo Starr. The version I have was published in 1991 by Sony.

In 2006, Bob Dylan also paid tribute to *Red Sails in the Sunset* in his *Modern Times* CD. The tune used for the seventh track, *Beyond the Horizon*, is the same as *Red Sails in the Sunset*, with Dylan's words, though in a very similar idiom to the original lyric. Though Kennedy and Grosz are not credited, a royalty is being paid; something that I am sure would have pleased both writers!

# 22: *The Jarvey*

Jimmy Kennedy knew from long experience that song writing success was very unpredictable. Time after time, luck and good contacts proved more valuable than talent. Average songs made the charts. Good ones ended up in desk drawers. How did you combat the problem? Despite being one of the best lyric writers around and with an unrivalled knowledge of the business, he used to say how important it was to keep on producing – the more songs you wrote, the more chance you had of catching the eye of a publisher, a record producer or, even, an artist – and this was a major reason for his prolific output of more than 2000 songs. But there was another reason – a creative impulsion: 'It's quite impossible, if you've been writing songs all your life, suddenly to stop. Ideas start coming into your head all the time – little bits of tunes, ideas, lyrics, they come along in series and the next thing you're writing them down.'

So, even though he was no longer expecting to get songs in the Top 20 from the mid 1960s on, he still went on dreaming them up, just as he had in all the decades before – *One Love For Me, Bless Your Heart, Pianist From Capri, Maggie May Not, She Took, Kanimambo, Romantic Love, The Lolly Theme, Bluebird, Morocco, Paris in the Snow, The House of Johann Strauss, Don't Leave Me Now, C'est Paris*...an endless stream of ideas, some good, some not so good, continued. I was amused by a comment in a Jimmy Phillips letter of 1962: 'I note that you are seeing Alex Alstone in Paris this week re *Valse Teeth*. What the Hell is that? At least *Dental Instrumental* rhymes.'

In 1962, Irish Television invited him to contribute some musical pieces for the first programmes performed by the new Radio Telefís Eireann Light orchestra. He composed music for three, including a folk-flavoured piece of music called *The Jarvey*, and these were specially arranged for the orchestra. They were well received and that encouraged him to write some comic words for *The Jarvey*, renaming it *The Jarvey was a Leprechaun*. The drivers of Irish jaunting cars (lightweight horse-drawn open carriages) were called 'Jarveys' and are usually regarded as figures of fun in Irish folklore, so the idea gave him scope for some amusing words. At that time, Irish entertainer Val Doonican, was on the threshold of a career that was to make him the biggest singing star on British television, with a Saturday peak-time TV show which ran for years, and a regular Christmas Show. In 1973 he also presented a BBC Radio 2 series of programmes about Jimmy Kennedy's life and songs in which he referred to *The Jarvey was a Leprechaun*:

Right back at the beginning of the 1960s, I myself was just getting the first whiff of the smell of success. I was doing my first ever solo broadcast on the BBC and working in the studio with Frank Chacksfield and his orchestra. During our coffee break, Frank produced a sheet of music and said, 'I was asked to give you this. It's called *The Jarvey was a Leprechaun*. Jimmy Kennedy wrote it with you especially in mind and thought you might like to broadcast it.'

Well, I was so flattered that a little known-singer like myself at the time could have this kind of personal attention from such a famous composer that I did broadcast the song – anyway, I loved it – and eventually I recorded it:

*A half a dozen tourists stood outside a Lim'rick bar,*
*And thought they'd like to take a trip by Irish jaunting car,*
*They jumped up on the side seats and it started down the street*
*But they never saw the character upon the driver's seat.*

*The Jarvey was a leprechaun and had some magic power,*
*He toured them thro' the Em'rald Isle at a thousand miles an hour,*
*A phantom horse was in the shafts and no one was surprised*

*For the Jarvey was a leprechaun and he had them hypnotised.*

*He showed them Connemara on the way to Ireland's Eye,*
*They heard him say that Galway Bay was frozen in July,*
*He had them kiss the Blarney Stone on Ballybunion Strand,*
*And a football team from Donegal was Macnamara's band.*

*The Jarvey was a leprechaun and really took them round,*
*They went thro Tipperary town at twice the speed of sound,*
*He told them it was Mullingar when passing by Clonmel,*
*For the Jarvey was a leprechaun and the truth he couldn't tell!*

*He told them it was Cromwell lost the battle of Clontarf*
*He said the famous Finn Mac'coul was nothing but a dwarf,*
*He swore the Giant's Causeway had been in the Phoenix Park,*
*And it was by Killarney's lakes that Noah built the ark!*

*The Jarvey was a leprechaun and did the trip so fast,*
*Although the horse had sprouted wings the pace just couldn't last,*
*He drove them up the airy mountain, down the rushy glen,*
*And the Jarvey and the passengers were never seen again.*

The penultimate line is a quote from William Allingham, the poet who was thought to be related to the Baskins, so my father almost certainly used it intentionally.

It was around this time that EMI, a conglomerate which concentrated mainly on record production, much of which had originally been devoted to the classical repertoire, started to wield enormous influence on the development of pop. EMI's musical power in part reflected its success in acquiring recording rights to the music of many of the new stars, including The Beatles, The Beach Boys, Queen and many others. During the 1960s and 1970s it also bought up all the significant music publishers which had lined the streets of Tin Pan Alley in its heyday, including Feldman's and Peter Maurice (which had already become part of Keith Prowse Music), and eventually wrapped them all up into a new entity,

EMI Music Publishing. With its catalogue of over a million songs reaching back to the early 1900s, it is now the most profitable part of the organization though, as I write, it seems EMI itself is about to be sold and broken up.

One reason why the EMI strategy of buying up the older music publishers worked for so long becomes plain from a letter Jimmy Phillips wrote to Jimmy Kennedy in 1968:

'I thought you might like to know of a few LPs (a couple of them are re-releases) which have come out in the last few months on your numbers – it is by no means complete:

*Did Your Mother Come from Ireland* (101 Strings)
*Harbour Lights* (The Bachelors, Dinah Washington, The Platters)
*Hometown* (David Lisbon)
*My Prayer* (Tommy Brennan, Anita Kerr)
*Poor Little Angeline* (Roy Fox)
*Roll Along Covered Wagon* (Jimmy Shand)
*South of the Border* (Wes Montgomery, Three Brass Buttons, Ambrose, Les Reed)
*Sunset Trail* (Jimmy Shand)

It was not just Jimmy Kennedy's standards that were still being recorded. So were the songs of other major writers from that era – even as The Beatles and an avalanche of other groups and individual stars – and styles - were taking popular music by storm.

# 23: Jimmy Kennedy on song writing

Jimmy Kennedy lived through the birth, adolescence, maturity, and some would say premature death, of the 20th-century commercial popular song. Commercial popular music has its origins long before modern times so, as a writer who grew up in Ireland, his first influences were initially home grown rather than American – from Irish and Scottish folk music and live entertainment, such as the music hall. However, early in the 20th century America was already producing eagerly awaited international hit songs which everyone wanted to hear and dance to. One of the most sensational early breakthroughs influencing him was ragtime. But he followed all the songs and dance crazes as they came out, spending his spare time learning all about them and the writers behind them via live performances, sheet music, radio, film and records. I think a significant reason why he has a place in the history of popular music in Britain is because, although he was rooted in folk music and British music hall, he moved ahead to very successfully blend these relatively parochial styles with the latest American cutting-edge popular song genres. In 1935, he reversed the America-to-Europe trend by being among the first British popular songwriters to have a catalogue of his songs sold to America in advance. Independent of this, *Isle of Capri*, *Red Sails in the Sunset*, *South of the Border* and other songs of his topped the US charts at a time when some of the greatest American songwriters were at their peak and America was dominating the whole of the popular song business. He was not entirely alone in his success but he was definitely a leader of the pack in London's Tin Pan Alley.

But what is it about Jimmy Kennedy's songs that have made them live so long? What did he think about popular music? He never wrote an extended article incorporating all his views, so his pronouncements on various subjects were usually in response to specific situations like radio or television interviews which took place 40 or 50 years ago. In these his views reflected the context of the time he was living in and his belief that the best of the golden age songs were as good as or better than anything else and, what is more, proved it because they stood the test of time. Why have they lasted? Because they were well crafted, professionally written, with a certain magic which captured the imagination of millions of people from all walks of life and have continued to do so ever since. Contrast that with typical hit parade material of later years, with unmemorable songs reaching No 1 for a day or a week and then going into the waste paper basket of pop history. Jimmy Kennedy complained about the level of this kind of material not only because it was manifestly of such poor quality but because it prevented established writers from getting their much better output accepted. It was a bit like being a highly qualified surgeon seeing your work done by a butcher. He would heartily have agreed with Sir Elton John who was quoted in the UK's Daily Telegraph (October 2010) as saying that he thought today's songwriters were 'awful.'... 'That is why everything sounds the same.' He added that artists needed to experience hard graft if they were to succeed in the long term.

But, in the far off days of the mid-20th century, what skills did Jimmy Kennedy think were needed to become a successful songwriter in his day? Where did the ideas come from? What kind of problems did they face in the music business? How did they write a memorable lyric? In no particular order, here are some of his thoughts.

I think an early revealing comment Jimmy Kennedy used to mention in his 1930s' heyday was that band leaders needed to be 'commercially melodic' to succeed. By that he meant that the girl next door, the butcher boy and the milkman are the ultimate judges of a good song and they want something they can whistle rather than a series of clever musical progressions with no melody. 'Stick to the tune' was a message he emphasised to bands, orchestras, performers and record producers in his magazine, *Feldmanism*. He was always at pains to say that the most important quality for a songwriter was the ability to work hard: 'How many songs I wrote before I had one accepted I could not say,' he once wrote. 'But I must have written hundreds (amateur writers, please note!). It is only by writing and writing that you can ever hope to reach the higher levels of the craft. Song writing is just like any other game of skill – you must put in a dickens of a lot of practice before you can be reasonably accomplished.' He also said: 'I am often asked how I get "inspiration" for a song. Well the answer is, I don't and never have. I've never been "inspired". I regard song writing as a skill or craft, not inspiration. It's rather like a newspaper man being asked to supply an article about the financial policy of Peru or something like that. He does his research, thinks it through and just sits down and writes it. It's exactly the same for a song. You sit down and write the song when it's needed. That way you supply the market with what it wants – from a children's song to a comedy number, from a hillbilly to a romantic ballad, from a hot rhythm number to something sophisticated.'

Jimmy Kennedy began polishing his skills as a schoolboy. As he said later: It was a lengthy apprenticeship stretching back to when I was 10 or 11. So I had a lot of self teaching behind me. And I continued to study the great contemporary writers both from America and in the UK even after I became successful myself. That helped me to produce consistently good results. Needless to say, writing a lyric is nearly always influenced by what other people, especially publishers, want you to produce for a particular situation. And sometimes their ideas can get in the way. My first publisher, Bert Feldman, who was thirty years older than me, was very old-fashioned. If I had a line beginning, 'It', Bert would say, 'Can't you write, 'Tis! That's why *The Isle of Capri* includes this convention.

I believe, regardless of how many people get involved and all the other influences that a writer is subject to, that there are some rules for a good lyric. I believe a lyric should be euphonious, easily remembered, something that trips off the tongue very easily and should be a good match for the tune. Every word should sit on every note: I think that is the most important thing. Having said all that, if I may be a little bit Irish, there is an art to writing almost anything. Call it a creative spark, if you like. I think getting the original idea for the song is the 'art' and its construction is the 'craft'. The way I write lyrics is best illustrated by taking one of my songs and analysing it. If you take *Isle of Capri*, for example, you can get an idea of how the chorus is built up lyrically by explaining the reasons behind each line.

So:

*'Twas on the Isle of Capri that I found her*
(Here you have located your story and established the title)

*Beneath the shade of an old walnut tree*
(Second line – supplementing the location – making it more definite. Even in 1934, a walnut tree is better than a palm or linden tree!)

*Oh! I can still see the flowers blooming round her*
(paints the picture – they can now see the girl surrounded by flowers – on a beautiful island with the sea in the distance)

*Where we met on the Isle of Capri*
(This rounds off the opening eight bars – completing the setting and the 'boy meets girl' situation – and you need to get the title in again.)

*She was as sweet as a rose at the dawning*
(This gives some detail about the girl – leading ladies must always be sweet and lovely!)

*But somehow fate hadn't meant her for me*
(Oh dear, this sounds as if it's going to be sad – getting to the heart stuff)

*And tho' I sail'd with the tide in the morning*
(This is a bit sudden – but they'll think he'll be back again for the happy ending!)

*Still my heart's on the Isle of Capri*
(There you are! He still loves her and the title again)
Now the middle:

*Summer time was nearly over*
(Idea here is that the end of summer fits in with the end of a romance)

*Blue Italian skies above,*
(Blue skies should go with happiness – but wait...)

*I said 'Lady I'm a rover*
(Our hero is obviously a vagabond lover – but, at least he's honest about it!)

*Can you spare a sweet word of love?'*
(For a fast worker, he really makes a very gentle approach and I'm sure it would sound very romantic in Italian!)

*She whisper'd softly 'It's best not to linger'*
(This is the start of the sob stuff. Note the value of 'She whispered <u>softly</u>' - she rather liked him!)

*And then as I kiss'd her hand I could see*
(She <u>must</u> have liked him - and wanted to be kind as she dismissed him - because she didn't say No, she just let him see that...)

*She wore a plain golden ring on her finger*
(What a shame! She must have been married!)

*'Twas goodbye on the Isle of Capri*
(So the sad little story comes to an end - they both behaved quite nicely - and the title again)

The song became popular because the public could grasp the idea and respond to the story. They could sing the words and dance to the many versions, with its unusual tune and rhythm. In short, it was commercially a good popular song.

Jimmy Kennedy understandably believed that popular song writing was reaching a peak in the 1930s golden age period. Standards had to be high, he argued, because of tremendous international competition between the writers and publishers who created the songs on the one hand, and the bands backed by their arrangers, who performed them. They all wanted to get the best and most distinctive sound they could to capture the public's imagination.

He was frequently scathing about performances of his songs. The reason was because so many performers tried to change the original concept he had in his own mind - it might be the tune, the rhythm, the tempo or the words. He was essentially coming from the old tradition of folk ballads which were sung exactly as heard, often with no accompaniment. Words were the heart of these songs. The irony is that he did not like many versions of his well-known songs even if they sold very well. But his asset was as a writer, not a performer, and it was always the public who decided which songs they liked and which they did not. However, sometimes his taste and the public agreed! Of all the hundreds of performers of his songs down the years, the one he admired most was Bing Crosby. Bing was the most influential singer of his time, perhaps of any time – the king of crooners – and sold more records in the 1930s, 40s and 1950s than anyone else. He made 12 recordings of Jimmy Kennedy songs, more than any other major artist. He made three different versions of *South of the Border* (one was for the film *Pepe*) and recorded *The Teddy Bears' Picnic* twice. But why did Kennedy rate Crosby so much as an interpreter? 'That's easy,' he once said on an Irish radio programme, 'I think he is the best interpreter of my songs because he sang them the way I wanted them sung. I think other writers would say the same thing. He was a wonderful song man. He sang a song the way you wrote it. He didn't try any fancy tricks or alter it or change the tempo or mess about with it like so many other performers. He didn't inject himself into the song. He had so much style, he didn't have to do that. He sang the song like you'd like to sing it yourself.' Apart from Bing's skill as a singer, he had a tremendous knowledge of song writing, something he revealed when they met for the first time in Dublin in the early 1970s. Recalling the occasion (which had been arranged by Dublin producer George O'Reilly), my father said: 'He knew all about my songs. He knew them all. In fact, he knew about all the writers – he could tell you who wrote this and who wrote that. When I asked him, for example, who arranged the special version of *Isle of Capri* that he did with Rosemary Clooney 40 years before in the 1930s, he said as quick as a flash, Jay Livingston and Ray Evans. He remembered their names after all those years.'

# 24: Back to Dublin

Jimmy Kennedy lived in Switzerland for most of the 1960s but he never liked the country. He used to say the reason he was there could be summed up in his interpretation of the French maxim: *reculer pour mieux sauter* – go back and regroup before returning to the music business fray. He always talked about going back to Ireland. Until he was able to do so, he had to content himself with being a visitor, albeit frequent – and these were usually announced in the social columns of *The Irish Times* so that his friends would know he was on his way. I sometimes met him in Dublin in those years when I was at Trinity College. He brought me over from England for my first term and took me out to my first meal with my cousin Ian, who was already at Trinity. We ate in a venerable French restaurant on Nassau Street called Jammets. Alistair Cooke, of the BBC's *Letter From America* fame was sitting at the next table. Jammets is now long gone, replaced by a pub, but was then among the top restaurants in Europe. In those days my father liked to stay at the Russell Hotel on the Harcourt Street corner of St Stephen's Green. The Russell, also now gone, had another of Dublin's top restaurants at the time to which I was also occasionally invited. My father could be quite an embarrassment in a restaurant if he thought it was below standard. I remember on one occasion we had just been served generous platefuls of Dublin Bay prawns and I was hopefully eyeing up the accompanying Gewürztraminer when, with a look of thunder, he summoned the waiter: 'How dare you serve these prawns!' There was a hush in the intimate hotel restaurant and I tried to make myself invisible. 'I beg your pardon, sir,' the waiter stammered.

'Why have they not been de-veined! ...' Our plates were hastily removed and returned with the offending parts eviscerated. It was typical of the man. He worked hard to give people what they wanted and expected everyone else to do the same.

A favourite haunt in the early 1960s was Hunter's Hotel in Rathnew, County Wicklow. He liked the hotel – a famous old coaching inn – not only because of its old world charm but because it was only some 20 miles from Dublin and he had friends who lived near-by. The hotel had lovely traditional décor and food and he got on very well with Mrs Hunter and the Gelletlie family who owned and managed the hotel. He used to visit it frequently and for quite extended periods, especially during the summer months in the 1960s. There he could be himself, prune the roses and keep in contact with the world through his favourite medium, letters. Despite his almost illegible handwriting, he must have written half a dozen a day.

Towards the end of the decade, he at last sold the family home in Somerset after his mother Anna died, aged 91, in 1965. She had always said she wanted to outlive Winston Churchill, who had been born in the same year as her, and she did it by a few months. After her death, Nell, continued to look after the house until they found a buyer, which turned out to be the Nuffield Trust. Now it is a hospital with a Kennedy ward. An early patient was my brother Derek's wife, Rosemary, who had a successful replacement hip operation there, so she helped keep the place in the family. With Staplegrove sold, my father was at last in a position to return to his roots and move back to Ireland. In 1971 he bought a country house called Springmount in Rathmichael, Shankill, for the relatively modest sum of £30,000. Springmount was a large house with a small lodge at the end of the drive for gardening or domestic staff. It was nine miles or so from Dublin, so it was easy to get from there into the city centre to keep up with music business and media contacts. It was also only a couple of miles from Bray and not far from Dun Laoghaire, so it was handy for the boat to Holyhead, too. I remember that by then he had put the faithful Dodge into long-term retirement in a garage near Staplegrove and had bought a Humber Imperial, quite an impressive car with real wood fascia and de luxe extras like courtesy reading lights for passengers. I once asked him what it had cost. 'Nothing!' he replied, 'I bought some shares in a new technology company and they went up so much I sold them and bought the car with the profits.' He was joined at Springmount by Nell, so they were able to keep each other company and she could share a little in the social world of Dublin, something she would have enjoyed because, like him, she was also a graduate of Trinity College. Springmount had an eight-acre field at the back and, being Ireland, the grass used to grow like mad and my father, who by now was seventy, could not cut it on his own. He tried several commercial contractors to do the job but they weren't very interested, despite the fact that eight acres of hay was quite valuable. They just did not fancy the work because the field was on a slope. Finally he asked a local farmer if he would do the job and what he would charge. He had expected a reasonable payment for it. What was he offered? '10 punts ...and a load of muck!'

My father occasionally used to talk of retiring to Connemara, but it was a romantic dream. It would have been too remote for him, despite the family connection with Donegal, not so much further up the coast. County Dublin was a far more practical place to be based and seemed to give him a new lease of creative life. Ideas for songs and for his new enthusiasm, instrumentals, kept coming along. He continued to develop these ideas and both RTE and the BBC put them into their programmes. As a result, he found himself with a string of instrumentals that many people seemed to like. The one that was most requested at the time was *Ski Girl*, inspired, so he told me, by a French redhead in a white ski-suit – the 'prettiest girl I ever saw!' Another, *The Swedish Can-Can*, was the result of a visit to an ice-show where a bevy of Scandinavian lovelies showed themselves as a challenge to the can-can dancers of the Folies-Bergère. The female of the species was as irresistible to him as ever! He loved the social life, making friends with many artists and others in the musical world of Dublin.

In 1970, in what was the first of its kind in the UK for a non-theatre songwriter, EMI produced a special LP called the Jimmy Kennedy *Golden Songbook* for him. It was devoted to twelve of his most famous songs, together with three of his later instrumentals, recorded by the orchestras of Neil Richardson and Frank Barber. 'It's a funny thing that it is either at the beginning of your career or at the end that you really notice if recording companies are taking any notice of you', he wrote, somewhat tongue-in-cheek, in the sleeve notes. He also produced various LPs on his own in Ireland, several by tenor Joseph Locke, for the Pickwick, Heritage, Demesne and EMI labels, and recorded with the Band of the Irish Guards, The Paddy McGinty Seven, The Dixie Dynamos and some of the contemporary stars of Irish television and radio.

But I think that of all the things he got up to in the 1960s and 1970s, he had most fun judging the many international Song Contests in Ireland and elsewhere – Castlebar, Dundalk, Wexford, Cavan, even Gibraltar (which inspired him to write *The Monkeys of Gibraltar*!). Cavan was an undoubted favourite. It used to be organized by Maire Maloney and singer Anne Lennon. Everyone had a good time at these contests since not only were there numerous aspiring acts of quality looking for quite decent prize money but they were being judged by influential people, not only Jimmy Kennedy himself, but people such as Terry Wogan and other leading professionals from the popular music industry. Terry recently said Jimmy Kennedy was Simon Cowell to his Louis Walsh. They clearly had some good times together as they judged some of these competitions. Here Sir Terry reminisces about those days:

I was fortunate enough to meet Jimmy Kennedy shortly after I took the emigrant route to Britain. You don't need a litany from me of the succession of huge hits he wrote that rang around the world, but a nicer, gentler man would be hard to find. Modest to a fault, he preferred tales of the quirky and funny people he had met along the way, rather than trumpeting his extraordinary popular music successes. We had some fun together in the 1970s when my supposed, and his undoubted, musical knowledge were called upon, as judges for the various Irish music festivals that seemed to spring up like weeds all over the country in those years. Don't talk to me about "X-Factor", Jimmy Kennedy and I were thirty years ahead of our time. He was Simon Cowell to my Louis Walsh..."

Tim Hollier, 1960s rock singer turned music businessman remembers another occasion when he was a judge. Tim had been given a lift to the Castlebar Song Festival by my father in his Humber Imperial during the same week that the Pope had visited the country:

Lo and behold! As we drove across Ireland we faced hordes of returning pilgrims who to a man had forgotten to dip their headlight. Jimmy and I arrived with headaches and in dire need of a drink to be met by our fellow judges, who included Terry Brown, head of a record company who had signed James Taylor and Joan

Baez. Terry, Jimmy and I voted our best and then decided to do a runner as our vote was not the most popular. Armed with very large gin and tonics, we retired to the Humber 'battle wagon' where we must have looked like the mafia – Jimmy 'the Don' in his camel coat and dinner jacket, Terry, with his ferret moustache and homburg, and me looking like a refugee from The Minder. We were just raising our glasses when there was a knock on the window. It was the Gardai, kindly asking who we were. 'The judges,' we intoned.' Ah!' said the officer, 'Enjoying a well-deserved drink, gentlemen?' Jimmy, trying to make witty conversation asked whether they had breathalysers in these parts.

'We did,' said the Gardai, 'But we don't now. People didn't seem to want them.'

Sigh of relief. Terry then piped up, 'When you did have it, what was the limit?'

'I think, sir, it was two litres.'

Lovely man...

In 1971, Jimmy Kennedy got his first Ivor Novello Award. For British songwriters, the Ivors are as important as Oscars or Emmys are to people in film or the theatre. The awards cover many different areas of musical creativity and achievement – for example, 'Best Song Musically and Lyrically', 'International Hit of the Year', 'Best Selling A Side', another for the 'Most Performed'. His award was the top one, for 'Outstanding Services to British Music'. If the Ivors had been around in the 1930s and 40s he might have had a mantelpiece full of them – but by the 1970s, with his hit writing days over, he was delighted with it – the first of two he would treasure.

A year later he wrote an anthem that was played all over Ireland and Britain by choral groups and schools, *Let There be Peace*. Explaining why he wrote it, he said:

'There have been so many songs of protest, I thought why should there not be one that conveys a message about peace. The present trouble in Ireland leaves one idea in everybody's mind: Let there be peace! So that was the idea. The Radio Telefís Eireann (R.T.E.) Radio Choir and orchestra took the song to America and even played it in St Patrick's Cathedral in New York.'

Then, in 1974, he was asked to write and compose the original music for Northern Irish playwright Stewart Parker's prize-winning play *Spokesong* which was first produced at the Dublin Theatre Festival. *Spokesong* dramatizes 80 years of Irish political history in the setting of a bicycle shop, a theatrical device which Parker used to interweave the life of John Dunlop, who developed the first practical pneumatic tyre whilst practising as a vet in Belfast. An unusual interpretation of the modern Irish saga, it was an entertainment which later ran for 6 months at the King's Head Theatre Club in London's Islington, moved to the Vaudeville in Victoria for a short run and is still played all round the world.

In 1977 he found his standards, the 'old indestructibles', as he called them, back in fashion once again. At the venerable age of 75, he was invited to Nashville, Tennessee, to receive an American Society of Composers, Authors and Publishers (ASCAP) plaque for *Red Sails in the Sunset* as the most played tune on US country music stations. And the next year, he did it again with *My Prayer.* This was a double first never before achieved by someone who was also a member of the UK's Performing Right Society and the Songwriters' Guild of Great Britain.

Then in 1978 came another honour, when he was awarded an Honorary Doctor of Letters (D.Litt) by the University of Ulster, in Coleraine, Northern Ireland – not more than a few miles from where he was brought up. It was in recognition of 'outstanding services to light music'

– the first time such a high award had been given to a popular songwriter. In his address, Professor Lilievre, the university's Public Orator, concluded by saying, 'In a great tradition that includes Moore and French he has given pleasure and raised the hearts, without exaggeration, of millions, and ... he has remained self-effacing.'

1978 also marked the 50th anniversary of Jimmy Kennedy's career in Tin Pan Alley and he celebrated it with another LP featuring two singers, Cavan International Song Festival organizer Anne Lennon, and Johnny Christopher, singing some of his unpublished songs, all unique in the sense that they had all been turned down by record companies. The L.P. was called *Hits You've Never Heard Till Now*!

By that time he was writing for fun rather than money, so he had more time to be able to develop and support one of his lifelong interests, the Songwriters' Guild. The Guild had been formed by songwriters Bruce Sievier and Eric Maschwitz, with other famous authors and composers who included Richard Addinsell, Eric Coates, Tommie Connor and Haydn Wood, at a time when Jimmy Kennedy was working almost exclusively in America. The founders wanted to champion the cause of British songwriters and musicians. There had been a tremendous influx of American music into Britain and Ireland during and after the War and it was strangling home-grown talent. At around that time only a fifth of the BBC's popular music output was British. In addition, by 1947, radio shows and films recorded in America were also being broadcast by the BBC. This trend increased from the 1950s onwards, when television began to replace radio as the main medium of home entertainment. The problem was that recorded shows publicised American rather than British songs and this meant that performance royalties and earnings from sales of records and sheet music were going to foreign rather than British writers in a way which was felt to be disproportionate, considering how much native talent there was on this side of the Atlantic. That was a big issue for the Guild. And there were many other matters, such as contracts and royalties and other forms of professional advice and assistance, where an organisation such as the Guild could work for the British songwriter. Jimmy Kennedy was in many ways lucky. He had so many best sellers that he was assured of a good income for life. But what about the many songwriters who had not had his talent or his luck? Many of them never had a hit at all and few managed more than one. The Guild was there to do what it could do for them too.

In 1972, shortly after he had resettled in Ireland, Jimmy Kennedy was invited to become the Guild's chairman, taking over from David Heneker (who wrote the lyrics for *Expresso Bongo, Irma la Douce, Half a Sixpence* and *Charlie Girl*). From his home outside Dublin he used to fly over to London to chair the monthly Guild Council meetings, keeping in touch with his colleagues and the younger generation of writers. Brian Willey, for many years vice-chairman of the Guild, told me he seldom missed a date: 'He had always tried to help and advise younger writers whenever he had the opportunity and was known throughout the industry not just as a successful man but as a caring man,' he said. Jimmy Kennedy remained chairman of the Guild for 12 years during which time it was renamed the British Academy of Songwriters, Composers and Authors (BASCA) and when he died in 1984, Oscar-winning lyric writer, Don Black (*Born Free, Diamonds are for Ever, Take that Look off Your Face* and a host of other show and hit songs) took over the chairmanship.

*Jimmy Kennedy with his third wife, Elaine, in the late 1970s at their home, Springmount, County Dublin.*

As he continued his creative life in Dublin, Jimmy Kennedy met an English woman called Elaine Pobjoy. He got to know Elaine in Ireland where her daughter was married to a peer, and they also socialised in England, where she had a house in Englefield Green, near Old Windsor. By now he really had reached the age to settle down and they were married in 1974. She had been married before but her husband had been killed in an air crash. Elaine joined him and sister Nell, who did not like her, at Springmount, but when Nell died of a heart attack in 1977, they decided the house was too big for two people and they moved to Greystones, a few miles down the coast in County Wicklow.

In July 1982 my father paid a last visit to his favourite London club, *Les Ambassadeurs*, in Park Lane. The occasion was the celebration of his eightieth birthday, and it was a purely family affair. But the day was marred by a savage act of terrorism when the IRA blew up two members of the Household Cavalry who were exercising in Hyde Park. Another 23 were injured and seven horses were also killed. How strange that this should occur on such a day. It was the IRA my father used to worry about when his father went out in the night all those years before when he was a child in County Tyrone and during the unrest of subsequent years.

Elaine had neither Irish roots nor musical interests and was bored in Ireland, so when her daughter decided to leave Ireland and move back to England, she said that she wanted to go back too. In 1983 she persuaded her reluctant husband to leave Ireland at the age of 81, and he bought Knap House, an elegant Cotswold stone home in the village of Broadway, near Evesham, Worcestershire. Denis Thatcher wrote a charming welcoming note to them from Number 10 Downing Street: 'We both send you our best wishes for your happiness and solace in your new home in Broadway. God willing, and time, I will avail myself of a visit to you ...'

# 25: *Kitty of Coleraine*

In the British New Year's Honours of 1984 Jimmy Kennedy was awarded an OBE, a rare honour for a songwriter at that time. The Beatles had been awarded only MBEs, a fact that amused him greatly. (John Lennon, of course, achieved some notoriety by sending his back). The trip to his investiture by The Queen at Buckingham Palace in February 1984 was nearly the last time he appeared in public. A month later he had to go into hospital for an operation to clear an obstruction. Though he had had a slight heart attack the year before, shortly before he left Ireland, and had also caught a nasty dose of shingles, he had never been seriously ill during his life so had been expected to emulate his mother and live to be over ninety. He seemed, like his songs, to be 'indestructible'. But his doctors told him his heart condition meant he was unlikely to survive the operation. So, he called in his eldest son, Derek, and made all the arrangements necessary for the family, including ensuring that Elaine was able to stay on at Knap House for the rest of her life. The doctors were right. He did not come round from the operation, dying a few days later on 5 April 1984. Elaine, who boasted her mother had lived to be '102 – and a half!' lived almost as long as her, remaining in the house until her death at the age of ninety-six, 12 years later.

Although Jimmy Kennedy had been awarded a second Ivor Novello Award in 1979, this time for 'Lifetime Achievement', the Ivor Novello tributes were far from over. The BASCA Committee members – the Ivors administrators – inaugurated a new category in his honour a year after he died. Called simply 'The Jimmy

Kennedy Award', it became an annual event within the main Ivors presentation ceremony for songwriters who had maintained the art and heritage of British song writing for at least 25 years. The first recipient was veteran songwriter Tommie Connor who, back in 1938, had helped to write *Underneath the Chestnut Tree* with Jimmy and his brother Hamilton Kennedy. Tommie was followed in 1986 by Hughie Charles, who with Ross Parker, wrote *We'll Meet Again.* The award was maintained annually until the year 2000 when it was deemed that the list of qualifying veterans had run out.

A fellow council member of BASCA, the late Ronnie Bridges, summed up Jimmy Kennedy: 'I remember him as a very gentle man, a very erudite man, a very quiet man. In his own way he could be quite dogmatic if he thought he had a point and wouldn't give in if he thought he was right, which I admire in anybody. He was so masterful with words and with the rhyme that he could hear a tune and invent a story – which in his case was sometimes the same story – but it didn't matter. The songs seemed different and they led to big hits.'

Though he had sent a note of welcome, Jimmy Kennedy's unexpected death meant Denis Thatcher never visited Knap House. However, he took time off from his public duties as Margaret's 'other half' to give the eulogy at a memorial service at St Giles-in-the-Fields, the songwriters' church, just behind Denmark Street – on 2 October 1984. This is what he said:

As we have said our prayers and sung the hymns here this morning, all of us have been remembering the first time we met Jim Kennedy. In my case, it was over 40 years ago, when he came into my office at the ninth Anti-Aircraft division in Cardiff and gave me the sloppiest salute I have ever seen before or since and with that wonderful smile said: 'I'm Kennedy – I'm told I'm to work here'. From that moment, I had a friend for life. Living and working in the same office with Jim I learnt and grew to love his remarkable qualities.

Even as a young man, as we all were, he has already an established songwriter of world-wide reputation. But his modesty was as sincere as it was natural to his whole character and he remained a modest man all his life. Those many of us who enjoyed his friendship – in my case for over half a lifetime – had a special privilege, for Jim was kind, thoughtful and he brought to his personal associations a generosity of spirit seldom to be found in any man.

The many honours he received in his artistic life, his doctorate and the honour from Her Majesty, the Queen, all rested lightly on him. To us, who knew him, these were honours well earned and deserved. To him, he was surprised, but nonetheless pleased that his work merited such high recognition. There are many here today whose expert knowledge of music and others whose appreciation of Jim Kennedy's contribution over 50 years, is far greater than mine. All will agree, however, that he was a master at catching the mood of the time for Jim understood and loved people – all people – ordinary people.

This understanding and feeling sprang from his earliest days as a child and a very young man in Northern Ireland when times were as troublous as they are now. There Jim's father was a policeman – in the Royal Irish Constabulary.

Examples of Jim's music which reflected the feeling of ordinary people are all too numerous but those of us who are now old will remember that when Churchill was roaring defiance at an evil enemy, Jimmy Kennedy wrote 'We're going to hang out the washing on the Siegfried Line' and thousands and thousands of soldiers and airmen sang it – and meant it – and their morale rose as they did so. For those days were dark.

We who mourn his passing and miss his presence have a consolation – of a memory as vivid and as close as if we had seen and talked to him this morning.

Jimmy Kennedy had an indefinable quality which made an irresistible appeal to those who came to know him.

And our lives have been enriched thereby.

In 1996, 12 by 16 feet bronze sailboat sculpture and a commemorative plaque were erected on the promenade at Portstewart, County Londonderry. The sculpture represents a sailing boat and celebrates the achievements of the town. The plaque commemorates Jimmy Kennedy's association with the resort through the writing of the lyrics for *Red Sails in the Sunset*. The event was linked to the story of the rediscovery and restoration of *Kitty of Coleraine*, the boat that had inspired the *Red Sails in the Sunset* lyric all those years before. This had come about when two enthusiasts of Jimmy Kennedy's songs, Dick and Pat Alexander, travel writers and broadcasters from El Granada in California, who used to visit Ireland regularly, found the boat in Cultra Folk Park (in Hollywood, County Down) in 1992, in very bad condition. They interested 'Speedy' Moore, a veteran Coleraine journalist, in the story of *Kitty's* sad state and its links with the song, and that inspired him to write an article about it. The upshot was that two local businessmen, Norman Hutchinson and Ivan Campbell, had it repaired at their own expense at the Portrush boatyard of Billy Gregg.

Following this, the late Leslie Mann, an enthusiast and promoter of the songs of Jimmy Kennedy, suggested to the Mayor of Coleraine, Alderman Pauline Armitage, that it would be appropriate to erect some sort of memorial to celebrate the song and symbolize the town and that led to a competition for the sculpture with the sailboat theme, sponsored by two local people, Jimmy and Barbara

Dempsey. The competition was won by Dublin sculptor Niall O'Neill. The sculpture has now been removed from the promenade but Portstewart has retained the link, renaming its annual summer festival the *Red Sails Festival*. At the time of writing, the boat, now owned by the Ulster Folk and Transport Museum, is undergoing further restoration in Coleraine and the intention is to put it on display when the Coleraine Museum eventually becomes a reality.

Leslie Mann worked tirelessly to strengthen the reputation of Jimmy Kennedy in Northern Ireland after he retired from a successful career as a singer and saxophonist in dance bands in Britain and America. He also wrote a miscellany of articles and other contributions about Jimmy Kennedy, entitled *My Song Goes Round the World*, the title of one of my father's earlier songs. Leslie probably did more than anyone in Northern Ireland to promote Jimmy Kennedy's life and works right up until his death following a stroke a few years ago.

He was also involved in proposing Jimmy Kennedy's posthumous induction in June 1997 into the American National Academy of Popular Music's Songwriters Hall of Fame – the only Irish-born writer at the time and one of only a handful of writers from the British Isles. There he joined a roll of honour which includes all the illustrious names of American song writing, names my father so much admired – from Irving Berlin, Jerome Kern, George and Ira Gershwin, Cole Porter, Richard Rodgers and Oscar Hammerstein II, to Burt Bacharach and Hal David, Simon and Garfunkel, Leiber and Stoller. As I write this book, there are less than 20 British and Irish inductees. They include Ray Noble, John Barry, Sir Noël Coward, John Lennon and Sir Paul McCartney, the Rolling Stones, Sir Tim Rice and Lord Andrew Lloyd Webber.

Entering the American Songwriters Hall of Fame was a fitting tribute to a man whose ideas and often poetic lyrics were formed in Ireland, honed in London's Tin Pan Alley and New York and whose songs are still played all over the world.

# APPENDIX: A SELECTION OF BRITISH POPULAR SONG BEST SELLERS 1930 – 1963

**compiled by the British Academy of Songwriters, Composers and Authors in 1972**

Jimmy Kennedy contributed 48 best sellers to British popular music from 1930 -1963, more than any other non-show writer. On top of that, and not included in the UK list below, were several American Top Ten revivals such as *Harbour Lights* (Guy Lombardo, Sammy kay and numerous other artists), *My Prayer* (The Platters and others), *Red Sails in the Sunset* (Fats Domino, Nat King Cole and others), *South of the Border* (Frank Sinatra, Patsy Cline and others) especially during the 1950s.

Songs by British writers listed with asterisks (*) were international hits at the time, though many are now forgotten.

# 1930

*Amy, wonderful Amy* - J. G. Gilbert & Horatio Nicholls
*Asleep in my heart (Silver Wings)*- D. Titheredge, Waller & Tunbridge
*Elizabeth (Wonderbar)* - Rowland Leigh & Robert Katscher
*Goodbye to all that* - Harry S. Pepper
*If your kisses can't hold the man* -Jack Yellen & Vivien Ellis
*Lazy day* - Martin & George Posford
*Let's be sentimental (Little Tommy Tucker)* - D. Carter & Vivian Ellis
*Moonbeams dance*- Carroll Gibbons
**Oh Donna Clara - Jimmy Kennedy & J. Petersburski**
*Oh maiden, my maiden (Frederica)* - Harry S. Pepper & Franz Lehar

*Over the garden wall* - Leslie Sarony & C. Harrington
*Sleepy Lagoon*- Eric Coates
*Someday I'll find you (Private Lives)* - Noel Coward
*Tell me I'm forgiven (Wonderbar)* - Rowland Leigh & Robert Katscher
**The Barmaid's Song - Jimmy Kennedy**
*The first weekend in June (Follow a star)* - D. Furber & Vivian Ellis
*The King's horses* - Harry Graham & Noel Gay
*The queen was in the parlour* - Errell Reaves & Sherman Myers
*There's a good time coming* - Ralph Butler & Raymond Wallace
*The sunshine of Marseilles* - J. G. Gilbert & Horatio Nicholls
*The wind in the willows* - Desmond Carter & Vivian Ellis
*Under the roofs of Paris* - Bruce Sievier & Raoul Moretti
*We all go 'oo ha ha' together* - Harrington, Moore & Wallace
*When the organ played at twilight* - R. Wallace, Campbell & Connelly
*You die if you worry* - S. J. Damerell & R. Hargreaves

# 1931

*Any little fish* - Noel Coward
*Don't tell a soul* - Harry S. Pepper
*Drink brothers, drink* - Harry S. Pepper & W. Lindemann
*Falling in love again* - Reg Connelly & F. Hollander
*Gipsy Moon* - Frank Eyton & I. Borganoff
*Goodbye (White Horse Inn)* - Harry Graham & Ralph Benatzky
*Good night sweetheart* - Campbell, Connelly & Ray Noble
*Half caste woman* - Noel Coward
*Her name is Mary* - Bruce Sievier & Harold Ramsay
*I found you* - Campbell, Connelly & Ray Noble

*I'm happy when I'm hiking* - Ralph Butler & R. Wallace

*Jolly good company* - Raymond Wallace

*Just once for all time* - Rowland Leigh & Werner Heymann

*Lady of Spain* - Errell Reaves & Tolchard Evans

*Laughing at the rain* - J. G. Gilbert & Noel Gay

*Life's desire* - Damerell, Hargreaves & Tolchard Evans

*Live, love and laugh* - Rowland Leigh & Werner Heymann

*Love what has given you this magic* - Harry Graham & Franz Lehar

*Mausie (Viktoria and her Hussar)* - Harry Graham & Paul Abraham

*Patiently smiling (Land of smiles)* - Harry Graham & Franz Lehar

*Pretty Kitty Kelly* - J. G. Gilbert & Nat Johns

*Rhymes* - Leslie Sarony

*Sally* - Harry Leon, Leo Towers & Bill Haines

*She's my secret passion* - Val Valentine & Arthur Young

*Slipping round the corner* - Harry Graham & Richard Addinsell

*Speak to me of love* - Bruce Sievier & Jean Lenoir

*The changing of the guard* - 'Flotsam' and 'Jetsam'(Malcolm McEachern & B. C. Hilliam)

*There's always tomorrow* - Douglas Furber & Philip Charig

*Today I feel so happy* - D. Carter, F. Eyton & Paul Abraham

*Tom Thumb's drum* - Leslie Sarony

*Vienna, city of my dreams* - Edward Lockton & R. Sieczynski

When the guards are on parade - Leslie Sarony & Horatio Nicholls

*White Horse Inn* - Harry Graham & Robert Stolz

*You are my heart's delight (Land of smiles)* - Harry Graham & Franz Lehar

# 1932

*After tonight we say goodbye* - Harry leon & Leo Towers
*Aint it grand to be blooming well dead* - Leslie Sarony
*Arm in arm* - Harry Leon & Leo Towers
*Brighter than the sun* - Anona Winn & Ray Noble
*Butterflies in the rain* - E. Reaves & Sherman Myers
*By the fireside* - Campbell, Connelly & Ray Noble
*Chinese laundry blues* - Jack Cottrell
*Dreaming* - Bud Flanagan & Reg Connelly
*Goodnight Vienna* - Holt Marvell & George Posford
*\*Got a date with an angel* - C. Grey, S. Miller & J. Tunbridge
*Here's to the next time* - Margery Lawrence & Henry Hall
*He's dead but he won't lie down* - Haines, Harper & Beresford
*Hoch Caroline (Tell her the truth)* - Weston, Lee, Waller & Tunbridge
*Iche liebe dich, my dear* - Jack Hart & Tom Blight
*I give my heart (The Dubarry)* - Rowland Leigh & Theo Mackeben
*I travel the road* - Donovan Parsons & Pat Thayer
*\*Let's all sing like the birdies sing* - Hargreaves, Damerell & Tolchard Evans
*Looking on the bright side* - Howard Flynn
*\*Love is the sweetest thing* - Ray Noble
*Lover of my dreams (Cavalcade)* - Noel Coward
*\*Mad about the boy (Words and music)* - Noel Coward
*Mad dogs and Englishmen (Words and music)* - Noel Coward
*Marching along together* - Eddie Pola & F. Steininger
*On the air* - Campbell, Connelly & Gibbons
*Please don't mention it* - Peter Wyse & Harry S. Pepper
*Round the Marble Arch* - Ralph Butler & Noel Gay
*Sing brothers (Tell her the truth)* - Weston, Lee, Waller & Tunbridge
*Tell me tonight* - Frank Eyton & Mischa Spoliansky

*The flies crawled up the window* - D. Furber & Vivian Ellis

*The old kitchen kettle* - Woods, Campbell & Connelly

*The party's over now (Words and music)* - Noel Coward

*The sun has got his hat on* - Ralph Butler & Noel Gay

*The younger generation (Words and music)* - Noel Coward

*Throw open wide your window* - Ralph Stanley & Hans May

*\*Try a little tenderness* - Woods, Campbell & Connelly

*20th Century Blues (Cavalcade)* - Noel Coward

*\*Underneath the arches* - Bud Flanagan

*What more can I ask?* - Anona Winn & Ray Noble

*You're blasé (Bow Bells)* - Bruce Sievier & Ord Hamilton

*You're more than the entire world to me* - Haines, Sumner & Beresford

# 1933

*All over Italy (They sing so prettily)* - Ralph Butler & Ronnie Munrow

*Happy ending* - Harry Parr Davies

*He was a handsome young soldier* - Eddie Pola & Michael Carr

*I took my harp to a party* - Desmond Carter & Noel Gay

*I was in the mood* - Eddie Pola & Michael Carr

*Just an echo in the valley* - Woods, Campbell & Connelly

*Let me give my happiness to you* - D. Furber & George Posford

*\*Love locked out* - Max Kester & Ray Noble

*Mary Rose* - Harry Parr Davies

*My heart's to let (He wanted adventure)* - Grey, Bert Lee, Jack Waller & Joe Tunbridge

*Old Father Thames* - Raymond Wallace & Betsy O'Hogan

*Roaming* - Bud Flanagan

*Si petite* - Bruce Sievier & Gaston Claret

*Sweep* - D. Furber & Vivian Ellis
**\*Teddy Bears' Picnic - Jimmy Kennedy & J. W. Bratton**
*The moment I saw you* - Clifford Grey & Noel Gay
*There's something about a soldier* - Noel Gay
*Three wishes* -D. Furber & George Posford
*Wanderer* - Bud Flanagan
*We all went up up up the mountain* - Box, Cox & Butler
*Wheezy Anna* - Leslie Sarony
*Without that certain thing* - Max & Harry Nesbitt

# 1934

*Angel on the loose* - William Walker & Fred Hartley
**Beside my caravan - Jimmy Kennedy & Karel Vacek**
**Café in Vienna - Jimmy Kennedy & Karel Vacek**
*Carry me back to green pastures* - Harry S. Pepper
*Come pretty one* - Leslie Sarony
*Faint harmony (Jack & Jill)* - D. Carter & Vivian Ellis
*Goodbye Hawaii* - Leon, Towers, Apollon & Robins
*\*If* - Damerell, Hargreaves & T. Evans
*\*I'll follow my secret heart (Conversation piece)*
- Noel Coward
**\*Isle of Capri - Jimmy Kennedy & Will Grosz**
*It's time to say good night* - Kate Gibson & Henry Hall
*La-di-da-di-da (That's a pretty thing)* - D. Carter & Noel Gay
*Lazin'* - I. Brunelle & Chas. F. Tovey
*Let's all go to the Music Hall* - Butler, Tilsley & Horatio Nicholls
*London Bridge March* - Eric Coates
*Love forever I adore you* - Sonny Miller & G. de Micheli
*Love is a song* - Max Kester & Ray Noble
*\*Love's last word is spoken* - Bruce Sievier & C. A. Bixio
*Love, wonderful love* - Harry Leon & Leo Towers
*My kid's a crooner* - Marion Harris & Reg Montgomery
**My song goes round the world - Jimmy Kennedy & Hans May**

*Ole Faithful* - Michael Carr & Hamilton Kennedy
**\*Play to me gypsy - Jimmy Kennedy & Karel Vacek**
**Roll along covered wagon - Jimmy Kennedy**
*Rolling in the hay* - Paul Boyle & George Posford
*\*Serenade for a wealthy widow* - Reginald Forsythe
*Sing as we go* - Harry Parr Davies
*Song of Paradise* - Bruce Sievier & Reginald King
*\*The very thought of you* - Ray Noble
*Things are looking up* - Clifford Grey & Noel Gay
*\*Unless* - Hargreaves, Damerell & T. Evans
*With her head tucked underneath her arm* - Bert Lee & Harris Weston
*Who's been polishing the sun?* - Ray Noble
*You turned your head (Streamline)* - Ronald Jeans & Vivian Ellis

# 1935

*All for a shilling a day* - Clifford Grey & Noel Gay
*Back to those happy days* - Horatio Nicholls
*\*Dinner for one please, James* - Michael Carr
*\*Dodging a divorcée* - Reginald Forsythe
*Fold your wings (Glamorous night)* - ChristopherHassall & Ivor Novello
*For love alone* - Bruce Sievier & Pat Thayer
*Gertie, the girl with the gong* - Ray Sonin & Ronnie Munro
*Glamorous night* - Christopher Hassall & Ivor Novello
*I'm on a see-saw (Jill Darling)* - Desmond Carter & Vivian Ellis
*I think I can* - D. Furber & Ray Noble
*It's my Mother's birthday today* - Eddie Lisbona & Tommie Connor
*Life begins at Oxford Circus* - Horatio Nicholls
*Love is ev'rywhere* - Harry Parr Davies
*Make it a party* - Raymond Wallace
*Many happy returns of the day* - Henry Hall

*One good turn deserves another* - D. Furber & Ray Noble
*Orchids to my lady* - Michael Carr
**\*Red sails in the sunset - Jimmy Kennedy & Hugh Williams**
*St James's Park* - Harry Leon & Tommie Connor
*Sarawaki* - Val Gordon (Harry Roy)
*Shannon River* - Kay Egan & Reginald Morgan
*She fell for a fella from Oopsala* -　　　Ralph Butler & Mark Strong.
*Song of the trees* - S. J. Damerell & Tolchard Evans
*Street in old Seville* - Rod Arden & Leo Towers
*The girl with the dreamy eyes* - Eddie Pola & Michael Carr
*\*There's a lovely lake in London* - Butler, Damerell & Tolchard Evans
*The wheel of the wagon is broken* - Box, Cox & Michael Carr
*The world is mine tonight* - Holt Marvell & George Posford
**Why did she fall for the leader of the band? -　Jimmy Kennedy & Michael Carr**
*Yip Neddy* - Michael Carr & Lewis Ilda
*Shine through my dreams (Glamorous night)*- Christopher Hassall & Ivor Novello

# 1936

*A feather in her Tyrolean hat* - Annette Mills
**\*At the Café Continental - Jimmy Kennedy & Will Grosz**
*Cuban Pete* - Jose Norman
**\*Did your Mother come from Ireland? - Jimmy Kennedy & Michael Carr**
*I once had a heart, Margarita* - E. Lisbona, T. Connor & J. Schmitz
*Let's have a tiddley at the milk bar* - Noel Gay

*Lonely road* - Eric Ansell

*Love's just a duet* - Christopher Hassall & G. Henman

*Me and my dog* - Vivian Ellis

**Misty islands of the highlands - Jimmy Kennedy & Michael Carr**

*Music from the movies* - Louis Levy

*Music in May (Careless Rapture)* - Christopher Hassall & Ivor Novello

*My first love song* - Harry Parr Davies

**O-Kay for sound - Jimmy Kennedy & Michael Carr**

*Play orchestra, play (Tonight at 8.30)*- Noel Coward

**Poor little Angeline - Jimmy Kennedy & Will Grosz**

**Serenade in the night - Jimmy Kennedy & C. A. Bixio**

*Sleepy river* - Eric Ansell

*Swing* - Vivian Ellis

*The duchess is learning the rumba* - Eddie Lisbona & Tommie Connor.

*The fleet's in port again (O-Kay for sound)* - Noel Gray

**There's a new world (O-Kay for sound) - Jimmy Kennedy & Michael Carr**

*\*These foolish things (Spread it abroad)* - Holt Marvell & Jack Strachey

*\*The touch of your lips* - Ray Noble

**We're tops on Saturday nights- Jimmy Kennedy & Michael Carr**

*When the poppies bloom again* - Towers, Morrow & Pelosi

*Why keep on hiding your heart?* - Christopher Hassall & G. Henman

*You can't do that there 'ere* - Jack Rolls & Raymond Wallace

# 1937

A bird sang in the rain - A. H. Lang-Ridge & Haydn Wood

*All alone in Vienna* - Towers, Morrow & Ilda

*A nice cup of tea (Home and beauty)* -　　A. P. Herbert & Henry Sullivan

*\*At the Balalaika (Balalaika)* -　Holt Marvell & George Posford

**Coronation Waltz - Jimmy Kennedy**

*Cowboy* - Michael Carr

*Empire Builders March* - Hubert Bath

*Girls were made to love and kiss (Paganini)* - A. P. Herbert & Franz Lehar

*Goodnight to you all*- Jack Denby & Muriel Watson

**\*Harbour lights - Jimmy Kennedy & Hugh Williams**

**Hometown (London Rhapsody) -　Jimmy Kennedy & Michael Carr**

*Horsey, Horsey* - Box, Cox, Butler & Roberts

*\*Leaning on a lamp post* - Noel Gay

*Let us be sweethearts over again* -Joseph G. Gilbert

*Little white room (Floodlight)* -Beverley Nichols

*Maybelle (Hide and seek)* - Vivian Ellis

*On the crest of the wave* - Ralph Reader

*Red, white and blue* - Noel Gay

*Rose of England (Crest of the wave)* - Christopher Hassall & Ivor Novello

*St Bernard Waltz* - H. O. Ward & D. Swallow

*She's my lovely (Hide and seek)* -Vivian Ellis

*Smile when you say goodbye* -Harry Parr Davies

*Song of the grateful heart* - Ord Hamilton

*\*The greatest mistake of my life* -James Netson

*The old house* - Frederick O'Connor

*The rhythm's O.K. in Harlem* -Michael Carr

**The spice of life - Jimmy Kennedy & Michael Carr**

*Walter, lead me to the altar* - Harper, Forrester and Haines

**Waltz of the gipsies (London Rhapsody) - Jimmy Kennedy& Michael Carr**
*When I'm cleaning windows* - F. E. Cliffe, H Gifford & G. Formby
*You're mine* - Bruce Sievier & Hero de Rance

# 1938

*Au revoir (J'attendrais)* - Bruce Sievier & D. Olivieri
*Biggest aspidistra in the world* - Connor, Harper and Haines
*Blue skies are around the corner* - Ross Parker & Hugh Charles
*Cherokee* - Ray Noble
**Cinderella, stay in my arms - Jimmy Kennedy & Michael Carr**
*Cinderella sweetheart* -Art Strauss & Bob Dale
*Dearest love (Operette)* - Noel Coward
*Dickie Bird Hop* - P. Gourlay
*Doing an Irish jig (Running Riot)* - Vivian Ellis
*Georgia's gotta moon* - Max & Harry Nesbit
*Girl in the Alice blue gown* - Ross Parker
*How do you do Mr Right? (Fleets lit up)* - Vivian Ellis
*I hadn't anyone till you* - Ray Noble
*I'll walk beside you* - Edward Lockton & Alan Murray
*In the mountains of the moon* - Box, Cox & Roberts
*It's in the air* - Harry Parr Davis
*Little boy that Santa Claus forgot* - M. Carr, T. Connor & J. Leach
*Little drummer boy* - Art Noel & Don Pelosi
*Love makes the world go round* -Noel Gay
*Me and my girl* - Douglas Furber & Noel Gay
*Merrily we roll along* - Michael Carr & Raymond Wallace
**On linger longer island - Jimmy Kennedy & Michael Carr**
*Rags, bottles and bones* - S. Holloway & Harry S. Pepper

*Sweetest song in the world* - Harry Parr Davies
**Ten pretty girls - Jimmy Kennedy & Will Grosz**
*The Army, the Navy and the Air Force* -Edward Lockton & H. Darewski
**The Chestnut Tree - Jimmy Kennedy, H. Kennedy & T. Connor**
*The down and out blues* - Sam Mayo
*\*The Lambeth walk (Me and my girl)* - Douglas Furber & Noel Gay
*The stately homes of England (Operette)* - Noel Coward
*The trek song* - Harry Parr Davies
*The windmill's turning* - Noel, Hardy & Jan van Laar
*Where are the songs we sung (Operette)*- Noel Coward
*With my shillelagh under my arm* - B. O'Brien & Raymond Wallace

# 1939

*\*Boomps a daisy* - Annette Mills
*Goodnight children everywhere* - Gaby Rogers & Harry Phillips
*I can give you the starlight (Dancing Years)* - C. Hassall & Ivor Novello
*I'll pray for you* - King, Hill, Gilbert & Gay
*I'm sending a letter to Santa Claus* - Lanny Rogers, T. Connor
& Spencer Williams
*I shall always remember you smiling* - Ross Parker & Hugh Charles
*I won't tell a soul* - Ross Parker & Hugh Charles
*Knees up Mother Brown* -Harris Weston & Bert Lee
*Lords of the air* - Davy Burnaby & Michael North
*Mine alone (Magyar Melody)* - Eric Maschwitz & George Posford
**\*My Prayer - Jimmy Kennedy & G. Boulanger**
*Nice people* - Nat Mills & Fred Malcolm

*On the outside looking in* - Michael Carr
*Run Rabbit run* - Ralph Butler & Noel Gay
**\*South of the Border - Jimmy Kennedy & Michael Carr**
*The girl who loves a soldier* - Noel Gay
**The Handsome Territorial - Jimmy Kennedy & Michael Carr**
*\*There'll always be an England* - Ross Parker & Hugh Charles
*Till the lights of London shine again* - Tommie Connor & Eddie Pola
*Transatlantic lullaby (Gate Revue)* - D. Morgan, R. Macdermot & Geoffrey ``Wright
*Waltz of my heart (Dancing Years* - C. Hassall & Ivor Novello
**Washing on the Siegfried Line - Jimmy Kennedy & Michael Carr**
*We'll meet again* - Ross Parker & Hugh Charles
*Wish me luck (as you wave me goodbye)* - Harry Parr Davies

# 1940

*All over the place* - Frank Eyton & Noel Gay
*\*A nightingale sang in Berkeley Square* - Eric Maschwitz & Manning Sherwood
*Bless 'em all* - Hughes & Lake
*Bubble Bubble (Black Velvet)* - Roma C. Hunter & Harry Parr Davies
*Crash bang (I want to go home)* - Ralph Butler & Harry Parr Davies
*Dancing is another name for love* - Roma C. Hunter & Freddy Grant
*Down ev'ry street* - Art Noel & Don Pelosi
*Franco-British Swing (New Faces)* - Eric Maschwitz & Jack Strachey
*If I should fall in love again* - Jack Popplewell
*If I only had wings* - Sid Colin & Ronnie Aldrich

*If you were Ginger Rogers and I were Fred Astaire (New Faces)* - Eric Maschwitz & Jack Strachey
*I'll always love you* - Jack Watson & Muriel Denby
*I'm spending Christmas with the old folks* - Tommie Connor
*In the quartermaster's stores* - Box, Cox & Bert Read
*I've got you where I want you (Up and doing)* - Tommie Connor & Manning Sherwin
Let the people sing (Lights up) - F. Eyton, Ian Grant & Noel Gay
*Only a glass of champagne (Lights up)* - Arthur Wimperis & Noel Gay
*Say a little prayer* - Gerry Mason (Billy Merrin)
*The badge from your coat* - Annette Mills & Horatio Nicholls
**There's a boy coming home on leave - Jimmy Kennedy**
*Tiggerty boo (6/8)* - Hal Halifax
*Walkin' thru Mockin' Bird Lane* - L. Peters, Clarence Jones & John Turner
*When the blackbird says bye, bye* - Art Noel & Don Pelosi
*When our dreams grow old* - Eddie Pola & V. Stellar
*Whitehall warriors (Up and doing)* - Phil Park
*Who's taking you home tonight?* - Tommie Connor & Manning Sherwin
*You've done something to my heart (Lights up)* - F. Eyton, Ian Grant & Noel Gay

# 1941

*A pair of silver wings* - Eric Maschwitz & Michael Carr
*Bow bells swinging the Broadway melody (More New Faces)* - Eric Maschwitz & Jack Strachey
*Cheeerio (Apple sauce)* - M. Carr, W. H. Kitchen & J. Westgarth

*Down Forget-me-not Lane* - C. Chester, H. Nicholls & Reg Morgan

*Hearts don't lie (Fun and Games)* - Val Guest & Manning Sherwin

*Hey little hen* - Ralph Butler & Noel Gay

*I'll think of you* - Gerry Mason (Billy Merrin)

*I've got sixpence* - Box, Cox & Hall

*\*Let there be love* - Lionel Rand & Ian grant

*London Pride* - Noel Coward

*Over the hill* - Gerry Mason (Billy Merrin)

*Rise and shine* - Gerry Mason (Billy Merrin)

*Room 504 (More new faces)* - Eric Maschwitz & George Posford

*Russian Rose* - Sonny Miller & Hugh Charles

**St Mary's in the twilight - Jimmy Kennedy.**

*She had those dark and dreamy eyes* - Jimmy Hughes & Ted Douglas

*Starlight serenade* - S. Miller, F. Tysh & Hans May

*That lovely week-end* - Moira & Ted Heath

*The first lullaby (Apple sauce)* - Jack Popplewell & Michael Carr

*The King is still in London* - Roma C. Hunter & Hugh Charles

*The London I love* - Harold Purcell & Harry Parr Davies

*There's a land of begin again* - Hugh Charles & Ross Parker

*This heart of mine (Rise above it)* - Tommie Connor & Manning Sherwin

*We both told a lie* - Art Noel & Jimmy Mesene

*What more can I say* - Art Noel

*When Big Ben chimes* - Kennedy Russell

*When eagles fly (Fun and Games)* - Tommie Connor & Manning Sherwin

*When they sound the last all clear* - Hugh Charles & Louis Elton

*When we're home sweet home again* - Annette Mills & Fred Prisker

*You don't have to tell me, I know* - Art Noel & Don Pelosi

# 1942

*Gotta bee in my bonnet (Scoop Revue)* - David Heneker &
Arthur Young
*Hey ho, the merry-o (The Big Top)* - B. Gordon, B.
Thomas
& Harry Parr Davies
*I hear your voice* - Ralph Butler & Tolchard Evans
**I'll just close my eyes - Jimmy Kennedy**
*I'm going to see you today* - Joyce Grenfell & Richard
Addinsell
*\*Jealousy* - Winifred May & Jacob Gade
*Just a little fond affection* - F. Eyton & Noel Gay
*Lilliburlero* - Trad: arr. Kenneth J. Alford
*My paradise (Gangway)* - B. Gordon, B. Thomas
*One love forever* - J. Dyrenforth & K. Leslie-Smith
*Sing everybody sing* - John P. Long
*Soft shoe shuffle* - Maurice Burman & Spencer Williams
*Some chicken, some neck* - David Heneker & Arthur
Young
*Stage Coach* - Eric Winstone
*Strange as it seems (Fine and Dandy)* - Val Guest & Manning
Sherwin
*Swing bugler (Gangway)* - Phil Park, B. Campbell & B.
Thompson
*Take the world exactly as you find it* - Phil Park & Harry
Parr Davies
**The Cokey-Cokey - Jimmy Kennedy**
*There'll come another day* - Alan Stranks & Pat Pattison
*The Thing-ummy-bob* - C. Thompson & David Heneker
*\*The Warsaw Concerto (from the film Dangerous Moonlight)*
- Richard Addinsell
*Three minutes of heaven* - D. Furber & Ivor Carmeli
*Waltz without end* - Eric Maschwitz & Bernard Grun
*When you know you're not forgotten* - Box & Cox

*Wrap yourself in cotton wool (Get a load of this)* - Val Guest & Manning Sherwin
*You're mine* - Jack Watson & Muriel Denby

# 1943

*A fine how-do-you-do* - al Guest & Manning Sherwin
**All our tomorrows - Jimmy Kennedy**
*Be like the kettle and sing* - T. Connor, D. O'Connor & W. Ridley
*I give thanks for you* - Linton & Peter Young
*I'm going to get lit up when the lights go up in London (Strike a new note)* - Hubert Gregg
*I'm looking for a melody (It's time to dance)* - Harry Roy, G. Rogers & A. Strauss
*I spy* - Arthur Brooks & Geoff Parks
*It costs so little* - A. Ritter, L. Smith & H. Nicholls
*I wonder why* - Art Noel
*Love must be free* -Max Kester & Alan Paul
*My heart and I (Old Chelsea)* - Fred s. Tysh & Richard Tauber
**My serenade - Jimmy Kennedy**
*Never say goodbye (Lisbon Story)* - H. Purcell & Harry Parr Davies
*Pedro the fisherman (Lisbon Story)* - H. Purcell & Harry Parr Davies
*Silver wings in the moonlight* - Charles, Towers & Miller
*Someday we shall meet again (Lisbon Story)* - H. Purcell & Harry Parr Davies
*Starlight souvenirs* - Connelly, Ilda & Ted Shapiro
*The homecoming waltz* - Musel, Sonin & Connelly
**The Pony Express - Eric Winstone (words by Jimmy Kennedy)**
*We'll smile again* - D. O'Connor & Kennedy Russell
*You happen once in a lifetime* - H. Purcell & manning Sherwin

# 1944

**An hour never passes - Jimmy Kennedy**
*Easy to live with (Arc de Triomphe)* - C. Hassall & Ivor Novello
*Happy days, happy months, happy years* - Frank Eyton & Noel Gay
*Hey ho it's love again* - Carl Yale & Peter Hart
*If you ever go to Ireland* - Art Noel
*I love to sing* - M. Carr, T. Connor & P. Misraki
*I'm sending my blessings* - J. Lubin, J. G. Gilbert & Noel Gay
*Just a little fond affection* - Box, Cox & Ilda
*\*Lilli Marlene* - T. Connor & N. Schultze
*Lover's lullaby* - M. Carr, T. Connor, Nat Temple & Ray Terry
*Man of my heart (Arc de Triomphe)* - C. Hassall & Ivor Novello
*Really and truly* - Jack Popplewell
*Roll me over* - Desmond O'Connor
*Sailor who are you dreaming of tonight* - Damerell, Butler & Evans
*Shine on Victory Moon* - Jos. Geo. Gilbert
*The happiest New Year of all* - D. O'Connor, Watson & Denby
*These you have loved* - Joseph Murrells & Alan Murray
*Waking or sleeping (Arc de Triomphe)* - C. Hassall & Ivor Novello
*Where the blue begins (Jenny Jones)* - Phil Park & Harry Parr Davies
*With all my heart* - J. Popplewell & Reginald King

# 1945

*A kiss in the night* - M. Mayne & P. de Carolis
*Boston Bounce* - B. Lamarr, A. Dallas & B. Harris

*Break of day* - Alan Stranks & Hans May
*Bye bye, so long for now* - Henry Hall, B. Elsdon & J. Hughes
*Carolina* - J. Stodel, Max & Harry Nesbitt
*Coming home* - Billy Reid
*Cruising down the river* - Eily Beadell & Nell Tollerton
*Dreaming* - D. O'Connor & Kennedy Russell
*Give me the stars* - D. O'Connor & Kennedy Russell
*I'll close my eyes* - Billy Reid
*I'll turn to you* - Howard Barnes & Louise Craven
*I'm gonna love that guy* - Frances Ash, Ted & Moira Heath
*I'm in love with two sweethearts* - Box, Cox & Ilda
*I want to sleep in fevers* - Box, Cox & Ilda
*Jamaican Rumba* - Arthur Benjamin
*Journey's end* - Hugh Charles & Sonny Miller
*Let's keep it that way* - O'Connor, Watson & Denby
*Love, here is my heart* (original 1915)- Adrian Ross & Lao Silesu
*Love is my reason (Perchance to dream)* - Ivor Novello
*Matelot (Sigh no more)* - Noel Coward
*My heart is in Vienna still* - Alan Murray
*Nina (Sigh no more)* - Noel Coward
*Only a few steps away* - Edith Temple & Reg Morgan
*One love* - Jack Popplewell
*Remember me* - Jose Bradley
*Sigh no more* - Noel Coward
*Soon it will be Sunday* - Buntin & Hart
*The gipsy* - Billy Reid
*The moment I saw you (Under the counter)* - H. Purcell & Manning Sherwin
*The sweetheart waltz* - Howard Barnes & Manning Sherwin
*The toorie on his bonnet* - George Brown & Noel Gay
*The wedding waltz* - Hugh Charles & Sonny Miller
*Those were the days* - Edith Temple & Meyer Lutz
*Till stars forget to shine* - Lubin, Miller & Charles

*Under the willow tree* - Billy Reid
*\*We'll gather lilacs (Perchance to dream)* - Ivor Novello
*You'll get used to it (Meet the Navy)* - V. Gordon & F. Grant
*You will return to Vienna* -Alan Stranks & Hans May

# 1946

*Apple honey* - Den Berry, D. O'Connor & B. Harris
*Bedelia* - Alan Stranks & Hans May
Give me the moon over London - Jason Matthews & Terry Shand
*Hope and pray* - Joseph Murrells & Peter Young
*I'll always love you (Sweetheart mine)* - Frank Eyton & Noel Gay
*I'll dance at your wedding* - Sonny Miller & Art Strauss
*\*It's a pity to say goodnight* - Billy Reid
*I want to see the people happy (Big Ben)*- A. P. Herbert & Vivian Ellis
*Kay-ud meelah falta* - Box, Cox & Ilda
*Let bygones be bygones (original 1933)* - Jos. Geo. Gilbert
*Let it be soon* - Hugh Wade & Dick Hurran
Love steels your heart - Alan Stranks & Hans May
*Make belief world* - Box, Cox & Ilda
*Mary Lou (High Time)* - Dick Hurran
*Primrose Hill* - Chas. Chester, E. Lynton & K. Morris
*Romance (from the film 'The Magic Bow')* - Paganini & Phil Green
*Runaway Rocking Horse* - Edward White
*Sweetheart we'll never grow old* - Muriel Watson & Jack Denby
Sweet Virginia (Fine Feathers) - Phil Park & Harry Parr Davies
*\*The bells of St Mary's (original 1917)* - D. Furber & A. Emmett Adams

*The green cockatoo* - Don Pellegro (Harold Geller)
*There's a harvest moon tonight* - Miller, Watson & Denby
*The trees in Grosvenor Square* - Bob Whittam
*Time cannot change a faithful heart* - Bruce Sievier & Rex Burrows

# 1947

**An apple blossom wedding - Jimmy Kennedy & Nat Simon**
**And Mimi - Jimmy Kennedy & Nat Simon**
*A thousand beautiful things* - Richard Corrin & Haydn Wood
*Bow Bells* - Harold Purcell & Ben Bernard
*\*Count your blessings* - Edith Temple & Reginald Morgan
*Danger ahead* - Billy Reid
*Don't fall in love* - Eddie Lisbona & Joe Lubin
**Down the old Spanish trail - Jimmy Kennedy & K. Leslie-Smith**
*Goodnight you little rascal you* - Art Noel
*\*Hear my song, Violetta* (original 1938 - Harry S. Pepper, Klose & Lukesch
*How lucky you are* - D. O'Connor & Eddie Cassen
*I'll make up for everything* - Ross Parker
*I was never kissed before (Bless the bride)* - A. P. Herbert & Vivian Ellis
*Little old mill* - Don Pelosi, L. Ilda & L. Towers
*Maybe it's because I'm a Londoner* - Hubert Gregg
*Ma belle Marguerite (Bless the bride)* - A. P. Herbert & Vivian Ellis
*May I call you sweetheart?* - Watson, Denby & Ilda
*My first love, my last love for always* - Billy Reid
*My love is only for you* - Clarkson Rose & Conrad Leonard
*My lovely world and you* - George Record
*Once upon a wintertime* - Johnny Brandon & Ray Martin

*Serenade to a beautiful day* - Hubert Sands & Peter Revell
*There is no end* - Bruce Sievier & Rex Burrows
*The shoemaker's serenade* - Joe Lubin & Eddie Lisbona
*The stars will remember* - Leo Towers & Don Pelosi
*This is a changing world (Pacific 1860)* - Noel Coward
*This is my lovely day (Bless the bride)* - A. P. Herbert & Vivian Ellis
*Too tired to sleep* - Alan Murray
*When China boy meets China girl* - Billy Reid

# 1948

*All my lifetime* - Edith Temple & Alan Murray
*Anything I dream is possible* - Billy Reid
*\*A tree in the meadow* - Billy Reid
**Ballerina - Jimmy Kennedy & E. Bootz**
*Cuckoo waltz* - Alan Stranks & J. E. Jonasson
*Far in the blue* - Dr. Arthur Colahan
*Hold it Joe (Starlight Roof)* - E. Maschwitz & George Melachrino
*I found my romance in Vienna* - Bruce Sievier & George de Jongh
*I'm happy right here* - Norman Newell & Leslie Baguley
*Jumping Bean* - Robert Farnon
*Miranda* - Jack Fishman & Peter Hart
*My own Darby and Joan* - Box, Cox & Kueleman
*\*Nice to know you care* - Norman Newell & Leslie Baguley
*\*No orchids for my lady* - Alan Stranks & Jack Strachey
*Portrait of a flirt* - Robert Farnon
*Reflections on the water* - Billy Reid
*\*Silver wedding waltz* - Max & Harry Nesbitt
*So little time (Starlight Roof)* - E. Maschwitz & George Melachrino
*Starlight serenade (Starlight Roof)* - E. Maschwitz & George Melachrino

*\*Take me to your heart (Vie en rose)* - Frank Eyton & Louiguy
*\*The dream of Olwen (from the film 'While I live')* - Charles Williams
*The wishing waltz* - Art Noel
*This is my Mother's day* - Billy Reid
*Time alone will tell (Cage me a peacock)* - Adam Leslie & Hugh Wade
*Time may change (Made to measure)* - Leigh Stafford & Hugh Wade
*Violins in the night (Starlight Roof)* - E. Maschwitz & George Melachrino
*When you're in love* - D. O'Connor, H. Fields & D. John
*Why is it only a dream?* - Arthur Henbury

# 1949

*A rose in a garden of weeds* (original 1926) - R. B. Saxe & Hubert W. David
*Blue ribbon gal* - Ross Parker & Irwin Dash
*Confidentially* - Reg Dixon
*Down in the Glen* - T. Connor & Harry Gordon
*Dusk* - C. Armstrong Gibbs
*Fly home little heart (King's Rhapsody)* - C. Hassall & Ivor Novello
*Hang on the bell, Nellie* - T. Connor, C. Erard & Ross Parker
*How can you buy Killarney?* - H. Kennedy, F. Grundland, G. Morrison & Ted Steele
*Is it too late?* - Leo Towers & Michael White
*I wish I could sing (Tough at the top)* - A. P. Herbert & Vivian Ellis
*Leicester Square Rag* - Harry Roy
*Mia Mantilla* - J. Morellio (Murrells) & E. Griffete (Griffiths)
*Monday, Tuesday, Wednesday* - Ross Parker
*On the 5.45* - Mark Warren

*Our love story* - Norman Newell & W. Harrison
*Scottish Samba* - Tommie Connor & Johnny Reine
*Snowy white and jingle bells* - Billy Reid
*Someday my heart will awake (King's Rhapsody)* - C. Hassall & Ivor Novello
*Song of the mountains (from the film 'Glass Mountain')* - Miller, Stana-Field & Pigarelli
*Story of the sparrows* - Norman Newell & Phil Green
*Sunday morning in England (Her Excellency)* - H. Purcell & Harry Parr Davies
*Take your girl (King's Rhapsody)* - C. Hassall & Ivor Novello
*The crystal gazer* - Frank Petch
*The echo told me a lie* - H. Barnes, H. Fields & D. John
*\*The Seine (Sauce Tartare)* - G. Parsons & Lafarge
*Till all our dreams come true* - D. O'Connor & H. C. Bonocini
*We all have a song in our hearts* - Carl & Reger Yale
*Wedding of Lilli Marlene* -Tommie Connor

# 1950

*A Gordon for me* - Robert Wilson
*All will come right (Golden City)* - John Toré
*Blue for a boy* - H. Purcell & Harry Parr Davies
*Cherry stones* - John Jerome
*Ferry Boat Inn* - Jimmy Campbell & Don Pelosi
**French Can-Can Polka - Jimmy Kennedy (adaption from Offenbach)**
*Hey neighbour (Knights of madness)* - Ross Parker
*Hors d'oeuvre (original 1915)* - Dave Comer
*If I were a blackbird* - Delia Murphy
*I leave my heart in an English garden (Dear Miss Phoebe)* - C. Hassall & Harry Parr Davies
*I remember the cornfields* - Martyn Mayne & Harry Ralston
*\*I've got a lovely bunch of coconuts* - Fred Heatherton

*Legend* - Robert Docker
*Let's do it again* - D. O'Connor & Ray Hartley
*Load of hay* - M. Feahy & Howard Barnes
*My thanks to you* - Norman Newell & Noel Gay
*Sail away (Ace of Clubs)* - Noel Coward
*We'll keep a welcome* - Lyn Joshua, James Harper & Mai Jones
*When there's love at home* - Tommie Connor
*Whisper while you waltz (Dear Miss Phoebe)* - C. Hassall & Harry Parr Davies
*Your heart and my heart (Knights of madness)* - Ross Parker

# 1951

*Forgive me Lord* - Ord Hamilton
*\*If you go (Si tu partais)* - Geoffrey Parsons & Michel Emer
*\*London by night (Fancy Free)* - Carroll Coates
*Love me little, love me long (And so to bed)* - Vivian Ellis
*\*Love's roundabout (La ronde)* - Harold Purcell & Oscar Straus
*\*Ma'moiselle de Paree* - Eric Maschwitz & Paul Durand
*Manzanilla* - Winifred Atwell
*Mary Rose* - T. Connor, Scheffer, Vogel & Dunk
*Ordinary people (Zip goes a million)* - E. Maschwitz, E. Littler & G. Posford
*Raise your voices* - W. Ridley, Peter Hart & J. Fishman
*\*Rose, Rose I love you* - Wilfred Thomas & (Chinese unknown)
*\*The green glens of Antrim* - Kenneth North & Archie Montgomery
*Tipperary Samba* - T. Connor & J. Johnston
*Tulips and heather* - Milton Carson
*Two little men in a flying saucer* - Arthur Pitt (Eric Spear)
*Vitality (Gay's the word)* - Alan Melville & Ivor Novello

# 1952

*Auf wiederseh'n, sweetheart* - J. Secton, J. Turner & E. Storch
*Britannia Rag* - Winifred Atwell
*Dixie Boogie* - Winifred Atwell
*Faith (original 1934)* - S. Damerell & Tolchard Evans
*Forget me not* - Reine, May & Sinclair
*Isle of Innisfree* - Dick Farrelly
*Jubilee Rag* - Winifred Atwell
*Meet Mister Callaghan* - Eric Spear
*My love and devotion* - Milton Carson
*The homing waltz* - T. Connor & Michael Reine
*Why worry* - Ralph Edwards

# 1953

**\*April in Portugal - Jimmy Kennedy & Raul Ferrao**
*Bridge of Sighs* - Billy Reid
*Broken wings* - John Jerome & Bernard Grun
*Celebration Rag* - Rodd Arden & Jimmy Harper
*Coronation Rag* -Winifred Atwell
*Ecstasy Tango* - Jose Belmonte (Phil Green)
*Elizabeth of England* - W. E. St. Lawrence Finney & Haydn Wood
*Eternally (Limelight, song version)* - G. Parsons, John Turner & Chas. Chaplin
*Five Finger Boogie* - Winifred Atwell
*Flirtation Waltz* - Leslie Sarony & R. Heywood (Joe Henderson)
*Genevieve (Film theme)* - Larry Adler
*Golden Tango* - Victor Silvester & Ernest Wilson
*I'm walking behind you* - Billy Reid
*In a golden coach* - Ronald Jamieson
*I saw Mommy kissing Santa Claus* - Tommie Connor
*Istanbul* - Jimmy Kennedy & Nat Simon

*It's a grand life in the army* - Joe Murrells & Charles Prentice
*Little Red Monkey* - Jack Jordan
*Melba waltz* - Norman Newell & M. Spoliansky
*Queen of Tonga* - Jack Fishman
*\*Theme from 'The last Rhapsody'* - Reynell Wreford
*\*Tobermory Bay* - J. Reine, J. Harper,& K. North(A. Montgomery)

# 1954

*\*Cara Mia* - Lee Lange, (Bunny Lewis) & Trulio Trapani (Mantovani)
*Don't ever leave me* - Rodd Arden, Max & Harry Nesbitt
*Don't laugh at me, 'cause I'm a fool* - Norman Wisdom
*Friends and neighbours* - Marvin Scott & Malcolm Lockyer
*Get well soon* - T. Harrison & Donald Phillips
*Homecoming waltz* - Musel, Sonin & Connelly
*I could be happy with you (The Boy Friend)* - Sandy Wilson
*I know you're mine* - Norman & Joe Murrells
*My son, my son* - Bob Howard, E. Calvert & M. Farley
*\*Oh my Papa* - John Turner, G. Parsons & P. Burkhard
*\*Smile (Modern Times, song version)* - John Turner, G. Parsons & Charlie Chaplin
*Someone else's roses* - Milton Carson
*The Book* - Paddy Roberts & Hans Gotwald
*\*The Happy Wanderer* - Antonia Ridge & F. W. Moller
*The little shoemaker* - John Turner, G. Parsons & Rudi Revil
*The Shadow Waltz* - Paul Dubois
*The story of Tina* - Christopher Hassall & D. Katrivanou

# 1955

*A blossom fell* - H. Barnes, H. Cornelius & D. John
*Arrivederci darling (Arrivederci Roma)* - Jack Fisherman & Renato Rasce
*Ev'rywhere* - Larry Kahn & Tolchard Evans
*He* - Richard Mullan & Jack Richards
*In love for the very first time* - Paddy Roberts & Jack Woodman
*John and Julie (theme from film)* - Philip Green
*Meet me on the corner* - Paddy Roberts & Peter Hunt
*Paper kisses* - John Jerome
*Softly, softly* - Paddy Roberts, P. Dudan & M. Paul
*Somebody* - Joe Henderson
*Stars shine in your eyes* - J. Turner, G. Parsons & Nino Rota
*That's how a love song was born* - N. Newell & Phil Green
*The Dam Busters March (from the film)* - Eric Coates
*The Engagement Waltz* - Joe Reidman, Joe Murrells, David Reid & Tommie Connor
*This is our secret (The Water Gipsies)* - A. P. Herbert & Vivian Ellis
*Three galleons* - Paddy Roberts & A. Alguero
*Tomorrow* - Peter Hart & Bob Geraldson
*With your love (Mes mains)* - J. Turner, G. Parsons & G. Becaud

# 1956

*Autumn concerto* - J. Turner, G. Parsons & G. Bargoni
*By the fountains of Rome* - Norman Newell & Matyas Seibeer
*Dreams can tell a lie* - Barnes, Cornelius & John
*Elizabethan Serenade* - Ronald Binge
*Lay down your arms* - Paddy Roberts, Land & Gerhard

*My September love* - Richard Mullan & Tolchard Evans
*My unfinished symphony* - Milton Carson
*Nellie the elephant* - Ralph Butler & Peter Hart
*Out of town* - Beaumont & Leslie Bricusse
*Pickin' a chicken* - Paddy Roberts, Bernfield & de Mortimer
*Rock with the cavemen* - M. Pratt, T. Steele & Lionel Bart
*Summer song* - Eric Maschwitz, Dvorak & arr. Grun
*The March hare* - Philip Green
*The old pi-anna Rag* - Elizabeth Brice & Don Phillips
*The snake (La Culebra)* - Jose Martinez & Norman Murrells
*Westminster Waltz* - Robert Farnon
*You are my first love* -Paddy Roberts & Lester Powell

# 1957

*A gnu* - Flanders & Swann
A handful of songs - T. Steel, M. Pratt & L. Bart
All - Allan Stranks & Reynell Wreford
*Cumberland Gap (new words and music)* - L. Donegan
*Don't you rock me Daddy'o* - Wally Whyton & F. W. Varley
*He's got the whole world in his hands* - Geoff Love
*I'll find you* - Richard Mullan & Tolchard Evans
*Puttin' on the style* (new words & arrangement) - Norman Cazden
*Shiralee* - Tommy Steele
*Swedish polka (Chickadee)* - Paddy Roberts & Hugo Alfven
*The hippopotamus* - Flanders & Swann
*The streets of Sorento* - Tony Osborne
*Wedding ring* - Ron Hulme (Russ Hamilton)
*We will make love* - Ron Hulme (Russ Hamilton)
*You me and us (adaptation from 'Cielito Lindo')* - John Jerome

# 1958

*Expresso Bongo* - J. More, D. Heneker & Monty Norman
*Grand Coolie Dam* - Woody Gutherie & Lonnie Donegan
*Hillside in Scotland* - S. Clayton, R. Roberts & Bill Katz
Carrie
*I need you* - Joe Henderson
*Josita* - Philip Green
*Lingering lovers* - Ron Goodwin
*Little one* - Ron Hulme (Russ Hamilton)
*Little serenade (Piccolissima serenata)* - G. Parsons, J. Turner & G. Ferrio)
*Love is (Lady at the wheel)* - Leslie Bricusse
*Melody from the sea* - Donald Phillips
*Midnight Cha-Cha* - Norman Murrells
*More than ever (Come primo)* - Mary Bond, (N. Newell), Taccani & di Paola
*Move it* - Ian Samwell
*Our language of love (Irma la Douce)* - Julian More & Marguete Monnot
*Siesta (Lady at the wheel)* - Leslie Bricusse & Robin Beaumont
*Song of the Clyde* - Bell & Gourlay
*The world goes around and around* - C. Charles & Tolchard Evans
*Trudie* - Joe Henderson
*Tulips from Amsterdam* - Gene Martyn & Ralf Arnie
*Why don't they understand* - Jack Fishman & Joe Henderson
*You need hands* - Roy Irwin (Max Bygraves)

# 1959

*Ballad of Bethnal Green* - Paddy Roberts
*Chick* - Joe Henderson
*China tea* - Trevor H. Stanford (Russ Conway)

*House of Bamboo* - W. Crompton & Norman Murrells
*If you love me (Hymn à l'amour)* orig. 1949 - G. Parsons & M. Monnot
*Jazzboat* - Joe Henderson
*Little white bull* - M. Pratt, J. Bennett & Lionel Bart
*Living doll* - Lionel Bart
*Lock up your daughters* - Lionel Bart & Laurie Johnson
*Meet the family (The crooked mile)* - P. Wildeblood & P. Greenwell
*Pixielated penguin* - Michael Carr
*Ring Ding* - Steve Race
*Roulette* - Trevor H. Stanford (Russ Conway)
*Side saddle* - Trevor H. Stanford (Russ Conway)
*Sing little birdie* - Syd Cordell & Stan Butcher
*Snow coach* - Trevor H. Stanford (Russ Conway)
*Strollin' (Clown Jewels)* - Ralph Reader
*The girl from Corsica* - Trevor Duncan
*The heart of a man* - Paddy Roberts & Peggy Cochrane
*The village of St. Bernadette* - Eula Parker
*This old man (Nick nack paddy wack)* - C. J. Sharp, S. B. Gould & M. Arnold
*Trampolina* - Geoff Love
*Treble chance* - Joe Henderson
*What do you want?* - Les Vandyke (Johnny Worth)
*Windows of Paris* - Tony Osborne

# 1960

*Apache* - Jerry Lordan
*As long as he needs me (Oliver)* - Lionel Bart
*A voice in the wilderness* - Bunny Lewis & Norrie Paramor
*Belle of Barking Creek* - Paddy Roberts
*Cinderella Jones* - Jerry Lordan & Thomas Mould
*Consider yourself (Oliver)* - Lionel Bart
*Do you mind* - Lionel Bart

*Fall in love with you* - Ian Samwell
*\*Fings aint wot they used t' be* - Lionel Bart
*\*Food glorious food (Oliver)* - Lionel Bart
*Goodness gracious me* - David Lee & Herbert Kretzmer
*Gurney Slade theme* - Max Harris
*Hit and Miss* - John Barry
*How about that?* - Les Vandyke (Johnny Worth)
*\*I'd do anything (Oliver)* - Lionel Bart
*Kickin' up the leaves* - Lionel Bart
*Little donkey* - Eric Boswell
*Look for a storm* - Mark Anthony (Tony Hatch)
*Looking high high high* - John Watson
**Love is like a violin - Jimmy Kennedy & M. Laparcerie**
*Mama (original 1941)* - G. Parsons, J. Turner & C. A. Bixio
*Milford* - Bunny Lewis & Marguerite Monnot
*My concerto for two* - Trevor H. Stanford (Russ Conway)
*My old man's a dustman* - P. Buchanan, B. Thorn & L. Donegan
*Please don't tease* - Bruce Welch & Peter Chester
*Poor me* - Les Vandyke (Johnny Worth)
*Royal event* - Trevor H. Stanford (Russ Conway
*Seashore* - Robert Farnon
*Someone else's baby* - Les Vandyke & Perry Ford
*Strawberry Fair (new words and arrangement)* -Anthony Newley
*Summer set* - Collett & Acker Bilk
*\*Theme from 'The Apartment'* - Charles Williams
*The singing piano* - Tolchard Evans
*\*Tie me kangaroo down sport* - Rolf Harris
*Tom Pillibi* - Marcel Stellman & André Popp

# 1961

*African Waltz* - Galt Macdermott
*A girl like you* - Jerry Lordan
*Are you sure?* - Allison Brothers

*A Scottish soldier* - Andy Stewart & Ian MacFadyen
*Don't treat me like a child* - John Schroeder
*Don't you know it* - Les Vandyke (Johnny Worth)
*F. B. I.* - Peter Gormley
*Ginchy* - Bert Weedon
*\*Gonna build a mountain (Stop the world)* - Anthony Newley & Leslie Bricusse
*I can't get enough of your kisses* - Larry Stone
*I'm shy Mary Ellen (original 1910)* - G. A. Stevens & Charles Ridgwell
*Johnny remember me* - Geoffrey Goddard
*Kon-Tiki* - Michael Carr
*Maigret Theme* - Ron Grainer
*Michael, row the boat (trad. Adaption)* - Lonnie Donegan
*Midnight in Moscow* - Soloviev & Matusovosky Arr. Kenny Ball
*My friend the sea* - Jack Fisherman & Ron Goodwin
*\*My kind of girl* - Leslie Bricusse
*No greater love* - Bunny Lewis & Michael Carr
*\*Once in a lifetime (Stop the world)* - Anthony Newley & Leslie Bricusse
*Pop goes the weasel (trad. Adaption)* - G. Hackney (Anthony Newley)
*\*Portrait of my love* - David West (N. Newell) & Cyril Ornadel
*Reach for the stars* - David West (N. Newell) & U. Jurgens
**Romeo (original 'Salome')** - **Jimmy Kennedy & R. Stolz**
*Sailor (Seaman)* - David West (N. Newell) & W. Scharfenberger
*Secrets of the Seine* - Tony Osborne
*\*Stranger on the shore* - Acker Bilk
*Theme from 'The frightened City'* - Norrie Paramor
*Theme from 'Whistle down the wind'* - Malcolm Arnold
*The Savage* - Norrie Paramor
*The wedding (La Novia)* - Fred Jay & J. Prieto
*Walking back to happiness* - Mike Hawker & John Schroeder

*What kind of fool am I? (Stop the world)* - Anthony Newley
& Leslie Bricusse
*Willow Waltz* - Cyril Watters
*You don't know* - John Schroeder & Mike Hawker

# 1962

*A picture of you* - Peter Oakman & J. Beveridge
*Bachelor Boy* - Bruce Welch & Cliff Richard
*Come dancing* - Hubert David & Ray Downes
*Come outside* - Charles Blackwell
*Concerto for dreamers* - Trevor H. Stanford (Russ Conway)
*Fanlight Fanny (original 1935)* - . Formby, F. Cliffe, H. Gifford & C. Ford
*Hole in the ground* - Myles Rudge & Ted Dicks
*Jeannie* - N. Newell & Trevor H. Stanford
*Lesson One* - Trevor H. Stanford (Russ Conway)
*Lonely* - Acker Bilk & Norrie Paramor
*March from A Little Suite* - Trevor Duncan
*Must be Madison* - Jack Woodman
Never goodbye - Jimmy Kennedy
*Nicola* - Steve Race
*Outbreak of murder* - Gordon Franks
*Right said Fred* - Myles Rudge & Ted Dicks
*Ring-a-ding girl* - Stan Butcher & Syd Cordell
*So do I (original 'Bel ami' 1939)* - Ian Grant & T. Mackeben
*Softly as I leave you* - John Harris (Hal Shaper) & de Vita
*Steptoe and Son Theme* - Ron Grainer
*Sun arise* - Rolf Harris & Harry Butler
*Telstar* - Joe Meek
*Tell me what he said* - Jeff Barry
*The day after tomorrow (Blitz)* - Lionel Bart
*The James Bond Theme-007* - John Barry
*The Mexican* - Morgan Jones & Arnold Murray
*Tiara Tahiti* - N. Newell & Phil Green

*Turkish Coffee* - Tony Osborne
*Wherever I go* - Chris Charles & Tolchard Evans
*White rose of Athens* - N. Newell & M. Hadjidakis
*Wonderful Land* - Jerry Lordan
*Z Cars Theme* - Bridget Fry

# 1963

*\*All my loving* - John Lennon & Paul McCartney
*Applejack* - Les Vandyke (Johnny Worth)
*Atlantis* - Jerry Lordan
*\*Bad to me* - John Lennon & Paul McCartney
*Carlos Theme* - Ivor Slaney
*Dance on* - Ray Adams, Elaine & Valerie Murtagh
*Dancing shoes* - Hank Marvin & Bruce Welch
*Diamonds* - Jerry Lordan
*Don't talk to him* - Cliff Richard & Bruce Welch
*\*Do you want to know a secret* - John Lennon & Paul McCartney
*Dream maker* - N. Newell & Phil Green
*Flash, bang, wallop (Half a sixpence)* - David Heneker
*Foot-tapper* - Bruce Welch & Brian Bennett
*\*Forget him* - Mark Anthony (Tony Hatch)
*\*From me to you* - John Lennon & Paul McCartney
*\*From Russia with love* - Lionel Bart
*Geronimo* - Hank B. Marvin
*\*Glad all over* - Mike Smith & Dave Clark

_J. J. Kennedy_

## BIBLIOGRAPHY

This book is made up almost entirely of conversations with my father towards the end of his life, coupled with his own comments on radio or in articles, letters etc he wrote, my own experiences, and on the comments of people who knew him – and the music business – well. It is therefore very much an aural history – much like a memoire.

However, I have used a number of external sources – reference books (Lissauer's and The Oxford Companion were especially helpful), biographies of other personalities and miscellaneous books of many kinds. Below is a brief selection of some I found most useful. Some, of course, may well now be out of print.

## 1. REFERENCE BOOKS

_Lissauer's Encyclopaedia of Popular Music in America, 1988 to the present._ Researched and written by Robert Lissauer. Paragon House, New York, 1991.

_The Oxford Companion to Twentieth Century Popular Music._ Compiled by Peter Gammond. Oxford University Press, 1991.

_The Faber Companion to Twentieth Century Popular Music._ By Phil Hardy and Dave Laing. Faber, 1990.

_Directory of Popular Music 1900 – 1965._ By Leslie Lowe. Peterson Publishing, 1975.

_Who's Who in Music_ (Fifth edition). Edited by W.J. Potterton. Burke's Peerage Limited, 1969.

_The Great Song Thesaurus._ By Roger Lax and Frederick Smith. Oxford University Press (New York), 1989.

_'You Must Remember This...' Popular Song writers 1900-_

298

*1980.* By Mark White. Frederick Warne, 1983.

*Sing us one of the Old Songs – a Guide to Popular Song 1860-1920.* By Michael Kilgarriff. Oxford University Press, 1998.

*First Hits – The book of sheet music 1946-1959.* By Brian Henson and Colin Morgan. Boxtree, 1989.

*British Dance Bands on Record 1911-1945.* By Brian Rust and Sandy Forbes. General Gramophone Publications, 1987.

## 2. GENERAL BOOKS ON TOPICS RELATED TO TWENTIETH CENTURY MUSIC AND THE JIMMY KENNEDY STORY

*Goodnight Sweetheart – songs and memories of the Second World War.* By Frank E. Huggett.W.H. Allen, 1979.

*'What a Lovely War' – British soldiers' songs from the Boer War to the present day.* By Roy Palmer. Michael Joseph, 1990.

*The Big Bands go to War.* By Chris Way. Mainstream, 1991

*Tin Pan Alley.* By Eddie Rogers. Robert Hale, 1964.

*The Dance Bands.* By Brian Rust. Ian Allen 1972

*You Must Remember This – Songs at the heart of the War.* By Steven Seidenberg, Maurice Sellar, Lon Jones. Boxtree, 1995

*After the Ball – Pop music from Rag to Rock.* By Ian Whitcombe. Allen Lane, The Penguin Press, 1972.

*The Rise and Fall of Popular Music.* By Donald Clarke. Penguin, 1995.

*The Lore and Language of Schoolchildren*. By Iona and Peter Opie. Oxford University Press, 1959

*Harmonious Alliance – A History of the Performing Right Society*. By Cyril Ehrlich. Oxford University Press, 1989.

*Sing a Song of England*. By Reginald Nettel Phoenix House, 1954.

*The Biggest Aspidistra in The World – a personal celebration of 50 years of the BBC*. By Peter Black. BBC, 1972.

*Radio Comedy 1938-1968*. By Andy Foster and Steve Furst. Virgin, 1996.

*My Song Goes Round the World*. By Leslie Mann. Ellen publications. 1997.

*William Allingham, a Diary, 1824 -1889*. Introduced by John Julius Norwich. Penguin Books, 1985.

*William Allingham, an introduction*. By Allen Warner. Dolmen Press, Dublin, 1971.

*Mid-Ulster Local History Journal, Number 3*. Edited by Eddie McCartney. Cookstown Printing Company, 1997.

## 3. BIOGRAPHIES

*Gracie Fields*. By Joan Moules. Summersdale, 1997

*Goodnight Sweetheart – Life and times of Al Bowlly*. By Ray Pallett. Spellmount, 1986.

*Goodbye, Dollie*. By Vivian Ellis. Fred Muller, 1970.

*Ivor Novello*. By Paul Webb. Stage Directions, 1999.

*Val Doonican – My Story, My Life*. JR Books, 2009

*Vocal Refrain. An Autobiogrpahy of Vera Lynn.* W.H. Allen, 1975.

*Gertrude Lawrence.* By Sheridan Morley. MCGRAW-HILL (New York), 1981

*Beatrice Lilly, the Funniest Woman in the World.* By Bruce Laffey. Robson Books, 1989

*The Greatest Billy Cotton Band Show.* By John Maxwell. Jupiter Books, 1976

*Lew Stone – a career in music.* By Kenneth Trodd. Joyce Stone, 1971.

*Patsy. The Life and Times of Patsy Cline.* By Margaret Jones. Harper Collins (New York), 1994.

*I Should Care – the Sammy Cahn Story.* By Sammy Cahn. W.H. Allen, 1975.

*Below the Parapet.* By Carol Thatcher. Harper Collins, 1996. (A biography of Denis Thatcher).

# INDEX

**Kennedy, Jimmy**

**1: A selection of best sellers:**

## 2: A selection of contemporary films and shows featuring Jimmy Kennedy songs:

## 3: Some major recording/performing artists of Jimmy Kennedy songs:

# The author

New York born J. J. Kennedy, who has both Irish and British nationalities, moderated in Modern History and Political Science at Trinity College, Dublin, in 1963. His songwriter father advised him against the music business so he pursued a career in the almost equally insecure fields of publishing, journalism and public relations. Now semi-retired, he lives near Céret in southern France.

Lightning Source UK Ltd.
Milton Keynes UK
UKOW05f1051210713

214119UK00001B/78/P